PERSONAL REMINISCENCES
OF
HENRY IRVING

Henry Irving making up.
from the Drawing by Paul Renouard.
in the possession of the Author

PERSONAL REMINISCENCES OF HENRY IRVING

BY

BRAM STOKER

VOLUME II

GREENWOOD PRESS, PUBLISHERS
WESTPORT, CONNECTICUT

Originally published in 1906
by William Heinemann, London

First Greenwood Reprinting 1970

SBN 8371-2845-5 (SET)
SBN 8371-2844-7 (VOL. 2)

PRINTED IN UNITED STATES OF AMERICA

CONTENTS

		PAGE
XLIII.	Irving's Philosophy of His Art	1
XLIV.	The Right Hon. William Ewart Gladstone	26
XLV.	The Earl of Beaconsfield	37
XLVI.	Sir William Pearce, Bart.	43
XLVII.	Stepniak	53
XLVIII.	E. Onslow Ford, R.A.	59
XLIX.	Sir Laurence Alma-Tadema, R.A.	65
L.	Sir Edward Burne-Jones, Bart.	73
LI.	Edwin A. Abbey, R.A.	79
LII.	J. Bernard Partridge	86
LIII.	Robert Browning	89
LIV	Walt Whitman	92
LV.	James Whitcomb Riley	112
LVI.	Ernest Renan	114
LVII.	Hall Caine	115
LVIII.	Irving and Dramatists	131
LIX.	Musicians	140
LX.	Ludwig Barnay	151
LXI.	Constant Coquelin	157
LXII.	Sarah Bernhardt	161
LXIII.	Geneviève Ward	167
LXIV.	John Lawrence Toole	177
LXV.	Ellen Terry	190
LXVI.	Fresh Honours in Dublin	208
LXVII.	Performances at Sandringham and Windsor	212

CONTENTS

		PAGE
LXVIII. PRESIDENTS OF THE UNITED STATES	. . .	229
LXIX. KNIGHTHOOD	. .	238
LXX. HENRY IRVING AND UNIVERSITIES	. . .	244
LXXI. ADVENTURES	. .	266
LXXII. BURNING OF THE LYCEUM STORAGE	. . .	297
LXXIII. FINANCE	. .	304
LXXIV. THE TURN OF THE TIDE	. . . .	321

ILLUSTRATIONS

	To face page
Irving Making Up. *Drawing by Paul Renouard* . *Frontispiece*	
Postcard from Mr. Gladstone	28
Statue of Henry Irving as Hamlet. *By E. Onslow Ford, R.A.* .	62
Letter, Walt Whitman to Bram Stoker	97
J. L. Toole. *Drawing by Fred Barnard*	177
Playbill, J. L. Toole and Henry Irving	178
Cast of "Dearer than Life"	182
Ellen Terry at 17	190
Ellen Terry as Lady Macbeth. *By John Sargent, R.A.* .	204
Ellen Terry and Dogs	206
Ellen Terry, 1906	207
Henry Irving and the Queen. *Drawing by Phil May* . .	214
Portrait of Henry Irving. *By McLuer Hamilton* . . .	241
Henry Irving, Portrait. *By Edwin A. Ward* . . .	275
Bram Stoker	321
Irving as Philip II. *By J. McNeil Whistler* . . .	323
Irving at Sea in 1905	342
Henry Irving and John Hare. *Last photograph taken* . .	352

XLIII

IRVING'S PHILOSOPHY OF HIS ART

The key-stone—The scientific process—Character—The Play—Stage Perspective—Dual Consciousness—Individuality—The True Realism

I

IRVING and I were alone together one hot afternoon in August 1889, crossing in the steamer from Southsea to the Isle of Wight, and were talking of that phase of Stage Art which deals with the conception and development of character. In the course of our conversation, whilst he was explaining to me the absolute necessity of an actor's understanding the prime qualities of a character in order that he may make it throughout consistent, he said these words:

"*If you do not pass a character through your own mind it can never be sincere!*"

I was much struck with the phrase, coming as it did as the crown of an argument—the explanation of a great artist's method of working out a conceived idea. To me it was the embodiment of an artistic philosophy. Even in the midst of an interesting conversation, during which we touched upon many subjects of inner mental working, the phrase presented itself as one of endless possibilities, and hung as such in my mind. Lest I should forget the exact words I wrote them then and there in my pocket-book, whence I entered them later in my diary.

I think that if I had interrupted the conversation at the above words and asked my friend to expound his philosophy and elaborate it, he would have been for an instant amused, and on the impulse of the moment would have deprecated the use of such an important word. Men untrained to Mental Science and unfamiliar with its terminology are apt to place too much importance on abstract, wide-embracing terms, and to find the natural flow of their true thought interrupted by disconcerting fears. His amusement would have been only momentary, however. I know now, after familiar acquaintance with his intellectual method for over a quarter of a century, that with his mental quickness—which was so marked as now and again to seem like inspiration—he would have grasped the importance of the theme as bearing upon the Art to which he had devoted himself and to his own part in it. And would have tried to explain matters as new and relevant subjects, consequences or causes, presented themselves. But such an exposition would have been—must have been confused and incomplete. The process of a creative argument is a silent and lonely one, requiring investigation and guesses ; the following up of clues in the labyrinth of thought till their utility or their falsity has been proved. The most that a striving mind can do at such a time is to keep sight of some main purpose or tendency; some perpetual recognition of its objective. If in addition the thinker has to keep eternally and consciously within his purview a lot of other subjects bearing on his main idea, each with its own attendant distractions and divergencies, his argument would to a listener seem but a jumble of undigested facts, deductions and imaginings. Moreover, it would leave in the mind of the latter a belief that the speaker is without any real conviction at all; a mere groper in the dark. If, on the other hand, the man in thinking out his problem tries to bear in mind his friend's understanding—with an eye to his ultimate approval and acceptance of his argument and conclusion—he is apt to limit himself to commonplace and accepted truths. In such case his thought is machine-made, and lacks the penetrative force which has its origin in intellectual or psychic fire. A whole history of such thought cannot equal a single glimpse or hint of an earnest mind working truly.

As Irving on that pleasant voyage spoke the words which seemed to explain his whole intellectual method I grasped instinctively the importance of the utterance, though the argument for present reticence did not present itself in its entirety.

To me the words became a text of which the whole of his work seemed the expounding. From him, as an artist, the thought was elementary and basic; explanatory and illuminative.

II

To "pass a character through your mind" requires a scientific process of some kind; some process which is natural, and therefore consistent. If we try to analyse the process we shall find that it is in accord with any other alimentative process. Nature varies in details, but her intents and objects are fixed: to fit and sustain each to its appointed task. In the animal or vegetable kingdoms, so in the mind of man. The hemlock and the apple take the juices of the earth through different processes of filtration; the one to noxious ends, the other to beneficence. Hardness and density have their purpose in the mechanism of the vegetable world; the wood rejects what the softer and more open valves or tissues receive. So too in the world of animal life. The wasp and the viper, the cuttle-fish and the stinging ray work to different ends from the sheep and the sole, the pheasant and the turtle. But one and all draw alimentative substance from common sources. But he who would understand character must draw varying results from common causes. And the only engine powerful enough in varying purposes for this duty is the human brain. Again, the worker in imagination is the one who most requires different types and varying methods of development. And still again, of all workers in imagination, the actor has most need for understanding; for on him is imposed the task of re-creating to external and material form types of character written in abstractions. It behoves him, then, primarily to understand what exactly it is that he has to materialise. To this end two forms of understanding are necessary: first that which the poet—the creator or maker of the play, sets down for him; second the truth of the given individual to the type or types which he is supposed to represent. This latter implies a

UNDERSTANDING OF CHARACTER

large knowledge of types; for how can any man judge of the truth of things when to him both the type and the instance are strange. Thus it happens that an actor should be a judge of character; an understander of those differences which discriminate between classes, and individuals of the class. This is an actor's study at the beginning of his work—when he is preparing to study his Art.

Let me say at the outset of this branch of my subject that I am in it trying to put into words, and the words into some sort of ordered sequence, that knowledge of his craft which in a long course of years Irving conveyed to me. Sometimes the conveyance was made consciously; sometimes unconsciously. By words, by inferences, by acting; by what he added to seemingly completed work, or by what he omitted after fuller thought or experience. One by one, or group by group, these things were interesting, though often of seeming unimportance; but taken altogether they go to make up a philosophy. In trying to formulate this I am not speaking for myself; I am but following so well as I can the manifested wisdom of the master of his craft. Here and there I shall be able to quote Irving's exact words, spoken or written after mature thought and with manifest and deliberate purpose. For the rest, I can only illustrate by his acting, or at worst by the record of the impression conveyed to my own mind.

III

We may I think divide the subject thus :
CHARACTER

A. Its Essence $\begin{cases} x.\text{—}\textit{The Dramatist's setting out of it} \\ y.\text{—}\textit{Its truth to accepted type} \\ z.\text{—}\textit{The Player's method of studying} \\ \phantom{z.\text{—}}\textit{these two} \end{cases}$

B. Reticence
C. Art. and Truth

THE PLAY
STAGE PERSPECTIVE
DUAL CONSCIOUSNESS
INDIVIDUALITY, AND THE KNOWLEDGE OF IT

IV

CHARACTER

A.—Its Essence

We think in abstractions ; but we live in concretions. In real life an individual who is not in any way distinguishable from his fellows is but a poor creature after all and is not held of much account by anybody. That law of nature which makes the leaves of a tree or the units of any genus, any species, any variety all different—which in the animal or the vegetable world alike makes each unit or class distinguishable whilst adhering to the type—is of paramount importance to man. Tennyson has hammered all this out and to a wonderful conclusion in those splendid stanzas of *In Memoriam* LIV to LVI beginning " Oh yet we trust that somehow good " to " Behind the veil, behind the veil."

Let it be sufficient for us to know and accept that there can be endless individual idiosyncrasies without violation of type. To understand these is the study of character. The *differentia* of each individual is an endless and absorbing study, not given to all to master. Some at least of this mastery is a necessary part of the equipment of an actor. Now there is a common saying that "the eyebrow is the actor's feature." This is largely true; but there is a double purpose in its truth. In the first place the eyebrow is movable at will; a certain amount of exercise can give mobility and control. It can therefore heighten expression to a very marked degree. But in addition it, when in a marked degree, is the accompaniment of a large frontal sinus—that bony ridge above the eyebrows which in the terminology of physiognomy implies the power to distinguish minute differences, and so is credited with knowledge of "character"—the difference between one and another; divergencies within a common type. With this natural equipment and the study which inevitably follows—for powers are not given to men in vain—the actor can by experience know types, and endless variants and combinations of the same. So can any man who has the quality. But the actor alone has to work out the ideas given to him by this study in recognisable material types and differentiated individual instances of the same type.

x

The dramatist having, whether by instinct or reason, selected his type has in the play to give him situations which can allow opportunity for the expression of his qualities; words in which he can expound the thoughts material to him in the given situations; and such hints as to personal appearance, voice and bearing as can assist the imagination of a reader. All these things must be consistent; there must be nothing which would show to the student falsity to common knowledge. "Do men gather grapes of thorns, or figs of thistles?" has a large application in art, and specially in stage art. It is the ignorance or neglect of this eternal law which is to my mind the weakness of some writers. Instance Ibsen who having shown in some character an essential quality through one or two acts makes the after action of the character quite at variance with it. A similar fault weakens certain of the fine work of "Ian Maclaren" when he proceeds to explain away in a later story some perfectly consistent and understandable quality of mind or action in one of his powerful and charming character stories. No after-explanation can supersede the conviction of innate character.

y

Now a dramatist is at perfect liberty to choose any type he likes and to deal with his individual creations just as he chooses. There is no law against it; however ridiculous it may be, it makes no breach of any code in accepted morals. But he should for his own sake be consistent; the character should at least be true to itself. It is by such qualities that posterity as well as the juries of the living judge. The track of literary progress is littered with wreckage from breaches of this truth.

A LESSON FROM THE BLIND

Of this we may be sure : if a character have in itself opposing qualities which cannot be reconciled, then it can never have that unity which makes for strength. Therefore the actor who has to represent the abstract idea as a concrete reality must at the beginning understand the dramatist's intention. He can by emphasis of one kind or another help to convey the dominant idea. There is an exact instance of this from Irving's own work ; one which at the same time illustrates how an actor, howsoever thoughtful and experienced he may be, can learn : For a good many years he had played Shylock to universal praise ; then, all at once, he altered it. Altered it in the manner of utterance of the first words he speaks : " Three thousand ducats,—well." He explained it to me when having noticed the change I asked him about it. He said that it was due to the criticism of a *blind* man —I think it was the Chaplain of the American Senate, Dr. Milburn.

"What did he say ? " I asked. He answered with a thoughtful smile :

"He said : 'I thought at first that you were too amiable. I seemed to miss the harsh note of the usurer's voice ! ' He was quite right ! The audience should from the first understand, if one can convey it, the dominant note of a character ! "

This was distinctly in accordance with his own theory ; and he always remembered gratefully the man who so enlightened him. The incident illustrates one phase of " passing a character through one's own mind." When it has gone through this process it takes a place as an actual thing—a sort of clothing of the player's own identity with the attributes of another. This new-seeming identity must have at first its own limitations; the clothing does not fit—somewhere too tight, elsewhere too loose. But at last things become easier. The individuality within, being of plastic nature, adapts itself by degrees to its surroundings. And then for purposes of external expression the mastery is complete.

Experience adds much to this power of mastery. When an actor has played many parts he learns to express the dominant ideas of various characters in simple form, so that each, through a sort of artistic metonymy, becomes a type. In fact, as he goes on studying fresh characters he gets a greater easiness of expression; he is not creating every time, but is largely combining things already created. This is true Art. The etymology of the word shows that its purpose is rather to join than to create. Were it not that each mind must create the units which have to be joined, histrionic art would not be primarily a creative art.

In Irving's own words:

" It is often supposed that great actors trust to the inspiration of the moment. Nothing can be more erroneous. There will, of course, be such moments when an actor at a white heat illumines some passages with a flood of imagination (and this mental condition, by the way, is impossible to the student sitting in his arm-chair); but the great actor's surprises are generally well weighed, studied, and balanced. . . . And it is this accumulation of such effects which enables an actor, after many

EXPRESSION AND SPEECH

years, to present many great characters with remarkable completeness."

And again when he insists upon the *intention* of effect :

"It is necessary that the actor should learn to think before he speaks. . . . Let him remember, first that every sentence expresses a new thought, and, therefore, frequently demands a change of intonation ; secondly, that the thought precedes the word. Of course, there are passages in which thought and language are borne along by the streams of emotion and completely intermingled. But more often it will be found that the most natural, the most seemingly accidental effects are obtained when the working of the mind is seen before the tongue gives it words."

I well remember at one of our meetings in 1876 when after dinner we had some "recitations," according to the custom of that time. Irving was very complimentary to my own work because I anticipated words by expression, particularly by the movement of my eyes.

z

So far, the study of natural types and the acceptance of the dramatist's ideas. But next the actor has to learn how to show best the development of character. It is not to the purpose of a high-grade play that each character can be at the start as though labelled thus or thus. As the story unfolds itself the new situations bring into view qualities hitherto unknown ; there has been heretofore no necessity for knowing them. Here it is that the dramatist must not make contradictions. He may show opposing qualities—such make the struggles of life and passions which it is the duty of the drama to portray; but the opposing forces, though they may clash, must not deny each other's very existence. Honour and baseness do not synchronously coexist; neither do patriotism and treachery; nor truth and falsehood; nor cruelty and compassion. If it be necessary in the struggles of good and bad—any of the common phases of human nature—in the same individual to show that now and again either dominates for a time, the circumstances must be so arranged as to show preponderating cause. If the dramatist acts up to this standard all can go well. But if his work be crude and not in itself illuminative, the actor's work becomes more complex and more difficult. He has in the manifold ways of his own craft to show from the first the *possibilities* of character which later on will have to be dealt with. He will have to suggest the faintest *beginnings* of things which later are to be of perhaps paramount importance.

This it is that Irving meant when he said that a character should be "sincere." It must not be self-contradictory. He put this point very definitely:

> ". . . the actor must before all things form a definite conception of what he wishes to convey. It is better to be wrong and consistent, than to be right, yet hesitating and uncertain."

And thus it is that the actor's skill can so largely

supplement that of the dramatist. He must add whatever the other has omitted or left undone. He must make straight the path which is in common to himself, the dramatist, and the public. He must prepare by subtle means—not too obtrusive to be distracting to the present purpose, nor too slight to pass altogether unnoticed—the coming of something as yet below the horizon. If this be done with care —and care implies both study and premeditation— the sincerity of the character will from first to last be unimpaired.

B. RETICENCE

On the other side of this phase of the Art of Acting is that fine undefinable quality of all art which is known as "reticence." Restraint is almost as rare as passion. The "reticence" of the actor is perhaps its most difficult phase. For he has to express that which has in the others to be concealed; and if his expression be too marked, not only does the restraint cease to exist, but a wrong idea—that of concealment—is conveyed.

C. ART AND TRUTH

All these things are parts of an integral whole; they all go to the formulation of an Art. Art is in itself only a part of the mechanism of truth. It is from the inner spirit that the outward seeming must derive. Rules and laws are but aids, restraints, methods of achievement: but it is after all to nature that the artist must look. In the words of Pope:

> "These laws of old discover'd, not deviz'd,
> Are nature still but nature methodiz'd."

Irving put the idea thus:

> " . . . merely to imitate is not to apply a similar method . . . the greatest of all the lessons that Art can teach is this: that truth is supreme and eternal. No phase of art can achieve much on a false basis. Sincerity, which is the very touchstone of Art, is instinctively recognised by all."

V

THE PLAY

The play as a whole is a matter of prime consideration for the actor, though it only comes into his province *quâ* actor in a secondary way. In the working of a theatre it is the province of the stage manager to arrange the play as an entity; the actor has to deal with it only with reference to his own scenes. But the actor must understand the whole scheme so as to realise the ultimate purpose; otherwise his limitations may become hindrances to this. Irving who was manager as well as actor, puts the matter plainly from the more comprehensive point of view:

> "It is most important that an actor should learn that he is a figure in a picture, and that the least exaggeration destroys the harmony of the composition. All the members of the company should work toward a common end, with the nicest subordination of their individuality to the general purpose."

THE ART OF ILLUSION

Here we have again the lesson of restraint—of reticence. There are also various other forms of the same need, to which he has at various times alluded. For instance, speaking of the presentation of a play he said:

> "You want, above all things, to have a truthful picture which shall appeal to the eye without distracting the imagination from the purpose of the drama."

In fact Irving took the broadest possible views of the aims and possibilities of his chosen art, and of the duties as well as of the methods of those who follow it. He even put it that the State had its duty with regard to the art of illusion:

> "The mere study of the necessities and resources of theatre art—the art of illusion—should give the theatre as an educational medium a place in State economy. Just think for a moment: a comprehensive art effort which consolidates into one entity which has an end and object and purpose of its own, all the elements of which any or all of the arts and industries take cognisance—thought, speech, passion, humour, pathos, emotion, distance, substance, form, size, colour, time, force, light, illusion to each or all of the senses, sound, tone, rhythm, music, motion. Can such a work be undertaken lightly or with inadequate preparation? Why, the mere patience necessary for the production of a play might take a high place in the marvels of human effort."

VI

STAGE PERSPECTIVE

One of the things on which Irving always insisted was a knowledge and understanding of stage perspective and of its application in the practice not only of the art of the stage in its scenic and illusive aspect but of the art of acting:

> "The perspective of the stage is not that of real life, and the result of seeming is achieved by means which, judged by themselves, would seem to be indirect. It is only the raw recruit who tries to hit the bull's eye by point-blank firing, and who does not allow for elevation and windage."

In pointing out the necessity of speaking more loudly on the stage than in a room, he puts the same idea in a different and perhaps a broader way:

> "This exaggeration applies to everything on the stage. To appear to be natural, you must in reality be much broader than natural. To act on the stage as one really would in a room would be ineffective and colourless."

He never forgot—and never allowed any one else to forget—that the purpose of stage art is illusion. Its aim is not to present reality but its semblance; not to be, but to seem. He put it thus:

> "The function of art is to do and not to create—it is to make to seem, and not to make to be, for to make to be is the Creator's work."

He had before said :

"It must never be forgotten that all art has the aim or object of seeming and not of being, and to understate is as bad as to overstate the modesty or the efflorescence of nature."

Thus we get the higher aim: to seem to be—but always in such wise that nature shall be worthily represented. Nature

"At once the end and aim and test of art."

So Pope. Irving put the value of nature as against mere pretence thus :

"To be natural on the stage is most difficult, and yet a grain of nature is worth a bushel of artifice. . . . Nature may be overdone by triviality in conditions that demand exaltation. . . . Like the practised orator, the actor rises and descends with his sentiment, and cannot be always in a fine frenzy."

How true this is; how consistent with eternal truth! Nature has her moods, why not man; has her means of expressing them, why not man also? Nature has her tones; and with these why may not the heart of man vibrate and express itself?

In this connection and with the same illustration —the orator compared with the actor—Irving put a new phase of the same idea :

"It matters little whether the actor sheds tears or not, so long as he can make his audience shed them; but if tears can be summoned at will and subject to his control it is true art to utilise such a power, and happy is the actor whose sensibility has at once such delicacy and discipline. In this respect the actor is like the orator. Eloquence is all the more moving when it is animated and directed by a fine and subtle sympathy which affects the spectator though it does not master him."

VII

DUAL CONSCIOUSNESS

The last-mentioned utterance of Irving's brings us at once to the deepest problem in the Art of Acting : the value and use of sensibility. Throughout his later life, from the time that he first entered the polemics of his art, he held consistently to one theory. To him the main disputants were Diderot and Talma ; any other was merely a supporter of the theory of either.

Diderot in his *Paradox of Acting* held that for good acting there must be no real feeling on the part of the actor :

> "Extreme sensibility makes middling actors; middling sensibility makes the ruck of bad actors ; in complete absence of sensibility is the possibility of a sublime actor."

Irving's comment on this theory is :

> "The exaltation of sensibility in Art may be difficult to define, but it is none the less real to all who have felt its power."

Talma[1] held quite the opposite view to that of Diderot. To him one of the first qualifications of an actor is sensibility, which indeed he considered the very source of imagination. To this quality, he held, there must be added intelligence:

> "To form a great actor ... the union of sensibility and intelligence is required."

---

[1] When Irving began to consider this branch of the "true inwardness" of his work he was so much struck with the argument of Talma that he had it translated and inserted in *The Theatre*. This was easy of accomplishment, for with regard to that magazine he had only to ask.

As a matter of fact *The Theatre* at that time belonged to him. He had long considered it advisable that there should be some organ in which matters deeply concerning the stage could be set forth. He accordingly arranged with the late Mr. F. W. Hawkins, then a sub-editor of the *Times*, to take the work in hand. Hawkins had already by his work shown his interest in the stage; Irving had a high opinion of his "Life of Edmund Kean" and of his book on the French stage which he had then well in hand. He trusted Hawkins entirely; gave him a free hand, and never interfered with him in any possible way except to suggest some useful article of a neutral kind. He would never even give a hint of his own opinion regarding any one of his own profession, but kept studiously out of the theatrical party-politics of the day. Hawkins had his own views which he was perfectly well able to support; he could take care of himself. Irving was content that the magazine should exist, and footed the bills. Later on when the editorship was vacant Irving made a present of the whole thing to Clement Scott who said that he would like to see what he could do with it.

The Talma articles appeared in *The Theatre* for the 30th January and 6th and 13th February 1877. This was before I came to Irving. It was long afterwards when I read them.

In 1883 Walter Herries Pollock, then editor of the *Saturday Review*, a great friend of Irving, produced an edition of the *Paradox of Acting* to which Irving wrote a preface. In this he set out his own views in his comments on the work of Diderot.

Irving used his knowledge of the controversy to this effect:

"I do not recommend actors to allow their feelings to carry them away . . .; but it is necessary to warn you against the theory, expounded with brilliant ingenuity by Diderot, that the actor never feels. . . . Has not the actor who can . . . make his feelings a part of his art an advantage over the actor who never feels, but makes his observations solely from the feelings of others? *It is necessary to this art that the mind should have, as it were, a double consciousness, in which all the emotions proper to the occasion may have full swing, while the actor is all the time on the alert for every detail of his method.* . . . The actor who combines the electric force of a strong personality with a mastery of the resources of his art, must have a greater power over his audiences than the passionless actor who gives a most artistic simulation of the emotions he never experiences."

The sentence printed in italics is a really valuable addition to the philosophy of acting. It is Irving's own and is, as may be seen, a development or corollary of Talma's conclusion. Talma required as a necessity of good acting both sensibility and intelligence. But Irving claimed that in the practice of the art they must exist and act synchronously. This belief he cherished, and on it he acted with excellent result. I have myself seen a hundred instances of its efficiency in the way of protective self-control; of conscious freedom of effort; of self-

DUAL CONSCIOUSNESS

reliance; of confidence in giving the reins to passion within the set bounds of art.[1]

In speaking of other branches of the subject Irving said:

> "An actor must either think for himself or imitate some one else."

And again:

> "For the purely monkey arts of life there is no future — they stand only in the crude glare of the present, and there is no softness for them, in the twilight of either hope or memory. With the true artist the internal force is the first requisite—the external appearance being merely the medium through which this is made known to others."

[1] I have seen a good many times Irving illustrate and prove the theory of the dual consciousness in and during his own acting: when he has gone on with his work heedless of a fire on the stage and its quelling: when a gas tank underneath the stage exploded and actually dispersed some of the boarding close to him, he all the time proceeding without even a moment's pause or a falter in his voice. One other occasion was typical. During a performance of *The Lyons Mail*, whilst Dubosc surrounded by his gang was breaking open the iron strong-box conveyed in the mail cart the horses standing behind him began to get restive and plunged about wildly, making a situation of considerable danger. The other members of the murderous gang were quickly off the stage, and the dead body of the postilion rolled away to the wings. But Irving never even looked round. He went calmly on with his work of counting the *billets-de-banque*, whilst he interlarded the words of the play with admonitions to his comrades not to be frightened but to come back and attend to their work of robbing. Not for an instant did he cease to be Dubosc though in addition he became manager of the theatre.

VIII

INDIVIDUALITY, AND THE KNOWLEDGE OF IT

If an actor has to learn of others—often primarily—through his own emotions, it is surely necessary that he learn first to know himself. He need not take himself as a standard of perfection—though poor human nature is apt to lean that way; but he can accept himself as something that he knows. If he cannot get that far he will never know anything. With himself then, and his self-knowledge as a foothold he may begin to understand others.[1]

Γνῶθι σεαυτόν : Know thyself! It is, after all, the base of all knowledge—the foothold for all forward thought. Commenting on the speech of Polonius: " To thine own self be true," Irving said:

> " But how can a man be true to himself if he does not know himself ? ' Know thyself ' was a wisdom of the Ancients. But how can a man know himself if he mistrusts his own identity, and if he puts aside his special gifts in order to render himself an imperfect similitude of some one else ? "

[1] As an instance of the efficacy of the method, let any one try to tell character by handwriting. It is very simple, after all. Let him take the strange writing, and after making himself familiar with it, measure it by himself, asking himself : " Under stress of what emotion would my own writing most nearly resemble that ? " Let him repeat this with each sign of divergence from his own caligraphy: and in a short time he will be astonished with the result. So it is with all studies of character. Without any standard the task is impossible ; but weigh each against your own self-knowledge and you at once begin to acquire comparative knowledge of simple qualities capable of being combined endlessly.

IX

Thus we have come back to Irving's original proposition :
"If you do not pass a character through your own mind it can never be sincere." The logical wheel has gone its full round and is back at the starting place. Begin with the argument where you will it must come sooner or later to the same end : "To know others know yourself." Your own identity is that which you must, for histrionic purposes, clothe with attributes not your own. You must have before your mind some definite image of what you would portray; and your own feeling must be ultimately its quickening force.

So far, the resolution of the poet's thought into a moving, breathing, visible, tangible character. But that is not the completion of the endeavour. In the philosophy of histrionic art are rarer heights than mere embodiment, mere vitality, mere illusion. The stage is a world of its own, and has its own ambitions, its own duties. Truth either to natural types or to the arbitrary creations of the dramatist is not sufficient. For the altitudes something else is required. Irving set it forth thus :

> "Finally in the consideration of the Art of Acting, it must never be forgotten that its ultimate aim is beauty. Truth itself is only an element of beauty, and to merely reproduce things vile and squalid and mean is a debasement of art."

Here he supports the theory of Taine that art, like nature, has its own selective power; and that in the wisdom of its choosing is its power for good. Does it not march with that sublime apothegm of Burke : " Vice itself lost half its evil by losing all its grossness " ?

Finally Irving summed up the whole Philosophy of his Art and of its place amongst the sister Arts in a few sentences :

" In painting and in the drama the methods of the workers are so entirely opposed, and the materials with which they work are so different, that a mutual study of the other work cannot but be of service to each. Your painter works in mouldable materials, inanimate, not sensitive but yielding to the lightest touch. His creation is the embodiment of the phantasm of his imagination, for in art the purpose is to glorify and not merely to reproduce. He uses forms and facts of nature that he may not err against nature's laws. But such natural facts as he assimilates are reproduced in his work, deified by the strength of his own imagination. Actors, on the other hand, have to work with materials which are all natural, and not all plastic, but are all sensitive—with some of the strength and all the weakness of flesh and blood. The actor has first to receive in his own mind the phantasmal image which is conveyed to him by the words of the poet ; and this he has to reproduce as he can with the faulty materials which nature has given to him. Thus the painter and the poet begin from different ends of the gamut of natural possibilities—the one starts from nature to reach imagination, the other from imagination to reach at reality. And if the means be not inadequate, and if the effect be sincere, both can reach that veritable ground where reality and imagination join. This is the true realism towards which all should aim—the holy ground whereon is reared the Pantheon of all the Arts."

XLIV

THE RIGHT HON. WILLIAM EWART GLADSTONE

Visits to the Lyceum—Intellectual stimulus and rest—An interesting post-card—His memory—" Mr. Gladstone's seat "—Speaks of Parnell—Visit to " Becket "—Special knowledge ; its application—Lord Randolph Churchill on Gladstone—Mrs. Gladstone

I

FOR fourteen years, from 1881 to 1895, Mr. Gladstone was a visitor at the Lyceum. The first occasion was on the First night of *The Cup*, January 3, 1881, of which I have already written. He had known Irving before, but this was the first time he had been behind the Lyceum scenes. He was very interested in everything, especially those matters of which up to then he knew little such as the setting of the scenes. His fund of information was prodigious and one could feel that he took a delight in adding to it. He was on that occasion very complimentary about all he saw and very anxious to know of the reality—as distinguished from the seeming—of things such as food and drink used, &c. That night his visit to the stage was only a passing one as he sat through the active part of the play in his own box, except during a part of one scene.

INTELLECTUAL STIMULANT

He seemed ever afterwards to take a great interest in Irving and all he did. At the end of June 1882 he invited Irving to one of his delightful " Breakfasts " in Downing Street. On 8th July of the same year he came to the Lyceum and brought Lord Northbrook with him. Whenever he visited the theatre after 1881 he always came and went by the private door in Burleigh Street, and he always managed to visit Irving on the stage or in his dressing-room or both. The public seemed to take a delight in seeing him at the theatre, and he appeared to take a delight in coming. I honestly believe that he found in it, now and again, an intellectual stimulant—either an excitement or a pausing time *before* some great effort, or a relief of change from fact to fancy *after* it. For instance: On 8th April 1886, Thursday, he made his great speech in the House of Commons introducing the Home Rule Bill—amid a time of great excitement. Two nights after, Saturday night, he came to the Lyceum—and received an immense ovation. Again, in the time of bitter regret and anxiety when Parnell made the violent attack on him in his Manifesto, November 29, 1890, Saturday, he took his earliest opportunity, Tuesday, 2nd December, of coming to the Lyceum.

This visit was a somewhat special one, for it was the first time that Mr. Gladstone came to sit behind the scenes in the O.P.[1] proscenium corner which then became known as " Mr. Gladstone's seat." The occasion of it was thus: I had the year previously written an Irish novel, *The Snake's Pass*,

[1] Opposite Prompt.

which after running as a serial through the London *People* and several provincial papers had now been published in book form. I had done myself the pleasure of sending an early copy to Mr. Gladstone whose magnificent power and ability and character I had all my life so much admired. Having met and conversed with him several times I felt in a way justified in so doing. He had at once written; I received his letter the same day—that of publication, 18th November 1890. I give his letter, which was in the post-card form then usual to him. I think it is a good example of his method of correspondence, kind and thoughtful and courteous—a model of style. I had as may be gathered written with some diffidence, or delicacy of feeling:

> "DEAR MR. BRAM STOKER,—My social memory is indeed a bad one, yet not so bad as to prevent my recollection of our various meetings. I thank you much for your work, and for your sympathy; and I hope to have perused all your pages before we meet again. When that will be I know not: but I am so fond a lover of *The Bride of Lammermoor* that I may take the desperate step of asking Mr. Irving whether he will some night, if it is on, let me sit behind the stage pillar—a post which C. Kean once gave me, and which alone would make me sure to hear.—Yours faithfully, W. E. GLADSTONE.
> N. 18. 90."

Some days later, after a most cordial invitation from Irving, it was arranged that he should choose exactly what date he wished and that all should be ready for him. There could be no difficulty, as *Ravenswood* was the only play then in the bill and would hold it alone till the beginning of the new

FACSIMILE POST-CARD FROM MR. GLADSTONE

year. When he did come I met him and Mrs. Gladstone at the private door and piloted them across the stage, which was the nearest way to Irving's box. The door to it was beside the corner where Mr. Gladstone would sit.

Possibly it was that as Mr. Gladstone was then full of Irish matters my book, being of Ireland and dealing with Irish ways and specially of a case of oppression by a "gombeen" man under a loan secured on land, interested him for he had evidently read it carefully. As we walked across the stage he spoke to me of it very kindly and very searchingly. Of course I was more than pleased when he said :

"That scene at Mrs. Kelligan's is fine—very fine indeed ! "

Now it must be remembered that, in the interval between his getting the book and when we met, had occurred one of the greatest troubles and trials of his whole political life. The hopes which he had built through the slow progress of years for the happy settlement of centuries-old Irish troubles had been suddenly almost shattered by a bolt from the blue, and his great intellect and enormous powers of work and concentration had been for many days strained to the utmost to keep the road of the future clear from the possibility of permanent destruction following on temporary embarrassment. And yet in the midst of all he found time to read—and remember, even to details and names—the work of an unimportant friend.

When it had been known on the stage that Mr. Gladstone was coming that night to sit behind the scenes the men seemed determined to make it a gala occasion. They had prepared the corner where he was to sit as though it were for Royalty. They had not only swept and dusted but had scrubbed the floor; and they had rigged up a sort of canopy of crimson velvet so that neither dust nor draught should come to the old man. His chair was nicely padded and made comfortable. The stage-men were all, as though by chance, on the stage and all in their Sunday clothes. As the Premier came in all hats went off. I showed Mr. Gladstone his nook and told him, to his immense gratification, how the men had prepared it on their own initiative. We chatted till the time drew near for the curtain to go up. Then I fixed him in his place and showed him how to watch for and avoid the drop scene, the great roller of which would descend guided by the steel cord drawn taut beside him. Lest there should be any danger through his unfamiliarity with the ways of theatres, I signalled the Master Carpenter to come to me and thus cautioned him.

"Would it not be well," I said, "if some one stood near here in case of accident?"

"It's all right, sir, we have provided for that. The two best and steadiest men in the theatre are here ready!" I looked round and there they were —alert and watchful. And there they remained all night. There was not going to be any chance of mishap to Mr. Gladstone *that* night!

I went always to join him between the acts, and Irving when he had opportunity from his dressing—of which there was a good deal in *Ravenswood* would come to talk with him. We were all, whatever our political opinions individually, full of the Parnell Manifesto and its many bearings on political life. For myself, though I was a philosophical Home-Ruler, I was much surprised and both angry at and sorry for Parnell's attitude, and I told Mr. Gladstone my opinion. He said with great earnestness and considerable feeling :

"I am very angry, but I assure you I am even more sorry."

I was pleased to think—and need I say proud also—that Mr. Gladstone seemed to like to talk politics with me. In March 1887 when the new Rules of Procedure for the House of Commons were introduced I ventured to write an exhaustive note on one of the suggested new Rules, No. XII., which I sent to him through the kindness of his friend James Knowles. He was good enough to send me a kind message regarding it through his son Mr. W. H. Gladstone. This suggested Rule was shortly dropped altogether, not of course in any way due to my suggestion. I felt, however, gratified that my view was correct. In my University days I had been something of a law maker in a small way, as I had revised and carried out the revision of the laws of order of the College Historical Society, Dublin University—our great debating society founded by Edmund Burke. I had also made the laws for the Actors' Benevolent Fund, for a hospital, and for numerous societies.

On that particular night he was very chatty, and in commenting on the play compared, strangely enough, Caleb Balderstone with Falstaff. He was interested and eager about everything round him and asked innumerable questions. In the course of conversation he said that he had always taken it for granted that the stage word "properties" included costumes.

He was seemingly delighted with that visit, and from that time on whenever he came to the theatre he always occupied the same place, Mrs. Gladstone and whoever might be with him sitting in Irving's box close at hand.

II

The next time he came, which was on 29th January of the next year, 1891, he generously brought Irving a cheque for ten pounds for the Actors' Benevolent Fund. That evening too he was delighted with the play, *Much Ado about Nothing*, which he had seen before in 1882, in the ordinary way. He applauded loudly, just as he used to do when sitting in the front of the house.

III

He came again in 1892, 11th May, when we were playing *Henry VIII.*, and in the course of conversation commented on Froude's estimate of the population of England in the sixteenth century, which according to his ideas had been stated much below the mark. He also spoke of Dante being in Oxford—a subject about which he wrote in the *Nineteenth Century* in the next month.

Another instance of Mr. Gladstone's visit to the Lyceum: on the evening of 25th February 1893 he came to see *Becket*. He had introduced his second Home Rule Bill on the thirteenth of the month, and as it was being discussed he was naturally full of it—so were we all. By the way, the Bill was carried in the Commons at the end of August of that year. That night when speaking of his new Bill he said to me:

"I will venture to say that in four or five years those who oppose it will wonder what it was that they opposed!"

He was delighted with *Becket*, and seemed specially to rejoice in the success of Tennyson's work.

IV

He was as usual much interested in matters of cost. Irving talked with him very freely, and amongst other things mentioned the increasing expenses of working a theatre, especially with regard to the salaries of actors which had, he said, almost been doubled of late years. Gladstone seemed instantly struck with this. When Irving had gone to change his dress, Gladstone said to me suddenly:

"You told me, I think, that you are Chancellor of the Exchequer here."

"Yes!" I said. "As in your own case, Mr. Gladstone, that is one of my functions!"

"Then would you mind answering me a few questions?" On my giving a hearty acquiescence he began to inquire exhaustively with regard to different classes of actors and others, and seemed to be weighing in his mind the relative advances.

In fact his queries covered the whole ground, for now and again he asked as to the quality of materials used. I knew he was omnivorous with regard to finance, but to-night I was something surprised at the magnitude and persistence of his interests. The reason came shortly. Three days after the visit, 28th February, Sir Henry Meysey-Thompson, M.P. for Handsworth, voiced in the House the wishes then floating of the Bi-Metallists for an International Monetary Conference. Mr. Gladstone replied to him in a great speech, the immediate effect of which was to relegate the matter to the Greek Kalends. In this speech he began with the standard of value, and by figures arrived at gold as the least variable standard. Then he went on to the values and change of various commodities, leading him to what he called " the greatest commodity of the world—human labour." This he broadly differentiated into three classes of work which were dependent on ordinary trade laws and conditions, and of a more limited class which seemed to illustrate the natural changes of the laws of value, inasmuch as the earners were not influenced to any degree by the course of events or the cost of materials. This, broadly speaking, was his sequence of ideas. When he had got so far he said :

> " Take also the limited class about whom I happened to hear the other day—the theatrical profession. I have it on unquestionable authority that the ordinary payments received by actors and actresses have risen largely."

With his keen instinct for both finance and argument he had seized at once on Irving's remark about the increase of salaries, recognising on the instant its suitability as an illustration in the setting forth of his views. And I doubt if he could have found any other class of wage-earning so isolated from commercial changes.

V

Irving told me of an interesting conversation which he had in those days with Lord Randolph Churchill in which the latter mentioned Gladstone in a striking way. Answering a query following on some previous remark, he said:

" The fact is we are all afraid of him!"

" How is that—and why ?" asked Irving.

" Well, you see, he is a first-class man. And the rest of us are only second-class—at best!"

Mr. Gladstone was a really good playgoer and he seemed to love the theatre. When he came he and Mrs. Gladstone were always in good time. I once asked him, thinking that he might have mistaken the hour, in which case I would have borne it in mind to advise him on another occasion, if he liked to come early, and he said:

" Yes. I have always made it a practice to come early. I like to be in my place, and composed, before they begin to tune the fiddles!"

This is the true spirit in which to enjoy the play. No one who has ever sat in eager expectation can forget the imaginative forcefulness of that acre of green baize which hid all the delightful mysteries of the stage. It was in itself a sort of introduction to wonderland, making all the seeming that came after as if quickened into reality.

VI

Like her great husband Mrs. Gladstone largely enjoyed the play. She too seemed to wish to be in good time and to be interested in everything. Like him she was incarnate memory and courtesy. I can give a little pleasing instance : Once when stepping from her carriage she dropped her cut glass smelling-bottle. I had met them coming in and saw her loss ; so I sent out and got another as like as possible to the fragments that lay on the path. She was greatly pleased at the little attention and did not forget it. Years afterwards, when I went to see her in her box, she held up the scent bottle and said :

" You see I have it still ! "

XLV

THE EARL OF BEACONSFIELD

His advice to a Court chaplain—Sir George Elliott and picture-hanging—As a beauty—As a social fencer—" A striking physiognomy "

I

I NEVER saw Benjamin Disraeli (except from the Gallery of the House of Commons) but on the one occasion, when he came to see *The Corsican Brothers*. Irving, however, met him often and liked to talk about him. He admired, of course, his power and courage and address; but it was, I think, the Actor that was in the man that appealed to him. I think also that Beaconsfield liked him, and gauged his interest and delight in matters of character. Somehow the stories which he told him conveyed this idea.

One was of an ambitious young clergyman, son of an old friend of the statesman, who asked him to use his influence in having him appointed a Chaplain to the Queen. This he had effected in due course. The Premier, to his surprise, some time afterwards received a visit from his protégé, who said he had, on the ground of the kindness already extended to him, to ask a further favour. When asked what it was he answered:

"I have through your kindness—for which I am eternally grateful—been notified that I am to preach before Her Majesty on Sunday week. So I have come to ask you if you would very kindly give me some sort of hint in the matter!" The Premier, after a moment's thought, had answered:

"Well, you see, I am not much in the habit of preaching sermons myself so I must leave that altogether to your own discretion. But I can tell you this: If you will preach for fifteen minutes the Queen will listen to you. If you will preach for ten minutes she will listen with interest. But if you will preach for five minutes you will be the most popular chaplain that has ever been at Court."

"And what do you think," he went on, "this egregious young man said:

"'But, Mr. Disraeli, how can I do myself justice in five minutes!'" Then came the super-cynical remark of the statesman-of-the-world:

"Fancy wanting to do himself justice — and before the Queen!"

II

Sir George Elliott, Bart., M.P., the great coal-owner, was a friend of Irving's and used to come to the Lyceum. One night—4th December 1890—at supper in the Beefsteak Room, he told us of a visit he paid to Lord Beaconsfield at Hughenden Manor. Disraeli had taken a fancy to the old gentleman, who was, I believe, a self-made man—all honour to him. He was the only guest on that week-end visit. His host took him over the house and showed him his various treasures. In the course of their going about, Beaconsfield asked him :

"How do you like this room ?" It was the dining-room, a large and handsome chamber; in it were two portraits, the Queen and the Countess Beaconsfield—Disraeli had had her title conferred whilst he was still in the Commons. At the time of Sir George's visit he was a widower.

"I thought it odd," said Sir George, "that the Queen's picture should hang on the side wall whilst another was over the chimney-piece, which was the place of honour, and asked Dizzy if they should not be changed. He smiled as he said, after a pause :

"'Well, her Majesty did me the honour of visiting me twice at Hughenden; but *she* did not make the suggestion !'

"He said it very sweetly. It was a gentle rebuke. I don't know how I came to make such a blunder."

There is another reading of the speech which I think he did not see.

III

Disraeli was always good to his Countess, who loved and admired him devotedly. She must, however, have been at times something of a trial to him, for she was outspoken in a way which must now and again have galled a man with his sense of humour; no man is insensitive to ridicule. One night at supper in the Beefsteak Room, a member of Parliament, who knew most things about his contemporaries, told us of one evening at a big dinner party at which Disraeli and Lady Beaconsfield were present. Some man had been speaking of a new beauty and was expatiating on her charms—the softness of her eyes, her dimples, her pearly teeth, the magnificence of her hair, the whiteness of her skin—here he was interrupted by a remark of Lady Beaconsfield made across the table :

" Ah ! you should see my Dizzy in his bath ! "

IV

James McHenry told me an anecdote of Disraeli which illustrates his astuteness in getting out of difficulties. The matter happened to a lady of his acquaintance. This lady was very anxious that her husband should get an appointment for which he was a candidate—one of those good things that distinctly goes by favour. One evening, to her great joy, she found that she was to sit at dinner next the Premier. She was a very attractive woman whom most men liked to serve. The opportunity was too good to lose, and as her neighbour " took " to her at once she began to have great hopes. Having " ground-baited " the locality with personal charm she began to get her hooks and tackle ready. She led the conversation to the subject in her mind, Disraeli talking quite freely. Then despite her efforts the conversation drifted away to something else. She tried again ; but when just close to her objective it drifted again. Thus attack and repulse kept on during dinner. Do what she would, she could not get on the subject by gentle

A STATESMAN'S DEFENCE

means. She felt at last that she was up against a master of that craft. Time ran out, and when came that premonitory hush and glance round the table which shows that the ladies are about to withdraw she grew desperate. Boldly attacking once more the arbiter of her husband's destiny, she asked him point blank to give the appointment. He looked at her admiringly; and just as the move came he said to her in an impressive whisper:

"Oh, you are a darling!"

V

Irving told me this:

He was giving sittings for his bust to Count Gleichen, who was also doing a bust of Lord Beaconsfield. One day when he came the sculptor, looking at his watch, said:

"I'm afraid our sitting to-day must be a short one—indeed it may be interrupted at any moment. You won't mind, I hope?"

"Not at all!" said Irving. "What is it?"

"The Premier has sent me word that he must come at an earlier hour than he fixed as he has a Cabinet Meeting." He had already unswathed the clay so as not to waste in preparation the time of the statesman when he should come. Irving was looking at it when something struck him. Turning to Count Gleichen he said:

"That seems something like myself—you know we actors have to study our own faces a good deal, so that we come to know them."

Just then Disraeli came in. When they had all shaken hands, the sculptor said to the new-comer:

"Mr. Irving says that he sees in your bust a resemblance to himself!"

Disraeli looked at Irving a moment with a pleased expression. Then he walked over to where Irving's bust was still uncovered. He examined it critically for a few moments; and then turning to Count Gleichen said:

"What a striking and distinguished physiognomy!"

XLVI

SIR WILLIAM PEARCE, BART.

A night adventure—The courage of a mother—The story of the " Livadia "—Nihilists after her—Her trial trip—How she saved the Czar's life

I

SIR WILLIAM PEARCE—made a Baronet in 1887—was a close friend of Irving. He was the head of the great Glasgow shipbuilding firm of John Elder & Co. In fact he *was* John Elder & Co. for he owned most of the whole great business. He was a " Man of Kent," which is a different thing from being a Kentish man. A Man of Kent is one born in the Isle of Thanet, where the old succession in cases of intestacy differs from the standard British law on the subject. He went to Glasgow as a shipwright and entered the works at Fairfield. He was a man of such commanding force and ability that he climbed up through the whole concern, right up to the top, and in time—and not a long time either for such a purpose—owned the whole thing. To him it is that we owe the great speed of ocean-going ships. For years all the great racers were built at his works on the Clyde. He also built many superb yachts, notably the *Lady Torfrida* and the *Lady Torfrida the Second*. The first-named was in his own use when we were playing in Glasgow in the early autumn of 1883. That provincial tour was a short one of six weeks previous to our leaving for America on our first Trans-Atlantic tour. We had commenced in Glasgow on 28th August. During the first week Irving, Loveday, and myself, and Ellen Terry, who had her little son with her, and one other young lady, Miss Macready, accepted Mr. Pearce's invitation to go on a week-end yachting tour, to begin after the play on the following Saturday night, 1st September.

II

The *Lady Torfrida* was berthed in the estuary of the Clyde off Greenock; so a little after eleven o'clock we all set off for Greenock.

It had been a blustering evening in Glasgow; but here in the open it seemed a gale. I think that the hearts of all the landsmen of our party sank when we saw the black water lashed into foam by the fierce wind. Pearce had met us at the station and came with us. Of the yachting party were his son the present Baronet, and a College friend of his, Mr. Bradbury. With the bluff heartiness of a yachtsman Pearce now assured us that everything was smooth and easy. At the stairs we found a trim boat with its oarsmen fending her off as with every rising wave she made violent dashes at the stonework. One of the men stood on the steps holding the painter; he dared not fasten it to the ring. From near the level of the water the estuary looked like a wide sea and the water so cold

MOTHERHOOD

and dark and boisterous that it seemed like madness going out on such a night in such a boat *for pleasure*. There were several of us, however, and we were afraid of frightening each other; I do not think that any of us were afraid for ourselves. Ellen Terry whispered to me to take her son, who was only a little chap, next to me, as she knew me and would have confidence in me.

We managed to get into the boat without any of us getting all wet, and pushed off. We drove out into the teeth of the wind the waves seeming much bigger now we were amongst them and out in the open Firth. Not a sign of yacht could be seen. To us strangers the whole thing was an act of faith. Presently Pearce gave an order and we burned a blue light, which was after a while answered from far off—a long, long distance off, we thought, as we looked across the waste of black troubled water looking more deadly than ever in the blue light—though it looked even more deadly when the last of the light fell hissing into the wave. By this time matters were getting really serious. Some one had to keep baling all the time, and on the weather side we had to sit shoulder to shoulder as close as we could so that the waves might break on our backs and not over the gunwale. It was just about as unpleasant an experience as one could have. I drew the lad next to me as close as I could partly to comfort him and more particularly lest he should get frightened and try to leave his place. And yet all the time we were a merry party. Ellen Terry with the strong motherhood in her all awake—a lesson and a hallowed memory—was making cheery remarks and pointing out to her boy the many natural beauties with which we were surrounded : the distant lights, the dim line of light above the shore line, the lurid light of the city of Greenock on the sky. She thought of only one thing, her little boy, and that he might not suffer the pain of fear. The place seemed to become beautiful in the glow of her maternity. He did not say much in answer—not in any enthusiastic way ; but he was not much frightened. Cold waves of exceeding violence, driven up your back by a fierce wind which beat the spray into your neck, make hardly a cheerful help to the enjoyment of the æsthetic !

Irving sat stolid and made casual remarks such as he would have made at his own fireside. His quiet calm, I think, allayed nervous tremors in some of the others. I really think he enjoyed the situation—in a way. As for Pearce, who held the tiller himself, he was absolutely boisterous with joviality, though he once whispered in my ear :

" Keep it up ! We will be all right ; but I don't want any of them to get frightened. It is pretty serious ! " I think we settled in time into a sort of that calm acceptance of fact which is so real a tribute to Belief. It certainly startled us a little when we heard a voice hailing us with a speaking trumpet—a voice which seemed close to us. Then a light flashed out and we saw the *Lady Torfrida* rising high from the water whereon she floated gracefully, just swaying with wave and wind. She was a big yacht with 600 h.p. engines, after the model of those of the *Alaska,* one of Pearce's building, then known as the " Greyhound of the ocean ! "

I think we were all rejoiced ; even Pearce, who told me before we went to our cabins in the early morning that all through that miserable voyage in the dark the sense of his responsibility was heavy upon him.

"Just fancy," he said, "if anything had happened to Irving or Ellen Terry! And it might have, easily! We had no right to come out in such a small boat on such a night; we were absolutely in danger at times!"

We were not long in getting aboard. The whole yacht seemed by comparison with the darkness we emerged from to be blazing with light and filled with alert, powerful men. We were pulled, jerked, or thrown on board, I hardly knew which; and found ourselves hurried down to our luxurious cabins where everything was ready for our dressing. Our things had fortunately been sent on board during the day; anything coming in the boat would have had a poor chance of arriving dry.

III

In a very short time we were sitting in the saloon, light and warm and doing ample justice to one of the most perfect meals I ever sat down to. It was now after one o'clock and we were all hungry. After supper we sat and talked; and after the ladies had retired we sat on still till the September sun began to look in through the silk curtains that veiled the ports.

Pearce was a man full of interesting memories and experiences, and that night he seemed to lay the treasures of them at the feet of his guests. But of all that he told—we listening eagerly—none was so fascinating as his account of the building and trial trip of the *Livadia*.

This was the great yacht which the Czar Alexander II. had built from the designs of Admiral Popoff of his own navy. It was of an entirely new pattern of naval construction : a turtle with a house on its back. The work of building had been entrusted to the Fairfield yard with *carte blanche* in the doing of it. No expense was to be spared in having everything of the best. Under the circumstances it could not be contracted for ; the builder was paid by a fixed percentage of the prime cost. The only thing that the builder had to guarantee was the speed. But that was so arranged that beyond a certain point there was to be a rising bonus ; the shipbuilder made an extra £20,000 on this alone. Pearce told us that it was the hope of the Czar to be able to evade the Nihilists, who were then very active and had attempted his life several times. The *Livadia* was really a palace of the sea whereon he could live in comfort and luxury for long periods ; and in which by keeping his own counsel he could go about the world without the knowledge of his enemies. It was known that the Nihilists regarded very jealously the building of the ship, and careful watch was kept in the yard. One day when the ship was finished and was partly coaled, there came a wire from the Russian Embassy that it was reported that there were two Nihilists in the shipyard. When the men were coming back from dinner, tally was kept at the gate where the Russian detectives were on watch. I have seen that return from dinner. Through the great gates seven thousand men poured in like a huge living

THE START

stream. On this occasion the check showed that *two men were missing*. The Nihilists also had their own Embassy and secret police!

It then became necessary to examine the ship in every part. Those were the days of the Thomassin " infernal machine," which was suspected of having been the means by which many ships had been sent to the bottom. These machines were exploded by clockwork set for a certain time, and were made in such fashion as would not excite suspicion. Some were in the form of irregularly shaped lumps of coal. The first thing to be done was therefore to take out all the coal which had already been put in. When the bunkers were empty and all the searchable portions of the ship had been carefully examined inch by inch, a picked staff of men opened and examined the watertight compartments. This was in itself a job, for there were, so well as I remember, something like a hundred and fifty of them. However, as each was done Pearce himself set his own seal upon it. At last he was able to assure the Grand Duke, who was in command and who had arrived to take the boat in charge, that she was so far safe from attack from concealed explosives. When she was starting the Grand Duke told Pearce that the Czar expected that he would go on the trial trip. In his own words:

" It is not any part of a shipbuilder's business to go on trial trips unless he so wishes. But in this case I could not have thought of refusing. The Czar's relations with me and his kindness to me were such that I could not do anything but what would please him!"

So the *Livadia* started from the Clyde with

sealed orders. Her first call was at Holyhead. There they met with a despatch which ordered an immediate journey to Plymouth. At Plymouth she was again directed with secret orders to go to Brest, whither she set out at once.

At Brest there was an " easy," and certain of the officers and men were allowed shore leave. The rest should have been for several days; but suddenly word was received to leave Brest at once; it was said that some suspected Nihilists were in the way. The men on shore were peremptorily recalled and in haste preparations were made for an immediate start for the south. Pearce's own words explain the situation :

" I went at once to the Grand Duke Nicholas and remonstrated with him. ' I can answer for the workmanship of the *Livadia*,' I said ; ' but the design is not mine, and so far as I know the principle on which she has been constructed has never been tested and there is no possibility of knowing what a ship of the pattern will do in bad weather, and that we have ahead of us. It is dirty now in the Bay and a storm is reported coming up. Does your Highness really think it wise to attempt the Bay of Biscay under the conditions ? ' To my astonishment not only the Grand Duke but some of his officers who were present, who had not hitherto shown any disposition to despise danger, spoke loudly in favour of going on at once. Of course I said no more. I had built the ship, and though I was not responsible for her I felt that if necessary I should go down in her. We had a terrible experience in the Bay, but got through safely to Ferrol. There she was laid up in a land-locked bay round

AN ESCAPE

the shores of which guards were posted night and day for months. It was necessary that she should lie up somewhere as the dock at Sebastopol—the only dock in the world large enough to hold her—was not ready.

"And whilst she lay there the Czar was assassinated, 13th March 1881."

IV

Then he went on to tell us how once already the *Livadia* had been the means of saving the Czar's life :

"When she was getting on I had a model of her made—in fact, two ; one of them," he said, turning to me, "you saw the other day in my office. These models are troublesome and costly things to make. The one which I intended as a present to the Czar cost five hundred pounds. It was my present to his Majesty on the twenty-fifth anniversary of his succession. It arrived the day before, 17th February—29th February old style. The Czar was delighted with it. That evening there was a banquet in the Winter Palace, where he was then in residence. He had been threatened for some time by means of a black-edged letter finding its way every morning into the Palace, warning him in explicit terms that if his oppression did not cease he would not live past the anniversary of his accession, which would be the following day. When he was leading the way to the dining-hall from the drawing-room he turned to the lady with him

—Princess Dolgoruki, his morganatic wife—and said :

"' By the way, I want to show you my new toy ! ' The model had been placed in the salon at the head of the grand staircase and they stopped to examine it.

"As they were doing so the staircase down which they would have been otherwise passing was blown up. The Nihilists knowing the exact routine of the Court and the rigid adherence to hours had timed the explosion for the passage of the staircase ! "

We spent a delightful Sunday going round Arran. We dined at anchor in Wemyss Bay and slept on board. On the forenoon of Monday we went back to Glasgow.

XLVII

STEPNIAK

A congeries of personalities—The " closed hand "—His appearance—" Free Russia"—The gentle criticism of a Nihilist—Prince Nicholas Galitzin—The dangers of big game

I

ON the evening of 8th July 1892, after the play, *Faust,* Irving had some friends to supper in the Beefsteak Room. I think that, all told, it was as odd a congeries of personalities as could well be. Sarah Bernhardt, Darmont, Ellen Terry and her daughter, Toole, Mr. and Mrs. T. B. Aldridge, of Boston, two Miss Casellas—and Stepniak. It was odd that the man was known only by the one name; no one ever used his first name, Sergius. Other men have second names of some sort; but this one, though he signed himself S. Stepniak, I never heard spoken of except by the one word. I sat next to him at supper and we had a great deal of conversation together, chiefly about the state of affairs in Russia generally and the Revolutionary party in especial. Hall Caine had been staying with me for a week, 20th to 27th June 1892, and he told me all about his coming journey to Russia. He had been studying the matter very carefully and trying to get back to the real cause of the " Exodus." To him it had begun in what was locally known as —the " closed hand." It was, so far as he could gather, on an economic basis. The Russian moujik was illiterate and as a rule a drunkard when he got the chance. In the endless steppes, which are so flat that the roads simply disappear on the horizon line, all the carriage of goods has to be by carts. There are no minor railways. The moujik with his load of corn would take his way to the nearest market centre and there stay in the tavern till he had drunk up all he had received for his crop. The Jew tavern-keeper was also the local usurer, and would make a certain advance on the man's labour for the coming year. When that credit had ended, since he never could get even, he would pledge the labour of his children. Thus after a time the children, practically sold to labour, would be taken away to the cities there to be put to work without remuneration. It was practically slavery. Then the Russian Government, recognising the impossibility of dealing with such a state of affairs, undertook to drive out the Jews altogether.

Such was the allegation made by the supporters of the Exodus, and there was at least a certain measure of truth in it. Caine had explained it all to me fully so that when I talked that night with Stepniak I had some foothold of information to rest on whilst I asked for more. He, who had presumably been in the very heart of the Revolutionary party and in all the secrets of Nihilism, told me some of his views and aspirations and those of the party— or rather the parties—of which he was a unit.

II

Stepniak was a very large man—large of that type that the line of the shoulders is high so that the bulk of the body stands out solid. He had a close beard and very thick hair, and strongly-marked features with a suggestion of the Kalmuck type. He was very strong and had a great voice. On 1st May of that year, 1892, I had heard him speak at the great meeting in Hyde Park for the "Eight-hour" movement. There were in the Park that day not far from a quarter of a million of people, so that from any of the tribunes—which were carts —no one could be heard that was not strong of voice. The only three men whom I could hear were John Burns, Stepniak, and Frederick Rogers—the latter a working bookbinder and President of the Elizabethan Society—also one of the very finest speakers—judged by any standard—I have ever heard.

In our conversation at supper that night he told me of the letters which they were receiving from the far-off northern shores of Siberia. It was a most sad and pitiful tale. Men of learning and culture, mostly University professors, men of blameless life and takers of no active part in revolution or conspiracy — simply theorists of freedom, patriots at heart—sent away to the terrible muddy shores of the Arctic sea, ill housed, ill fed, over worked—where life was one long, sordid, degrading struggle for bare life in that inhospitable region. I could not but be interested and moved by his telling. He saw that I was sympathetic, and said he would like to send me something to read on the subject. It came some weeks later, as the following letter will show :

<p style="text-align:center">"31 BLANDFORD ROAD,
"BEDFORD PARK, W.,
"<i>August</i> 2, 1892.</p>

"DEAR MR. STOKER,—It is a long time that I wanted to write to you since that delightful party at the Lyceum. But I was so busy, and the parcel I wanted to send to you for one reason or another could never be ready, and so it dragged on. What I send to you is the paper, *Free Russia*, I am editing. Since you have read all my books and have been so kind and indulgent for them, and so interested in the Russian Cause, I suppose you will be interested in the attempt to give a practical expression to English sympathies. Unfortunately the collection of *Free Russia* is incomplete (No. 1 is quite out of print). But what you will have is quite sufficient to give you an idea of the whole.

"May I ask whether you live permanently in London and whether I may hope to see you some day once again?—Yours very truly, S. STEPNIAK."

III

In February 1893 Stepniak saw Irving and Ellen Terry play in *King Lear*. The following excerpts are from a letter which he sent to Irving—a long letter of fourteen pages. I was so struck with it when Irving showed it to me that I asked leave to make a copy. Whereupon he gave me the letter.

This was after a habit of his of which I shall speak later. In the letter he said :

"The actor is a joint creator with the author—even with such an author as Shakespeare. He has a right of his own in interpretation, and the only point is

A GENTLE NIHILIST

how far he made good his claims, and that you have done to a wonderful extent. Yours was not acting: it was life itself, so true, natural and convincing was every word, every shade of expression upon your face or in your voice. The gradual transformation of the man, his humbling himself, the revelation of his better, sympathetic self—it was all a wonder of realism, nature and subtlety. Your acting reminded me of the pictures of the great Flemish master who seems to paint not with a brush but with a needle. Yet this astonishing subtlety was in no way prejudicial to the completeness and the power and masterliness of the great whole. . . . I cannot forbear from asking you to transmit my compliments and admiration to Miss Ellen Terry—if you think that she may care about such a humble tribute. There is a passage from ' I love your Majesty according to my bonds, not more or less ' and the following monologue, which I am bold enough to say are the weakest in the play: too cold and dry and forward and elaborate for Cordelia. But in her rendering there was nothing of that: it was all simplicity, tenderness, spontaneous emotion. The charm of her personality and character, which she has such a unique gift of infusing into everything, has partially improved the original text. I hope you will not consider my saying so too sacrilegious. There are spots upon the sun. And the scene in the French camp! Her ' No cause, no cause! ' was quite a stroke of genius. I would not believe before I saw her in that, that words can produce such an emotion."

And this was the man who stood for wiping tyrants from the face of the earth; who aided in the task, if *Underground Russia* be even based on truth. This gentle, appreciative, keenly critical, sympathetic man!

Strange it was that he who must have gone through such appalling dangers as beset hourly the workers in the Nihilist cause and come through them all unscathed was finally killed in the commonplace way of being run over by a train on the underground railway.

IV

It reminds me of another experience with Irving and a surprising *dénouement*. When we were in California in 1893 a gentleman called to see Irving at his hotel. He was a countryman of Stepniak, but of quite the opposite degree—a Prince claiming blood kin with the Czar, Nicholas Galitzin. He supped with Irving and some others, forty-five in all, at the Café Riche, 13th September, when he gave Irving a very charming souvenir in the shape of a gold match-box set with gems. Several times after we met at supper and came to be quite friends. Prince Galitzin was a mighty hunter and had slain much big game, including many bears and some grizzlies. He told us many interesting hunting adventures. He had lost one arm. He had not mentioned any adventure bearing on this, and one time Irving asked him if it was by a mischance in a hunting adventure that he had suffered the loss. He said with a laugh:

"No! No! Nothing of the kind. It was a damn stupid fellow who let a Saratoga trunk fall on me over the staircase of a hotel!"

XLVIII

E. ONSLOW FORD, R.A.

Fatherly advice—The design—The meeting—Sittings—Irving's hands

ONE morning—it was 12th January 1880—I got a note from Irving sent down by cab from his rooms. In it he said:

"There is a certain Mr. Onslow Ford coming to the theatre this morning. Please see him for me and give him some fatherly or brotherly advice."

I left word with the hallkeeper to send for me whenever the gentleman came. I did not know who he was or what he wanted: but I did know what "fatherly or brotherly advice" meant. At that period of his life the demands made on Irving's time were fearful. He used to get shoals of letters every day asking for appointments. Nearly all the writers wanted something—money, advice, free tickets, engagements for self or friend, to sell work of their own or of others, to read plays, to get him to sit for photographs, to ask him for sittings for pictures. There was no end to them; no limit to the range of their wants. Of all the classes three were naturally within the range of his own work: authors of plays, actors wanting engagements, artists of all kinds. Rarely indeed did any one of secured position come in that way; such usually sent letters of introduction. Even then they had in most cases to see me; it was a physical impossibility that Irving could give the time; rehearsals, production, and his work at night and in the day took up the whole possible working hours.

A little after noon I was sent for; the expected stranger had arrived. In those days the stage door in Exeter Street was very small and absolutely inconvenient. There was comfortable room for Sergeant Barry, the hallkeeper, who was a fine, big, bulky man; two in the room crowded it. Barry waited outside and I went in. The stranger was a young man of medium height, thin, dark haired. His hair rose back from his forehead without parting of any kind, in the way which we in those days associated in our minds with French artists. His face was pale, a little sallow, fine in profile and moulding; a nose of distinction with sensitive nostrils. He had a small beard and moustache. His eyes were dark and concentrated—distinctly "seeing" eyes. My heart warmed to him at once. He was young and earnest and fine; I knew at a glance that he was an artist, and with a future. Still I had to be on guard. One of my functions at the theatre, as I had come to know after a year of exceedingly arduous work, was to act as a barrier. I was "the Spirit that denies!" In fact I had to be. No one likes to say "no!"—a very few are constitutionally able to. I had set myself to help Irving in his work and this was one of the best ways I could help him. He recognised gratefully the utility of the service, and as he trusted absolutely in my discretion I gradually fell into the habit of using my own decision in the great majority of cases. " First fire ! Then enquire ! " was an old saying of an Irish sergeant instructing recruits on sentry duty. He was pretty right !

When Mr. Onslow Ford told me that he wished to make a statuette of Henry Irving as Hamlet I felt that the time for " advice " had come, and began to pave the way for a *non possumus* strong in intention though gentle in expression. The young sculptor, however, had thought the matter all over for himself. He knew the demands on Irving's time and how vastly difficult it would be to get sittings so many and so long as would be required for the work he had projected. I listened of course and thought better of him and his chance in that he knew his difficulties at the beginning.

Presently he put his hand in his pocket and took out something rolled in paper—a parcel about as big as a pork pie. When he had unrolled it he held up a rough clay model of a seated figure.

" This," said he, " is something of the idea. I have been several times in the front row of the stalls watching as closely as I could. One cannot well model clay in the stalls of a theatre. But I did this after the first time, and I have had it with me on each other occasion. I compared it on such opportunities as I had—you do keep the Lyceum dark all but the stage ; and I think I can see my way I don't want to waste Irving's time or my own opportunities if I am so fortunate as to get sittings ! "

That was the sort of artist that needed none of my " advice "—fatherly, brotherly, or otherwise. My mind was already made up.

"Would you mind waiting here a while?" I asked. In those early days we had only the one office and no waiting room except the stage. He waited gladly, whilst I went back to the Office. Irving had by this time arrived. I told him I had seen Mr. Ford.

"I hope you put it nicely to him that I can't possibly give him sittings," he said.

"That is why I came to see if you had arrived."

"How do you mean," he asked again. So I said:

"I think you had better see him, and if you think as I do you will give him sittings!"

"Oh, my dear fellow, I can't. I am really too pressed with work."

"Well, see him any way!" I said; "I have asked him to wait on purpose." He looked at me keenly for an instant as though I had somehow "gone back" on him. Then he smiled:

"All right. I'll see him now!"

I brought Onslow Ford. When the two men met, Irving *did* share my opinion. He did give sittings for a bronze statuette. The result was so fine that he gave quite another series of sittings for him to do the life-size marble statue of "Irving as Hamlet" now in the Library of the London Guildhall. It is a magnificent work, and will perhaps best of all his works perpetuate the memory of the great Sculptor who died all too young.

Irving gave many sittings for the statue. With the experience of his first work Onslow Ford could begin with knowledge of the face so necessary in portrait art. I often went with him and it was an intense pleasure to see Onslow Ford's fine hands

Henry Irving as Hamlet.
Marble Statue by E. Onslow Ford.
in the Guildhall.

at work. They seemed like living things working as though they had their own brains and initiation.

I was even able to be of some little assistance. I knew Irving's face so well from seeing it so perpetually under almost all possible phases of emotion that I could notice any error of effect if not of measurement. Often either Irving or Onslow Ford would ask me and I would give my opinion. For instance:

"I think the right jowl is not right!" The sculptor examined it thoughtfully for quite a while. Then he said suddenly:

"Quite right! but not in that way. I see what it is!" and he proceeded to add to the left of the forehead.

After all, effect is comparative; this is one of the great principles of art!

On 31st March last, one of the Academy view days of those not yet Royal Academicians, I went to Onslow Ford's old studio in Acacia Road, now in possession of his son, Wolfram the painter, to see his portrait of his beautiful young wife, the daughter of George Henschel. Whilst we were talking of old days he unearthed treasures which I did not know existed: casts from life of Henry Irving's hands.

No other such relics of the actor exist; and these are of supreme interest. Irving had the finest man's hands I have ever seen. Later on he sent me a cast of one of them in bronze; a rare and beautiful thing which I shall always value. Size, and shape, proportion and articulation were all alike beautiful and distinguished and distinctive. It would be hard to mistake them for those of any other man. With them he could *speak*. It was not possible to doubt the meaning which he intended to convey. With such models to work on a few lines of pencil or brush made for the actor an enlightening identity of character. The weakness of Charles I., which not all the skill of Vandyck could hide; the vulture grip of Shylock; the fossilised age of Gregory Brewster; the asceticism of Becket.

What, after the face, can compare with the hand for character, or intention, or illustration. It can be an index to the working of the mind.

XLIX

SIR LAURENCE ALMA-TADEMA, R.A.

"Coriolanus"—Union of the Arts—Archæology—The re-evolution of the toga—Twenty-two years' delay—Alma-Tadema's house—A lesson in care—"Cymbeline"

I

IN his speech at the close of the second "season" at the Lyceum, 25th July 1879, Irving announced amongst the old plays which he intended to do, *Coriolanus*. He never announced any play, then or thereafter, without having thought it well over and come to some conclusion as to its practicability. In this instance he had already made up his mind to ask Laurence Alma-Tadema to make designs for the play and to superintend its production. The experience of having a free hand in such matters, now that he was his own master in regard to stage productions, had shown to him the great possibilities of effect to be produced by the great masters of technique. There had in the past been great painters who had worked for the stage. Loutherbourg and Clarkson Stanfield, for instance, had made fame in both ways of picturesque art, the Gallery and the Stage. But the idea was new of getting specialists in various periods to apply their personal skill as well as their archæological knowledge to stage effect. Indeed up to that time even great painters were not always historically accurate. A survey of the work of most of the painters of the first half of the Victorian epoch will show such glaring instances of anachronism and such manifest breaches of geographical, ethnological, and technological exactness as to illustrate the extraordinary change for the better in the way of accuracy in the work of to-day. The National Gallery and Holland House have instances of errors in costumes incorrect as to alleged nationality and date. Irving wanted things to be correct, well knowing that as every age has its own suitabilities to its own need that which is accurate is most likely to convince. Alma - Tadema had made a speciality of artistic archæology of Ancient Rome. In working from his knowledge he had reformed the whole artistic ideas of the time. He had so studied the life of old Rome that he had for his own purposes reconstructed it. Up to his time, for instance, the toga was in art depicted as a thin linen robe of somewhat scanty proportions. Look at the picture of Kemble as Cato by Lawrence, or indeed of any ancient Roman by any one. Irving had become possessed of the toga of Macready, and anything more absurd one could hardly imagine; it was something like a voluminous night-shirt. Of course the audience also were ignorant of the real thing, and so it did not matter; the great actor's powers were unlessened by the common ignorance. In his studying for his art Alma-Tadema had taken from many statues and fragments the folds as well as the texture of the toga. With infinite patience he had gathered up details of various kinds, till at last, with a mind stored with knowledge, he set to himself the task of reconstruction; to restore the toga so that it would answer all the conditions evidenced in contemporary statuary. And the result? Not a flimsy covering which would have become draggle-tailed in a day or an hour of strenuous work; but a huge garment of heavy cloth which would allow of infinite varieties of wearing, and which would preserve the body from the burning heat of the day and the reacting chills of night. Even for the purposes of pictorial art the revived toga made a new condition of things, in all ways harmonising with the accepted facts. There is in record plenty of marble and stone work of old Rome; of work in bronze and brass and iron and copper; in silver and gold; in jewels and crystals—in fact in all those materials which do not yield to the ravages of time. All this Alma-Tadema had studied till he *knew* it. He was familiar with the kinds of marble and stone used in Roman architecture, statuary, and domestic service. The kinds of glass and crystal; of armour and arms; of furniture; of lighting; sacerdotal and public and domestic service. He knew how a velarum should be made and of what, and how adorned; how it should be put up and secured. He was learned of boats and chariots; of carts and carriages, and of the trappings of horses. Implements of agriculture and trade and manufacture and for domestic use were familiar to him. He was a master of the many ceremonial undertakings which had such a part in Roman life. . . . . In fact, Alma-Tadema's artistic reconstruction was like that of Owen; he reconciled fragments and brought to light proof of the unities and harmonies and suitabilities of ancient life.

II

Irving felt that with such an artist to help—archæologist, specialist, and genius in one—he would be able to put before an audience such work as would not only charm them by its beauty and interest them in its novelty, but would convince by its suitability. For there is an enormous aid to conviction in a story when those who follow it accept from the beginning in good faith the things of common knowledge and use which are put before them. I often say myself that the Faith which still exists is to be found more often in a theatre than in a church. When an audience go into a playhouse which is not connected in their minds with the habit of deceit they are unconsciously prepared to accept all things *ab initio* in the simple and direct manner of childhood. When therefore what they see is *vraisemblable*—with the manifest appearance of truth to something—all the powers of intellectual examination and working habit come into force in the right direction.

In that summer of 1879 when Irving announced *Coriolanus* he also announced several other plays.

It was not, of course, his intention to produce these plays all at once but one by one as occasion served. As has been seen, the putting on of *The Merchant of Venice* and its phenomenal success shelved or postponed most of the plays then announced; but Irving did not lose sight of *Coriolanus*. One morning in the following winter, whilst Sir Laurence Alma-

Tadema, as he has himself told me, was in his studio in his house at North Gate, Regent's Park, he heard the sound of sleigh bells coming over the bridge. Naturally his thoughts went back to *The Bells* and Irving, for no one who has seen the play can hear the sound unexpectedly without the thought. He heard the sound stop at his own gate; and whilst wondering what it could mean Irving was announced. He was accompanied by Mr. W. L. Ashmead Bartlett, who afterwards took his present name on his marriage to the Baroness Burdett-Coutts. Irving at once entered upon the subject of his visit; and the great painter was charmed to entertain it. As was usual with him when working on a new play, Irving had a rough scenario in his mind; and he and Alma-Tadema spoke of it then and there. Irving could tell him of the scenes he wanted and give some hints not only as to their practical use but of the ideas which he wished them to convey. When he had gone Alma-Tadema took down his Shakespeare and began his own study of the play. The continuous success of *The Merchant of Venice* gave him ample time, and his studies and designs were unique and lovely.

III

As we know, the production of *Coriolanus* did not take place till twenty-two years later; but all through 1880 and 1881 Alma-Tadema had the matter in hand. In those years the high policy of his theatre management was a good deal changed. When Irving had experience of Ellen Terry's remarkable powers and gifts he wisely determined to devote to them, so far as was possible, the remaining years of her youth. She had now been twenty-five years on the stage; and though she began in her very babyhood—at eight years old—the flight of time has to be considered, for the future if not for the past. She was now thirty-three years of age; in the very height of her beauty and charm, and to all seeming still in her girlhood. He therefore arranged *Romeo and Juliet* as the next Shakespearean production. This was followed in time by *Much Ado about Nothing; Twelfth Night, Olivia, Faust*—all plays that showed her in her brightness and pathos; and so *Coriolanus* was kept postponed. But well into 1881 it was still being worked on, and in those days I had many visits to the studio of Alma-Tadema. The house he then occupied was Townshend House, North Gate, Regent's Park, which he had so exquisitely fitted up after his previous home had been almost entirely destroyed by the blowing up of a barge carrying explosives on the Regent's Canal.

I have never forgotten — no one who had seen it could ever forget—that wonderful house; its windows of hammered bronze in Roman design, with panes of onyx and marble cut so thin as to be translucent, almost transparent; its dado rail of the Elgin marbles reproduced *in petto* in carved ivory; its tesselated floors, its wood carvings, its golden alcoves, its Chinese draperies, its Japanese bronzes. All the exquisite adornment and things of beauty with which a great and successful artist can surround himself in the many years of devotion to his art. It is surely no wonder that Alma-Tadema has prospered. Even with a lesser measure of genius than his, labour and application and such devotion to work could not but achieve success in so marked a degree.

IV

Let me give an instance of his thoroughness in his art work.

Once when in his studio I saw him occupied on a beautiful piece of painting, a shrub with a myriad of branches laden with berries and but few leaves, through which was seen the detail of the architecture of the marble building beyond. The picture was then almost finished. The next time I came I found him still hard at work on the same painting; but it was not nearly so far advanced. Dissatisfied with the total effect, he had painted out the entire background and was engaged on a new and quite different one. The labour involved in this stupendous change almost made me shudder. It needs but a small amount of thought to understand the infinite care and delicacy of touch to complete an elaborate architectural drawing between the gaps of those hundreds of spreading twigs.

V

This devotion to his art is often one of the touchstones of the success of an artist in any medium; the actor, or the singer, or the musician as well as the worker in any of the plastic arts.

I remember Irving telling me of a conversation

he had with the late W. H. Vanderbilt when, after lunch in his own house in Fifth Avenue, the great millionaire took him round his beautiful picture gallery. He was pointing out the portrait of himself finished not long before by Meissonier, and gave many details of how the great painter did his work and the extraordinary care which he took. Vanderbilt used to give long sittings, and Meissonier, to aid the tedium of his posing, had mirrors fitted up in such a way that he could see the work being executed. "Do you know," the millionaire concluded, " that sometimes after a long sitting he would take his cloth and wipe out everything he had done in the day's work. And I calculated roughly that every touch of his brush cost me five dollars ! "

VI

When in 1896 Irving produced *Cymbeline*, Alma-Tadema undertook to design and supervise the picturesque side ; or, as it was by his wish announced in the programme : " kindly acted as adviser in the production of the play."

He chose a time of England when architecture expressed itself mainly in wood ; natural enough when it was a country of forest. It is not a play allowing of much display of fine dresses, and Irving never under any circumstances wished a play to be unsuitably mounted. The opportunities of picturesque effect came, in this instance, in beautiful scenery.

L

SIR EDWARD BURNE-JONES, BART.

"King Arthur"—The Painter's thought—His illustrative stories from child life

I

It was to Irving an intense pleasure to work with Sir Edward Burne-Jones. The painter seemed to bring to whatever he had in hand a sort of concentration of all his great gifts, and to apply them with unsparing purpose and energy. His energy was of that kind which seems to accomplish without strenuous effort; after all it is the waste of force and not its use which proclaims itself in the doing. This man had such mighty gifts that in his work there was no waste; all the creations of his teeming brain were so fine in themselves that they simply stood ready for artistic use. His imagination working out through perfected art peopled a whole world of its own and filled that world around them with beautiful things. This world had been opened to Irving as to the rest of the world who admired it. But when the player came adventuring into it, the painter displayed to him a vast of hidden treasures. There was simply no end to his imaginative ideas, his artistic efforts, his working into material beauty the thoughts which flitted through his mind. As a colourist he was supreme, and he could use colour as a medium of conveying ideas to the same effect as others used form. His own power of dealing with the beauties of form was supreme.

To work with such an artist was to Irving a real joy. He simply revelled in the task. Every time they met it was to him a fresh stimulation. Burne-Jones, too, seemed to be stimulated; the stage had always been to him a fairyland of its own, but he had not had artistic dealings with it. Now he entered it with full power to let himself run free. The play which he undertook for Irving, *King Arthur*, was of the period which he had made his own: that mystic time when life had single purposes and the noblest prevailed the most; when beauty was a symbol of inner worth; when love in some dainty as well as holy form showed that even flesh, which was God's handiwork, was not base.

In the working out of the play each day saw some new evidence of the painter's thought; the roughest sketch given as a direction or a light to scene painter or property maker or costumier was in itself a thing of beauty. I veritably believe that Irving was sorry when the production of the play was complete. He so enjoyed the creative process that the completion was a lesser good.

Regarding human nature, which was Irving's own especial study, Burne-Jones had a mind tuned to the same key as his own. To them both the things which were basic and typal were closest. The varieties of mankind were of lesser importance than the species. The individual was the particular method and opportunity of conveyance of an idea;

A SEARCHING QUERY

and, as such, was of original importance. To each of the two great artists such individual grew in his mind, and ever grew ; till in the end, on canvas or before the footlights, the being lived.

II

It would be hard to better illustrate the mental attitude of both to man and type and individual than by some of the stories which Burne-Jones loved to tell and Irving to hear. The painter had an endless collection of stories of all sorts ; but those relating to children seemed closest to his heart. In our meetings on the stage or at supper in the Beefsteak Room, or on those delightful Sunday afternoons when he allowed a friend to stroll with him round his studio, there was always some little tale breathing the very essence of human nature.

I remember once when he told us an incident in the life of his daughter, who was then a most beautiful girl and is now a most beautiful woman, Mrs. J. W. Mackail. When she was quite a little girl, she came home from school one day and with thoughtful eyes and puckered brows asked her mother :

"Mother, can you tell me why it is that whenever I see a little boy crying in the street I always want to kiss him; and when I see a little girl crying I want to slap her ?"

III

Another story was of a little boy, one of a large family. This little chap on one occasion asked to be allowed to go to bed at the children's tea time, a circumstance so unique as to puzzle the domestic authorities. The mother refused, but the child whimpered and persevered—and succeeded. The father was presently in his study at the back of the house looking out on the garden when he saw the child in his little night-shirt come secretly down the steps and steal to a corner of the garden behind some shrubs. He had a garden fork in his hand. After a lapse of some minutes he came out again and stole quietly upstairs. The father's curiosity was aroused, and he too went behind the shrubs to see what had happened. He found some freshly turned earth, and began to investigate. Some few inches down was a closed envelope which the child had buried. On opening it he found a lucifer match and a slip of paper on which was written in pencil in a sprawling hand :

" DEAR DEVIL,—Please take away Aunt Julia."

IV

Another story related to a little baby child, the first in the household. There was a dinner party, and the child, curious as to what was going on, lay awake with torturing thoughts. At last, when a

AN OBEDIENT CHILD

favourable opportunity came through the nurse's absence, she got quietly from her cot and stole downstairs just as she was. The dining-room door was ajar, and before the agonised nurse could effect a capture she had slipped into the room. There she was, of course, made much of. She was taken in turn on each one's knees and kissed. Mother frowned, of course, but father gave her a grape and a wee drop of wine and water. Then she was kissed again and taken to the waiting nurse. Safe in the nursery her guardian berated her :

"Oh, Miss Angy, this is very dreadful. Going down to the dining-room!—And in your nighty!—And before strangers!—*Before gentlemen!* You must never let any gentleman see you in your nighty!—Never! Never! Never! Never! That is Wicked!—Awful!" And so on.

A few nights afterwards the father, when going from his dressing-room for dinner, went into the nursery to say another "good-night" to baby. When he went in she was saying her prayers at nurse's knee, in long night-robe and with folded hands like the picture of the Infant Samuel. Hearing the footstep she turned her head round, and on catching sight of her father jumped up crying: "Nau'ty—nau'ty—nau'ty!" and ran behind a screen. The father looked at the nurse puzzled :

"What is it, nurse?"

"I don't know, sir! I haven't the faintest idea!" she answered, equally puzzled.

"I'll wait a few minutes and see," he said, as he sat down. Half a minute later the little tot ran from behind the screen, quite naked, and running over to him threw herself on his knee. She snuggled in close to him with her arms round his neck, and putting her little rosebud of a mouth close to his ear whispered wooingly :

" Pap-pa, me dood girl now ! "

LI

EDWIN A. ABBEY, R.A.

*"Richard II."—" The Kinsmen "—Artistic collaboration
—Mediæval life—The character of Richard*

I

WHEN Irving was having the enforced rest consequent to the accident to his knee in December 1896, he made up his mind that his next Shakespearean production should be *Richard II*. For a long time he had had it in view and already formed his opinion as to what the leading features of such a production as was necessary should be. He knew that it could not in any case be made into a strong play, for the indeterminate character of Richard would not allow of such. The strong thing that is in the play is, of course, his suffering; but such when the outcome of one's own nature is not the same as when it is effected by Fate, or external oppression. He knew therefore that the play would want all the help he could give it. Now he set himself to work out the text to acting shape as he considered it would be best. Despite what any one may say to the contrary, and it is only faddists that say it, there is not a play of Shakespeare's which does not need arranging or cutting for the stage. So much can now be expressed by pictorial effect—by costume, by lighting and properties and music—which in Shakespeare's time had to be expressed in words, that compression is at least advisable. Then again, the existence of varied scenery and dresses requires time for changes, which can sometimes be effected only by the transposition of parts of the play. In his spare time, therefore, of 1897 he began the arrangement with a definite idea of production in 1899. When he had the general scheme prepared—for later on there are always changes in readings and minor details —he approached the man who in his mind would be the best to design and advise concerning the artistic side: Edwin A. Abbey, R.A.

II

Irving and Abbey were close friends; and I am proud to say I can say the same of myself and Abbey for the last twenty-five years. Irving had a great admiration for his work, especially with regard to Shakespeare's plays, many of which he illustrated for *Harper's Magazine*. The two men had been often thrown together as members of " The Kinsmen," a little dining club of literary and artistic men of British and American nationality. Abbey and George Boughton and John Sargent represented in London the American painters of the group. Naturally in the intimate companionship which such a club affords, men understand more of the wishes and aims and ambitions of their friends. Irving had instinctive belief that the painter who thought out his work so carefully and produced effects at once so picturesque and so illuminative of character would or might care for stage work where everything has to seem real and regarding which there must be an intelligent purpose somewhere. Irving, having already produced *Richard III.* with the limited resources of the Bateman days, knew the difficulties of the play and the effects which he wished to produce. When afterwards Abbey painted his great picture of the funeral of Henry VI., Irving recognised a master-hand of scenic purpose. Years afterwards when he produced the play he availed himself, to the best of his own ability and the possibilities of the stage, of the painter's original work. It was not possible to realise on the stage Abbey's great conception. It is possible to use in the illusion of a picture a perspective forbidden on the stage by limited space and the non-compressible actuality of human bodies.

When he came to think over *Richard II.*, he at once began to rely on Abbey's imagination and genius for the historical aspect of the play. He approached him ; and the work was undertaken.

III

Abbey has since told me of the delight he had in co-operating with Irving. Not only was he proud and glad to work with such a man in such a position which he had won for himself, but the actual working together as artists in different media to one common end was pleasure to him. Irving came to him with every detail of the play ready, so that he could get into his mind at one time both the broad dominating ideas and the necessary requirements and limitations of the scenes. The whole play was charted for him at the start. Irving could defend every position he had taken; knew the force and guidance of every passage; and had so studied the period and its history that he could add external illumination to the poet's intention.

In addition, the painter found that his own suggestions were so quickly and so heartily seized that he felt from the first that he himself and his work were from the very start prime factors in the creation of the *mise-en-scene*. In his own words :

" Irving made me understand him; and he understood me! We seemed to be thoroughly at one in everything. My own idea of the centre point of the play was Richard's poignant feeling at realising that Bolingbroke's power and splendour were taking the place of his own.

> "'O God! O God! that ere this tongue of mine,
> That laid the sentence of dread banishment
> On yon proud man, should take it off again
> With words of sooth! O, that I were as great
> As is my grief, or lesser than my name!
> Or that I could forget what I have been!
> Or not remember what I must be now!
> Swell'st thou, proud heart? I'll give thee scope to beat,
> Since foes have scope to beat both thee and me.'

" This seemed to be exactly Irving's view also —only that he seemed to have thought out every jot and tittle of it right down to the 'nth.' He had been working out in his own mind the realisation of everything whilst my own ideas had been scattered, vague, and nebulous. As we grew to know the play together it all seemed so natural that a lot of my work seemed to do itself. I had only to put down in form and colour such things as were requisite. Of course there had to be much consulting of authorities, much study of a technical kind and many evasive experiments before I reached what I wanted. But after I had talked the play over with Irving I never had to be in doubt."

To my humble mind this setting out of Abbey's experience—which is in his own words as he talked on the subject with me—is about as truthful and exhaustive an illustration of the purpose and process of artistic co-operation as we are ever likely to get.

IV

In his designs Abbey brought home to one the *cachet* of mediæval life. What he implied as well as what he showed told at a glance the conditions and restrictions — the dominant forces of that strenuous time: the fierceness and cruelty; the suspicion and distrust; the horrible crampedness of fortress life; the contempt of death which came with the grim uncertainties of daily life. In one of his scenes was pictured by inference the life of the ladies in such a time and place in a way which one could never forget. It was a corner in the interior of a castle, high up and out of reach of arrow or catapult; a quiet nook where the women could go in safety for a breath of fresh air. Only the sky above them was open, for danger would come from any side exposed. The most had been made of the little space available for the cultivation of a few plants. Every little "coign of vantage" made by the unequal tiers of the building was seized on for the growth of flowers. The strictness of the little high-walled bower of peace conveyed forcefully what must have been the life of which this was the liberty. It was exceedingly picturesque; a grace to the eye as well as an interest to the mind. There was a charming effect in a great copper vase in a niche of rough stonework, wherein blossomed a handful of marigolds.

V

In this play Irving was very decided as to the " attack." He had often talked with me about the proper note to strike at the beginning of the play. To him it was one of what should seem to be stately seriousness. In Richard's time the " Justice " of the King was no light matter; not to take it seriously was to do away with the ultimate power of the Monarch. Richard, as is afterwards shown, meant to use his kingly power unscrupulously. He feared both Bolingbroke and Norfolk, and meant to get rid of them. So meaning, he would of course shroud his unscrupulous intent in the ermine of Justice. A hypocrite who proclaims himself as such at the very start is not so dangerous as he might be, for at once he sounds the note of warning to his victims. This, *pace* the critics, makes the action of Bolingbroke simple enough. *He* saw through the weaker Richard's intent of treachery, and knew that his only chance lay in counter-treachery. A King without scruple was a dangerous opponent in the fourteenth century. It was not until Richard had violated his pledge regarding the succession and right of Lancaster—thus further intending to cripple the banished Duke—that the new Lancaster took arms as his only chance.

In Irving's reading of the character of Richard this intentional hypocrisy did not oppose his florid, almost flamboyant, self-torturing vapourings of his pain and woe. He is a creature of exaggerations of his own greatness, as of his own self-surrender.

As the production of the play progressed Irving began to build greater and greater hopes on it. Already when he was taken ill at Glasgow in 1898 he had expended on the scenery alone—for the time for costumes and properties had not arrived— a sum of over sixteen hundred pounds. It was a bitter grief to him that he had to abandon the idea of playing the part. But he still cherished the hope that his son Harry might yet play it on the lines he had so studiously prepared. To this end he wished to retain the freshness of Abbey's work, and when during his long illness, when another manager, believing that he intended abandoning the production, wished to secure Abbey's co-operation, the painter refused the offer so that Irving might later use the work for his son. Abbey, though no fee or reward for all his labour had yet passed, considered the work done as in some way joint property. This generous view endeared him more than ever to Irving, who up to the day of his death regarded him as one of the best and kindest and most thoughtful of his friends.

LII

J. BERNARD PARTRIDGE

Lyceum souvenirs—Partridge's method—" Putting in the noses "—The last picture of Irving

For a good many years Bernard Partridge was a *persona grata* at the Lyceum Theatre. He made the drawings of Irving and Ellen Terry for the souvenirs which we issued for the following plays, *Macbeth, The Dead Heart, Ravenswood, Henry VIII., King Lear, Becket,* and *King Arthur.* He has a wonderful gift of " remembering with his eyes." This was particularly useful in working any drawing of Henry Irving, whose expression altered so much when anything interested him that he became the despair of most draughtsmen. Partridge used to stand on the stage and watch him; or sit with him in his dressing-room for a chat. He would make certain notes with pen and pencil, and then go home and draw him. In the meantime Hawes Craven, the scene painter, would make sketches in monochrome of the scenes chosen for the souvenir, putting in the figures but leaving the faces vacant. Then would come Bernard Partridge with his own fine brushes and Hawes Craven's palette and put in the likeness of the various actors. These were so admirably done that any one taking up any of the souvenirs can say who were the actors—if, of course, the individuality of the latter be known to him. He used to laugh whenever I spoke of his "putting in the noses." Of course, the single figures were his own work entirely. I think in all the years of Irving's management Bernard Partridge was the only person outside the personnel of the company or staff who was allowed to pass in and out of the stage door just as he wished. He used to be present at rehearsals from which all others were forbidden.

Thus he came to have an exceptional knowledge of Irving's face in pretty well all its moods and phases. For this reason, too, the coloured Frontispiece of this book is of exceptional interest. It was the last work of art done from Irving before his death. Later on, he was, of course, photographed; the last sun picture done of him was of him sitting alongside John Hare, with whom he was staying at his place in Overstrand two months before he died. But Partridge's pastel was the last art study from life. On the evening of 17th July 1905 he was dining with Mr. and Mrs. Partridge in their pretty house in Church Street, Chelsea. Sir Francis and Lady Burnand were there and Anstey Guthrie, and Mr. Plowden, the magistrate. Irving enjoyed the evening much—one can see it by the happy look in his face. Partridge, in the fashion customary to him, made his "eye notes" as Irving sat back in his armchair with the front of his shirt bulging out after the manner usual to such a pose. Early next morning Partridge did the pastel.

To me it is of priceless worth, not only from its pictorial excellence, but because it is the last artistic record of my dear friend; and because it shows him in one of the happy moods which alas! grew rarer with his failing health. It gives, of course, a true impression of his age—he was then in his sixty-eighth year; but all the beauty and intelligence and sweetness of his face is there.

LIII

ROBERT BROWNING

Browning and Irving on Shakespeare—Edmund Kean's purse—Kean relics—Clint's portrait of Kean

It was quite a treat to hear Irving and Robert Browning talking. Their conversation, no matter how it began, usually swerved round to Shakespeare ; as they were both excellent scholars of the subject the talk was on a high plane. It was not of double-endings or rhyming lines, or of any of the points or objects of that intellectual dissection which forms the work of a certain order of scholars who seem to always want to prove to themselves that Shakespeare was Shakespeare and no one else— and that he was the same man at the end of his life that he had been at the beginning. These two men took large views. Their ideas were of the loftiness and truth of his thought ; of the magic music of his verse ; of the light which his work threw on human nature. Each could quote passages to support whatever view he was sustaining. And whenever those two men talked, a quiet little group grew round them ; all were content to listen when they spoke.

We used to meet Browning at the houses of George Boughton, the Royal Academician, and of

Arthur Lewis, the husband of Kate, the elder sister of Ellen Terry. Both lived on Campden Hill, and the houses of both were famous for hospitality amongst a large circle of friends radiating out from the artistic classes.

Robert Browning once made Irving a present which he valued very much. This was the purse, quite void of anything in the shape of money, which was found, after his death, in the pocket of Edmund Kean. It was of knitted green silk with steel rings. Charles Kean gave it to John Foster who gave it to Browning who gave it to Irving. It was sold at Christie's at the sale of Irving's curios, with already an illustrious record of possessors.

Irving loved everything which had belonged to Edmund Kean, whom he always held to be the greatest of British actors. He had quite a collection of things which had been his. In addition to this purse he had a malacca cane which had come from Garrick, to Kean; the knife which Kean wore as Shylock; his sword and sandals worn by him as Lucius Brutus; a gold medal presented to him in 1827; his Richard III. sword and boots; the Circassian dagger presented to him by Lord Byron.

He had had also two Kean pictures on which he set great store. One of large size was the scene from *A New Way to Pay Old Debts*, in which Kean appeared as Sir Giles. The other was the portrait done by George Clint as the study for Kean in the picture. This latter was the only picture for which Edmund Kean ever sat, and Irving valued it accordingly. He gave the large picture to the

Garrick Club ; but the portrait he kept for himself. It was sold at the sale of his effects at Christie's where I had the good fortune to be able to purchase it. To me it is of inestimable value, for of all his possessions Irving valued it most.

LIV

WALT WHITMAN

Irving meets Walt Whitman—My own friendship and correspondence with him—Like Tennyson—Visit to Walt Whitman, 1886—Again in 1887—Walt Whitman's self-judgment—A projected bust—Lincoln's life-work—G. W. Childs—A message from the dead

I

In the early afternoon of Thursday, 20th March 1884, I drove with Irving to the house of Thomas Donaldson, 326 North 40th Street, Philadelphia. We went by appointment. Thomas Donaldson it was who had, at the dinner given to Irving by the Clover Club on December 6, 1883, presented him with Edwin Forrest's watch.

When we arrived Donaldson met us in the hall. Irving went into the "parlour"; Hatton, who was with us, and I talked for a minute or so with our host. When we went in Irving was looking at a fine picture by Moran of the Great Valley of the Yellowstone which hung over the fireplace. On the opposite side of the room sat an old man of leonine appearance. He was burly, with a large head and high forehead slightly bald. Great shaggy masses of grey-white hair fell over his collar. His moustache was large and thick and fell over his mouth so as to mingle with the top of the mass of the bushy flowing beard. I knew at once who it was, but just as I looked Donaldson, who had hurried on in front, said :

"Mr. Irving, I want you to know Mr. Walt Whitman." His anxiety beforehand and his jubilation in making the introduction satisfied me that the occasion of Irving's coming had been made one for the meeting with the Poet.

When he heard the name Irving strode quickly across the room with outstretched hand. " I am delighted to meet you ! " he said, and the two shook hands warmly. When my turn came and Donaldson said " Bram Stoker," Walt Whitman leaned forward suddenly, and held out his hand eagerly as he said ·

"Bram Stoker—Abraham Stoker is it ? " I acquiesced and we shook hands as old friends—as indeed we were. " Thereby hangs a tale."

II

In 1868 when William Michael Rosetti brought out his Selected Poems of Walt Whitman it raised a regular storm in British literary circles. The bitter-minded critics of the time absolutely flew at the Poet and his work as watch-dogs do at a ragged beggar. Unfortunately there were passages in the *Leaves of Grass* which allowed of attacks, and those who did not or could not understand the broad spirit of the group of poems took samples of detail which were at least deterrent. Doubtless they thought that it was a case for ferocious attack;

as from these excerpts it would seem that the book was as offensive to morals as to taste. They did not scruple to give the *ipsissima verba* of the most repugnant passages.

In my own University the book was received with homeric laughter, and more than a few of the students sent over to Trübner's for copies of the complete *Leaves of Grass*—that being the only place where they could then be had. Needless to say that amongst young men the objectionable passages were searched for and more noxious ones expected. For days we all talked of Walt Whitman and the new poetry with scorn—especially those of us who had not seen the book. One day I met a man in the Quad who had a copy, and I asked him to let me look at it. He acquiesced readily :

"Take the damned thing," he said; "I've had enough of it!"

I took the book with me into the Park and in the shade of an elm tree began to read it. Very shortly my own opinion began to form; it was diametrically opposed to that which I had been hearing. From that hour I became a lover of Walt Whitman. There were a few of us who, quite independently of each other, took the same view. We had quite a fight over it with our companions who used to assail us with shafts of their humour on all occasions. Somehow, we learned, I think, a good deal in having perpetually to argue without being able to deny—in so far as quotation went at all events—the premisses of our opponents.

However, we were ourselves satisfied, and that was

much. Young men are, as a rule, very tenacious of such established ideas as they have—perhaps it is a fortunate thing for them and others; and we did not expect to convince our friends all at once. Fortunately also the feeling of intellectual superiority which comes with the honest acceptance of an idea which others have refused is an anodyne to the pain of ridicule. We Walt-Whitmanites had in the main more satisfaction than our opponents. Edward Dowden was one of the few who in those days took the large and liberal view of the *Leaves of Grass*, and as he was Professor of English Literature at the University his opinion carried great weight in such a matter. He brought the poems before the more cultured of the students by a paper at the Philosophical Society on May 4, 1871, on " Walt Whitman and the Poetry of Democracy." To me was given the honour of opening the debate on the paper.

For seven years the struggle in our own circle went on. Little by little we got recruits amongst the abler young men till at last a little cult was established. But the attack still went on. I well remember a militant evening at the " Fortnightly Club "—a club of Dublin men, meeting occasionally for free discussions. Occasionally there were meetings for both sexes. This particular evening— February 14, 1876—was, perhaps fortunately, not a " Ladies' Night." The paper was on " Walt Whitman " and was by a man of some standing socially; a man who had had a fair University record and was then a county gentleman of position in his own county. He was exceedingly able; a good scholar, well versed in both classic and English literature, and a brilliant humorist. His paper at the "Fortnightly" was a violent, incisive attack on Walt Whitman; had we not been accustomed to such for years it would have seemed outrageous. I am bound to say it was very clever; by confining himself almost entirely to the group of poems, "Children of Adam," he made out, in one way, a strong case. But he went too far. In challenging the existence in the whole collection of poems for mention of one decent woman—which is in itself ridiculous, for Walt Whitman honoured women—he drew an impassioned speech from Edward Dowden, who finished by reading a few verses from the poem "Faces." It was the last section of the poem, that which describes a noble figure of an old Quaker mother. It ends:

> " The melodious character of the earth,
> The finish beyond which philosophy cannot go, and does not wish to go,
> The justified mother of men."

I followed Dowden in the speaking and we carried the question. I find a note in my diary, which if egotistical has at least that merit of sincerity which is to be found now and again in a man's diary—when he is young:

"Spoke—I think well."

III

That night before I went to bed—three o'clock—I wrote a long letter to Walt Whitman. I had written to him before, but never so freely; my

431 Stevens st.
cor West.

Camden,
U.S. America, N. Jersey.
March 6/76

Bram Stoker,
 My dear young man,
  Your letters have been most welcome to me — welcome to me as Person & then as Author — I don't know which most — you did well to write to me so unconventionally, so fresh, so manly, & so affectionate, too. I too hope, (though it is not probable) that we shall one day personally meet each other. Meantime I send you my friendship & thanks.

 Edward Dowden's letter containing among others your subscription for a copy of my new edition has just been rec'd. I shall send the books very soon by express in a package to his address. I have just written to E. D.

 My physique is entirely shatter'd — doubtless permanently — from paralysis & other ailments. But I am up & dress'd, & get out every day a little — live here quite lonesome, but hearty, & good spirits. Write to me again.
     Walt Whitman

LETTER FROM WALT WHITMAN

letters were only of the usual pattern and did not call for answer. But this letter was one in which I poured out my heart. I had long wished to do so but was, somehow, ashamed or diffident—the qualities are much alike. That night I spoke out; the stress of the evening had given me courage.

Mails were fewer and slower thirty years ago than they are to-day. My letter was written in the early morning of February 15. Walt Whitman wrote in answer on March 6, and I received it exactly two weeks later; so that he must have written very soon after receipt of my letter. Here is his reply:

"431 STEVENS ST.   "CAMDEN, N. JERSEY,
"COR. WEST.   "U.S. AMERICA,
         "*March* 6, '76.

" BRAM STOKER,—My dear young man,—Your letters have been most welcome to me—welcome to me as a Person and then as Author—I don't know which most. You did well to write to me so unconventionally, so fresh, so manly, and so affectionately too. I, too, hope (though it is not probable) that we shall one day personally meet each other. Meantime I send you my friendship and thanks.

" Edward Dowden's letter containing among others your subscription for a copy of my new edition has just been recd. I shall send the book very soon by express in a package to his address. I have just written to E. D.

" My physique is entirely shatter'd—doubtless permanently—from paralysis and other ailments. But I am up and dress'd, and get out every day a little, live here quite lonesome, but hearty, and good spirits.— Write to me again.   WALT WHITMAN."

The books alluded to, which I received on 9th April, are the two volumes of the Centennial Edition of his poems. These were published by subscription as a means through which a party of friends could help him through a bad time.

In 1871 a correspondence had begun between Walt Whitman and Tennyson which lasted for some years. In the first of Tennyson's letters, July 12, 1871, he had said :—

> " I trust that if you visit England, you will grant me the pleasure of receiving and entertaining you under my own roof."

This kind invitation took root in Walt Whitman's mind and blossomed into intention. He was arranging to come to England, and Edward Dowden asked him to prolong his stay and come to Ireland also. This was provisionally arranged with him. When he should have paid his visit to Tennyson he was to come on to Dublin, where his visit was to have been shared between Dowden and myself. Dowden was a married man with a house of his own. I was a bachelor, living in the top rooms of a house, which I had furnished myself. We knew that Walt Whitman lived a peculiarly isolated life, and the opportunity which either one or other of us could afford him would fairly suit his taste. He could then repeat his visit to either, and prolong it as he wished. We had also made provisional arrangements for his giving a lecture whilst in Dublin ; and as the friends whom we asked were eager to take tickets, he would be assured of a sum of at least a hundred pounds sterling—a large sum to him in those days.

But alas!

> "The best laid schemes o' mice an' men
> Gang aft agley."

At the very beginning of 1873 Walt Whitman was struck down by a stroke of paralysis which left him a wreck for the rest of his days. He could at best move but a very little; the joys of travel and visiting distant friends were not to be for him.

IV

At the meeting in 1884 he and Irving became friends at once. He knew some at least of Walt Whitman's work, for we often spoke of it; I myself gave him a two-volume edition. Walt Whitman was sitting on a sofa and Irving drew up a chair, a large rocker, beside him. They talked together for a good while and seemed to take to each other mightily. Irving doubtless struck by his height, his poetic appearance, his voice, and breadth of manner, said presently:

"You know you are like Tennyson in several ways. You quite remind me of him!" Then knowing that many people like their identity to be unique and not comparable with any one else, however great, he added:

"You don't mind that, do you?" The answer came quickly:

"Mind it! I like it!—I am very proud to be told so! I like to be tickled!" He actually beamed and chuckled with delight at the praise. He always had a lofty idea of Tennyson and respect as well as love for him and his work; and he was hugely pleased at the comparison. He stood up so that Irving might gauge his height comparatively with Tennyson's.

Donaldson in his book on Walt Whitman, published after the Poet's death, wrote of the interview:

> "Mr. Whitman was greatly pleased with Mr. Irving, and remarked to me how little of the actor there was in his manner or talk. Frequently, after this, Mr. Whitman expressed to me his admiration for Mr. Irving, now Sir Henry Irving, for his gentle and unaffected manners and his evident intellectual power and heart."

Be it remembered that Walt Whitman was fond of the theatre and went to it a good deal before he was incapacitated by his paralysis; but he did not like the vulgarity of certain actors in their posing off the stage. In his day in parts of the Southern States—and even to this day with a certain class of actors in some places—a travelling company on its arrival had a "parade." They all had loud costumes for the purpose, and the whole company, men and women, would strut through the streets. It was most undignified, and naturally offended one who, like the Poet, had the real artistic sensitiveness. When he met the great actor with whose praise the whole country was then ringing and found that he was gentle and restrained and unassuming in manner the whole craft rose in his estimation.

When it came to my own turn to have a chat with Walt Whitman I found him all that I had ever dreamed of, or wished for in him: large-minded, broad-viewed, tolerant to the last degree;

incarnate sympathy; understanding with an insight that seemed more than human. Small wonder, I thought, that in that terrible war of '61–5 this man made a place for himself in the world of aid to the suffering which was unique. No wonder that men opened their hearts to him—told him their secrets, their woes and hopes and griefs and loves! A man amongst men! With a herculean physical strength and stamina; with courage and hope and belief that never seemed to tire or stale he moved amongst those legions of the wounded and sick like a very angel of comfort materialised to an understanding man. When it is remembered that in that awful war six millions of men went through the hospitals, when the calls for medical attendance and hospital accommodation could never be adequately answered, no wonder that men were grateful to one who devoted himself to helping not only their bodies but their minds. He *lived* amongst the suffering, distributing such comforts as were supplied to him by the charitable; writing letters to home for those who were helpless; sympathising, encouraging, spreading hope and comfort in the way only possible to one who walks in the steps of the Master!

To me he was an old friend, and on his part he made me feel that I was one. We spoke of Dublin and those friends there who had manifested themselves to him. He remembered all their names and asked me many questions as to their various personalities. Before we parted he asked me to come to see him at his home in Camden whenever I could manage it. Need I say that I promised.

V

It was not till after two years that I had opportunity to pay my visit to Walt Whitman. The cares and responsibilities of a theatre are always exacting, and the demands on the time of any one concerned in management are so endless that the few hours of leisure necessary for such a visit are rare.

At last came a time when I could see my way. On 23rd October 1886 I left London for New York, arriving on 31st. I had come over to make out a tour for *Faust* to commence next year. On 2nd November I went to Philadelphia by an early train. There after I had done my work at the theatre I met Donaldson, and as I had time to spare we went over to Camden to pay the visit to which I had looked forward so long.

His house, 328 Mickle Street, was a small ordinary one in a row, built of the usual fine red brick which marks Philadelphia and gives it an appearance so peculiarly Dutch. It was a small house, though large enough for his needs. He sat in the front room in a big rocking chair which Donaldson's children had given him; it had been specially made for him, as he was a man of over six feet high and very thick-set. He was dressed all in grey, the trousers cut straight and wide, and the coat loose. All the cloth was a sort of thick smooth frieze. His shirt was of rather coarse cotton, unstarched, with a very wide full collar open low—very low in the neck and fastened with a big white stud. The old lady who cared for him and nursed him had for him a manifest admiration. She evidently liked to add on her own account some little adornment; she had fastened a bit of cheap narrow lace on his wide soft shirt-cuffs and at the neck of his collar. It was clumsily sewn on and was pathetic to see, for it marked a limited but devoted intelligence used for his care. The cuffs of his coat were unusually deep and wide and were stuck here and there with pins which he used for his work. His hair seemed longer and wilder and shaggier and whiter than when I had seen him two years before. He seemed feebler, and when he rose from his chair or moved about the room did so with difficulty. I could notice his eyes better now. They were not so quick and searching as before; tireder-looking, I thought, with the blue paler and the grey less warm in colour. Altogether the whole man looked more worn out. There was not, however, any symptom of wear or tire in his intellectual or psychic faculties.

He seemed genuinely glad to see me. He was most hearty in his manner and interested about everything. Asked much about London and its people, specially those of the literary world; and spoke of Irving in a way that delighted me. Our conversation presently drifted towards Abraham Lincoln for whom he had an almost idolatrous affection. I confess that in this I shared; and it was another bond of union between us. He said:

" No one will ever know the real Abraham Lincoln or his place in history ! "

I had of course read his wonderful description of the assassination by Wilkes Booth given in his *Memoranda during the War*, published in the volume called *Two Rivulets* in the Centennial Edition of his works in 1876. This is so startlingly vivid that I thought that the man who had written it could tell me more. So I asked him if he were present at the time. He said :

"No, I was not present at the time of the assassination; but I was close to the theatre and was one of the first in when the news came. Then I afterwards spent the better part of the night interviewing many of those who were present and of the President's Guard, who, when the terrible word came out that he had been murdered, stormed the house with fixed bayonets. It was a wonder that there was not a holocaust, for it was a wild frenzy of grief and rage. It might have been that the old sagas had been enacted again when amongst the Vikings a Chief went to the Valhalla with a legion of spirits around him!"

The memory of that room will never leave me. The small, close room—it was cold that day and when we came in he had lit his stove, which soon grew almost red-hot; the poor furniture; the dim light of the winter afternoon struggling in through the not over large window shadowed as it was by the bare plane tree on the sidewalk, whose branches creaked in the harsh wind; the floor strewn in places knee-deep with piles of newspapers and books and all the odds and ends of a literary working room. Amongst them were quite a number of old hats—of the soft grey wide-brimmed felt which he always wore.

I was more interested than I can say and was loth to leave. I had to catch the 4.30 train to New York, there to meet General Horace Porter, with whom I was to travel that night to Boston, where he was to lecture at the Tremont Temple on " General Grant " to the Loyal Legion. We were to sup with the Loyal Legion afterwards. Donaldson and I had arrived at Mickle Street about three, and at four we left. I think Walt Whitman was really sorry to have us go. Indeed Thomas Donaldson describes the visit. I venture to give it *in extenso*, even at the cost of seeming vain. But I was and am proud of it—and I humbly think I have good reason to be :

" Mr. Bram Stoker, a man of intelligence and cultivation, having had the advantage of association with the most cultivated in all walks of contemporary English life, was at his best. Mr. Whitman was captivated. Mr. Stoker had previously met Mr. Whitman at my house in Philadelphia in 1884. We remained an hour, and then left in spite of his protest. Many days after this visit he referred to it by saying : ' And friend Stoker ; where is he now ? ' I replied, ' In Chicago.' [In this, by the way, Donaldson,'writing ten years after the event, made a slight error. We paid two visits together, 1886 and 1887—it is to the latter that Chicago referred.] ' Well, well ; what a broth of a boy he is ! My gracious, he knows enough for four or five ordinary men ; and what tact ! Henry Irving knows a good thing when he sees it, eh ? Stoker is an adroit lad, and many think that he made Mr. Irving's path, in a business way, a smooth one over here.' I replied ' Indeed ! ' ' I should say so,' was his answer. ' See that he comes over again to see me before he leaves the country. He's like a breath of good, healthy, breezy sea air.' "

I can only ask pardon for the quotation. But I think it justifies itself and bears out all that I have already said. It was contemporary and not even in my knowledge till Donaldson sent me his book in 1896.

VI

The opportunity for my next visit to Walt Whitman came in the winter of 1887 when we were playing in Philadelphia. On the 22nd December Donaldson and I again found our way over to Mickle Street. In the meantime I had had much conversation about Walt Whitman with many of his friends. The week after my last interview I had been again in Philadelphia for a day, on the evening of which I had dined with his friend and mine, Talcott Williams of the *Press*. During the evening we talked much of Walt Whitman, and we agreed that it was a great pity that he did not cut certain lines and passages out of the poems. Talcott Williams said he would do it if permitted, and I said I would speak to Walt Whitman about it whenever we should meet again. The following year, 1887, I breakfasted with Talcott Williams, 19th December, and in much intimate conversation we spoke of the subject again.

We found Walt Whitman hale and well. His hair was more snowy white than ever and more picturesque. He looked like King Lear in Ford Madox Brown's picture. He seemed very glad to see me and greeted me quite affectionately. He said he was "in good heart," and looked bright though his body had distinctly grown feebler.

I ventured to speak to him what was in my mind as to certain excisions in his work. I said:

"If you will only allow your friends to do this —they will only want to cut about a hundred lines in all—your books will go into every house in America. Is not that worth the sacrifice?" He answered at once, as though his mind had long ago been made up and he did not want any special thinking:

"It would not be any sacrifice. So far as I am concerned they might cut a thousand. It is not that—it is quite another matter:"—here both face and voice grew rather solemn—" when I wrote as I did I thought I was doing right and right makes for good. I think so still. I think that all that God made is for good—that the work of His hands is clean in all ways if used as He intended! If I was wrong I have done harm. And for that I deserve to be punished by being forgotten! It has been and cannot not-be. No, I shall never cut a line so long as I live!"

One had to respect a decision thus made and on such grounds. I said no more.

When we were going he held up his hand saying, "Wait a minute." He got up laboriously and hobbled out of the room and to his bedroom overhead. There we heard him moving about and shifting things. It was nearly a quarter of an hour when he came down holding in his hand a thin green-covered volume and a printed picture of himself. He wrote on the picture with his indelible blue pencil. Then he handed to me both book and picture, saying:

"Take these and keep them from me and Goodbye!"

The book was the 1872 edition of the *Leaves of Grass*—" As a Strong Bird on Pinions Free "—and contained his autograph in ink. The picture was a photograph by Gutekunst, of Philadelphia. On it he had written:

> *To*
> Bram Stoker.
> Walt Whitman.   Dec. 22, '87.

That was the last time I ever saw the man who for nearly twenty years I had held in my heart as a dear friend.

VII

When I had come to New York after my visit to Walt Whitman in 1886 I made it my business to see Augustus St. Gaudens, the sculptor, regarding a project which had occurred to me. That was to have him do a bust of Walt Whitman. He jumped at the idea, and said it would be a delight to him —that there ought to be such a record of the great Poet and that he would be proud to do it. I arranged that I should ask if he could have the necessary facilities from Walt Whitman. We thought that I could do it best as I knew him and those of his friends who were closest to him. I made inquiries at once through Donaldson, and when business took me again to Philadelphia, on 8th and 9th November, we arranged the matter. Walt Whitman acquiesced and was very pleased at the idea. I wrote the necessary letters and left addresses and so forth with St. Gaudens. He was at that time very busy with his great statue of Abraham Lincoln for Chicago. Incidentally I saw in his studio the life mask and hands of Lincoln made by the sculptor Volk before he went to Washington for his first Presidency. The mould had just been found by the sculptor's son twenty-five years after their making. Twenty men joined to purchase the models and present them to the nation. St. Gaudens made casts in bronze of the face and hands with a set for each of the twenty subscribers with his name in each case cut in the bronze. Henry Irving and I had the honour of being two of the twenty. The bronze mask and hands, together with the original plaster moulds, rest in the Smithsonian Institute in Washington with a bronze plate recording the history and the names of the donors. I felt proud when, some years later, I saw by chance my own name in such a place, in such company, and for such a cause.

Before leaving New York, which I did on November 1886, I saw a good many friends, and arranged with them that we should each pay a certain sum towards a fund which would at least defray out-of-pocket expenses of casting the bronze bust of Walt Whitman when St. Gaudens should have done it.

Unhappily, for want of time—for he was overwhelmed with work—and other causes, St. Gaudens could not get to Philadelphia for a long time. Then Walt Whitman got another stroke of paralysis early in 1888. Before the combination of possibilities came when he could sit to the sculptor and the latter could give the time to the work he died.

Happily he did not in the last years of his life want for anything. He earned enough for his wants, and if anything were lacking for comforts it came. He had good friends. In 1889 Irving sent him a cheque for which he was grateful. But there was one friend as willing as able to help; that was George W. Childs, owner and editor of the Philadelphian *Ledger*. He was always doing kind and generous things, and used to ask certain of his friends to suggest good cases for help. Once he asked me if there was anything of the kind which I wished him to do. This was in his office on December 14, 1887. Irving and I had been to see him. Irving stayed for only a short while, but I remained as I was going with Mr. Childs to lunch with "Tony" Drexel in the Bank parlour of his great bank in Chestnut Street. When he asked me if I wished him to do anything, I said:

"Yes, Mr. Childs, there is Walt Whitman! A lot of us are anxious about him for he is old and feeble and in bad health. Moreover, though he is not in want, he is poor. His needs are very small, but in his state of health they are likely to be continuous. We are all willing to help, but we are scattered about and may not know. It will be very good of you if you will have an eye on him." He was sitting down, but he rose up as he said very sweetly:

"Thank you very much, my dear Bram Stoker, for speaking to me about him. But be quite assured and easy in your mind. Walt Whitman will never want. That is already seen to." It was only after his death and Walt Whitman's that Donaldson, who looked after the Poet's affairs for him, knew that the $1200, which had relieved the mortgage on Whitman's house in Mickle Street, had been secretly paid by Mr. Childs.

Let me lay the memory of this kindness as a flower on the grave of a good man.

VIII

I was not in America between the spring of 1888 and the early fall of 1893 at which time Irving opened the tour in San Francisco. We did not reach Philadelphia till towards the end of January 1894. In the meantime Walt Whitman had died, March 26, 1892. On 4th February I spent the afternoon with Donaldson in his home. Shortly after I came in he went away for a minute and came back with a large envelope which he handed to me:

"That is for you from Walt Whitman. I have been keeping it till I should see you."

The envelope contained in a rough card folio pasted down on thick paper the original notes from which he delivered his lecture on Abraham Lincoln at the Chestnut Street Opera House on April 15, 1886.

With it was a letter to Donaldson, in which he said:

> "Enclosed I send a full report of my Lincoln Lecture for our friend Bram Stoker."

This was my Message from the Dead.

LV

JAMES WHITCOMB RILEY

Supper on a car—A sensitive mountaineer—" Good-bye, Jim "

IRVING, like all who have ever known him, loved the " Hoosier " poet. We saw a great deal of him when he was in London; and whenever we were in Indianapolis, to meet him was one of the expected pleasures. Riley is one of the most dramatic reciters that live, and when he gives one of his own poems it is an intellectual delight. I remember two specially delightful occasions in which he was a participant. Once in Indianapolis when he came and supped on the car with us whilst we were waiting after the play for the luggage to be loaded. He was in great form, and Irving sat all the time with an expectant smile whilst Riley told us of some of his experiences amongst the hill folk of Indiana where conditions of life are almost primitive. One tale gave Irving intense pleasure—that in which he told of how he had asked a mountaineer who was going down to the nearest town to bring him back some tobacco. This the man had done gladly; but when Riley went to pay him the cost of it he drew his gun on him. When the other asked the cause of offence, which he did not intend or even understand, the mountaineer answered :

A SENSITIVE MOUNTAINEER

"Didn't I do what ye asked me! Then why do you go for to insult me. I ain't a tobacker dealer. I bought it for ye, an' I give it to ye free and glad. I ain't sellin' it!"

The other occasion was a dinner at the Savoy Hotel, July 29, 1891, to which Irving had asked some friends to meet him. "Jamesy"—for so his friends call him—recited several of his poems, most exquisitely. His rendering of the powerful little poem, "Good-bye, Jim," made every one of the other eight men at the table weep.

LVI

ERNEST RENAN

Renan and Haweis—How to converse in a language you don't know

ON April 3, 1880, when we were playing *The Merchant of Venice,* Ernest Renan came to the Lyceum ; the Rev. H. R. Haweis was with him. At the end of the third act they both came round to Irving's dressing-room. It was interesting to note the progress through the long Royal passage of that strangely assorted pair. Haweis was diminutive, and had an extraordinary head of black hair. Renan was ponderously fat and bald as a billiard ball. The historian waddled along with an odd rolling gait, whilst the preacher, who was lame, hopped along like a sort of jackdaw. The conversation between Irving and Renan was a strange one to listen to. Neither knew the other's language ; but each kept talking his own with, strange to say, the result that they really understood something of what was said. When I was alone with Irving and remarked on it he said :

" If you don't know the other person's language, keep on speaking your own. Do not get hurried or flustered, but keep as natural as you can ; your intonation, being natural, will convey something. You have a far better chance of being understood than if you try to talk a language you don't know ! "

LVII

HALL CAINE

*A remarkable criticism—Irving and " The Deemster "—
" Mahomet "—For reasons of State—Weird remembrances
—" The Flying Dutchman "—" Home, Sweet Home "—
" Glory and John Storm "—Irving and the chimpanzee
—A dangerous moment—Unceremonious treatment of a
lion—Irving's last night at the play*

I

THE early relations between Irving and Hall Caine are especially interesting, considering the positions which both men afterwards attained. They began in 1874. On the 16th of October in that year Irving wrote to him a very kindly and friendly letter in answer to Hall Caine's request that he should allow his portrait to be inserted in a monthly magazine which he was projecting.

A fortnight later Hall Caine, as critic of the Liverpool *Town Crier*, attended the first night of *Hamlet* at the Lyceum—31st October 1874. His criticism was by many friends thought so excellent that he was asked to reprint it. This was done in the shape of a broad-sheet pamphlet. The critique is throughout keen and appreciative. The last two paragraphs are worthy of preservation :

> " To conclude.—Throughout this work (which is not confined to the language of terror and pity, the language of impassioned intellect, but includes also

the words of everyday life), every passage has its proper pulse and receives from the actor its characteristic mode of expression. Every speech is good and weighty, correct and dignified, and treated with feeling. The variety, strength and splendour of the whole conception have left impressions which neither time nor circumstance can ever efface. They are happy, indeed, who hear Hamlet first from Mr. Irving. They may see other actors essay the part (a very improbable circumstance whilst Mr. Irving holds his claim to it), but the memory of the noble embodiment of the character will never leave them.

"We will not say that Mr. Irving is the Betterton, Garrick, or Kemble of his age. In consideration of this performance we claim for him a position altogether distinct and unborrowed. Mr. Irving will, we judge, be the leader of a school of actors now eagerly enlisting themselves under his name. The object will be— the triumph of *mental* over *physical* histrionic art."

This critical forecast is very remarkable considering the writer's age. At that time he was only in his *twenty-second* year. He had been writing and lecturing for already some time and making a little place for himself locally as a man of letters.

Two years later they had a meeting by Irving's request. This was during a visit to Liverpool whilst the actor was on tour. There began a close friendship which lasted till Irving's death. Caine seemed to intuitively understand not only Irving's work but his aim and method. Irving felt this and had a high opinion of Caine's powers. I do not know any one whose opinions interested him more. There was to both men a natural expression of intellectual frankness, as if they held the purpose as well as the facts of ideas in common. The two men were very much alike in certain intellectual ways. To both was given an almost abnormal faculty of self-abstraction and of concentrating all their powers on a given subject for any length of time. To both was illimitable patience in the doing of their work. And in yet one other way their powers were similar: a faculty of getting up and ultimately applying to the work in hand an amazing amount of information. When Irving undertook a character he set himself to work to inform himself of the facts appertaining to it; when the time for acting it came, it was found that he knew pretty well all that could be known about it. Hall Caine was also a "glutton" in the same way. He absorbed facts and ideas almost by an instinct and assimilated them with natural ease. For instance, when he went to Morocco to get local colour before writing *The Scapegoat* he so steeped himself in the knowledge of Jewish life and ideas and ritual that those who read his book almost accepted him as an authority on the subject.

II

When Hall Caine published *The Deemster* in 1887 Irving was one of its most appreciative admirers. We were then on tour in America and he naturally got hold of the book a little later than its great and sudden English success. Still he read it unprejudiced by its success and thought it would make a fine play. When we got back to England early in April 1888, he took his earliest opportunity of approaching the author; but only to find that he had already entered into an arrangement with

Wilson Barrett with regard to dramatisation of the novel.

Irving's view of this was different to that of both Caine and Barrett. To him the dramatic centre and pivotal point of the play that would be most effective was the Bishop. Had the novel been available he would—Caine being willing to dramatise it or to allow it to be dramatised by some one else—have played it on those lines.

I think it was a great pity that this could not be, for Irving and Hall Caine would have made a wonderful team. The latter was compact of imagination and — then undeveloped — dramatic force. With Irving to learn from, in the way of acting needs and development, he would surely have done some dramatic work of wonderful introspection and intensity.—As he will do yet; though his road has been a rough one.

From that time on, Irving had a strong desire that Caine should write some play that he could act. Time after time he suggested subjects; theories that he could deal with; characters good to act. But there seemed to be always some *impasse* set by Fate. For instance, Irving had had for a long time a desire to act the part of Mahomet, and after the publication in France of the play on the subject by De Bornier it seemed to be feasible. Herein too came the memory of the promptings and urging of Sir Richard Burton of some three years before as to the production of an Eastern play. De Bornier's play he found would not suit his purpose; so he suggested to Hall Caine that he should write one on the subject. Caine jumped at the idea—he too had a desire to deal with an

A MEMORY

Eastern theme. He thought the matter out, and had before long evolved a scenario. Well do I remember the time he put it before me. At that time he was staying with me, and on the afternoon of Sunday, January 26, 1890, he said he would like to give his idea of the play. He had already had a somewhat trying morning, for he had made an appointment with an interviewer and had had a long meeting with him. Work, however, was—is—always a stimulant to Hall Caine. The use of his brain seems to urge and stimulate it "as if increase of appetite had grown by what it fed on." Now in the dim twilight of the late January afternoon, sitting in front of a good fire of blazing billets of old ship timber, the oak so impregnated with salt and saltpetre that the flames leaped in rainbow colours, he told the story as he saw it. Hall Caine always knows his work so well and has such a fine memory that he never needs to look at a note. That evening he was all on fire. His image rises now before me. He sits on a low chair in front of the fire; his face is pale something waxen-looking in the changing blues of the flame. His red hair, fine and long, and pushed back from his high forehead, is so thin that through it as the flames leap we can see the white line of the head so like to Shakespeare's. He is himself all aflame. His hands have a natural eloquence—something like Irving's; they foretell and emphasise the coming thoughts. His large eyes shine like jewels as the firelight flashes. Only my wife and I are present, sitting like Darby and Joan at either side of the fireplace. As he goes on he gets more and more afire till at the last he is like a living flame. We sit quite still; we fear to interrupt him. The end of his story leaves us fired and exalted too. . . .

He was quite done up; the man exhausts himself in narrative as I have never seen with any one else. Indeed when he had finished a novel he used to seem as exhausted as a woman after childbirth. At such times he would be in a terrible state of nerves—trembling and sleepless. At that very time he had not quite got through the nervous crisis after the completion of *The Bondman*. At such times everything seemed to worry him; things that he would shortly after laugh at. This is part of the penalty that genius pays to great effort.

III

The next day, January 27, 1890, in the office at the Lyceum, Caine told—not read—to Irving the story of his play on Mahomet. Irving was very pleased with it, and it was of course understood that Caine was to go on and carry out the idea. He set to work on it with his usual fiery energy, and in a few months had evolved a scenario so complete that it was a volume in itself. By this time it was becoming known that Irving had in mind the playing of Mahomet. The very fact of approaching De Bornier regarding his play had somehow leaked out. As often happens in matters theatrical there came a bolt from the blue. None of us had the slightest idea that there *could* be any objection in a professedly Christian nation to a play on the subject. A letter was received from the Lord Chamberlain's department, which controls the

THE EMPIRE AND THE STAGE

licences of theatres and plays, asking that such a play should not be undertaken. The reason given was that protest had been made by a large number of our Mahometan fellow-subjects. The Mahometan faith holds it sacrilege to represent in any form the image of the Prophet. The Lord Chamberlain's department does its spiriting very gently; all that those in contact with it are made aware of is the velvet glove. But the steel hand works all the same—perhaps better than if stark. It is an understood thing that the Lord Chamberlain's request is a command in matters under his jurisdiction. Britain with her seventy millions of Mahometan subjects does not wish—and cannot afford—to offend their sensibilities for the sake of a stage play. Irving submitted gracefully at once, of course. Caine was more than nice on the matter; he refused to accept fee or reward of any kind for his work. He simply preserved his work by privately printing, three years later, the scenario as a story in dramatic form. He altered it sufficiently to change the personnel of the time and place of Mahomet, laying the story of *The Mahdi* in modern Morocco.

This was not Irving's first experience of the action on a political basis of the Lord Chamberlain. I shall have something to say of it when treating of Frank Marshall's play, *Robert Emmett*.

IV

During the visit to me in Edinburgh in 1891 Irving and Caine saw much of one another. On the 18th we took supper with Dr. Andrew Wilson, an old friend of us all, at the Northern Club. That night both Irving and Caine were in great form and the conversation was decidedly interesting. It began with a sort of discussion about Shakespeare as a dramatist—on the working side ; his practical execution of his own imaginative intention. Hall Caine held that Shakespeare would not have put in his plays certain descriptions if he had had modern stage advantages to explain without his telling. Irving said that it would be good for moderns if they would but take Shakespeare's lesson in this matter. Later on the conversation tended towards weird subjects. Caine told of seeing in a mirror a reflection not his own. Irving followed by telling us of his noticing an accidental effect in a mirror, which he afterwards used in the *Macbeth* ghost : that of holding the head up. The evening was altogether a fascinating one ; it was four o'clock when we broke up.

V

On November 19, 1892, Hall Caine supped with Irving in the Beefsteak Room, bringing his young son Ralph with him. The only other guest was Sir (then Mr.) Alexander Mackenzie. It was a delightful evening, a long, pleasant, home-like chat. Irving was very quiet and listened attentively to all Caine said. The latter told us the story of the novel he had just then projected. The scene was to be laid in Cracow to which he was shortly to make his way.

Irving was hugely interested. Any form of oppression was noxious to him; and certainly the Jewish "Exodus" that was just then going on came under that heading. I think that he had in his mind the possibilities of a new and powerful play. As I said he was most anxious to have a play by Hall Caine, and after the abortive attempt at Mahomet, he was more set on it than ever.

He had before this suggested to Caine that he should do a play on the subject of the "Flying Dutchman." The play which he had done in 1878, *Vanderdecken*, was no good as a play, though he played in it admirably. For my own part I believed in the subject and always wanted him to try it again—the play, of course, being tinkered into something like good shape, or a new play altogether written. The character, as Irving created it, was there fit for any setting; and so long as the play should be fairly sufficient the result ought to be good. Irving had a great opinion of Caine's imagination, and always said that he would write a great work of weirdness some day. He knew already his ability and his fire and his zeal. He believed also in the convincing force of the man.

VI

In 1894 Hall Caine wrote a poem called *The Demon Lover*, in which he found material for a play. He made a scenario, which he told rather than read to Irving after supper in the Beefsteak Room on St. Valentine's day of the next year, 1895. Irving was much impressed by it but thought that the part would of necessity be too young for him—he was then fifty-six. He asked Caine again to try the "Flying Dutchman."

In the June of next year 1896 we were in Manchester in the course of a tour. Hall Caine came over from the Isle of Man to stay with me, bringing with him the scenario of a play on the "Flying Dutchman" and also the scenario of a new play which he had just completed, *Home, Sweet Home*. He read, or rather told, me the latter with the MS. open before him. He never, however, turned the pages! The next forenoon we went by previous arrangement to Irving's rooms at the Queen's Hotel. There he read—or told from his script—the scenario of his play on the "Flying Dutchman." We discussed it then, and afterwards during a carriage drive, Irving asked Caine if he could not make the character of Vanderdecken more sympathetic and less brutal at the start. Caine having promised to go into this and see what he could do, then told the story of *Home, Sweet Home*. Irving feared from the description that the play would not do for him. In Act I. the character was too young; in Act II. too rough; and in Act III. too tall. For his objection in the last case he gave a reason, enlightening in the matter of stage craft:

"There is no general sympathy on the stage for tall old men!"

Finally Caine told us the story of his coming novel, which was afterwards called *The Christian*. He knew it in his own mind by the tentative title which he used, "Glory and John Storm."

VII

In the afternoon we all went to the Bellevue Gardens to see a wonderful chimpanzee, "Jock," a powerful animal and more clever even than "Sally," who was then the great public pet at the "Zoo" in Regent's Park. Ellen Terry came with us and also Comyns Carr, who had arrived from London. Jock was certainly an abnormal brute. He rode about the grounds on a tricycle of his own! He ate his food from a plate with knife and fork and spoon! He slept in a bed with sheets and blankets! He smoked cigarettes! And he drank wine—when he could get it! His favourite tipple was port wine and lemonade, and he was very conservative in his rights regarding it. Indeed in this case it was very nearly productive of a grim tragedy.

We went into a little room close to the keeper's house; a sort of general refreshment room with wooden benches round it and a table in the centre. Jock had his cigarette; then his grog was mixed to his great and anxious interest. The keeper handed him the tumbler, which he held tight in both hands whilst he went through some hanky-panky pantomime of thanks—usually, I took it, productive of pennies. Irving said to the keeper:

"Would he give you some of that, now?" The man shook his head as he answered:

"He doesn't like to, but he will if I ask him. I have to be careful though." He asked Jock, who very unwillingly let him take the tumbler, following it with his hands. The arms stretched out as it went farther from him; but the hands always remained close to the glass. The man just put the edge of the glass to his mouth and then handed it back quickly. The monkey had acted with considerable self-restraint, and looked immensely relieved when he had his drink safe back again. Then Irving said :

"Let me see if he will let me have some!" The keeper spoke to the monkey, keeping his eye fixedly on him. Irving took the glass from his manifestly unwilling hands and raised it to his own lips. Being a better actor than the keeper he did his part more realistically, actually letting the liquid rise over his shut lips.

The instant the monkey saw his beloved liquor touch the mouth he became a savage—a veritable, red-eyed, restrainless demon. With a sudden hideous screech he dashed out his arms, one of them catching Irving by the throat, the other seizing the glass. It made us all gasp and grow pale. The brute was so strong and so savage that it might have torn out his windpipe before a hand could have been raised. Fortunately Irving did instinctively the only thing that could be done; he yelled just as suddenly in the face of the monkey—an appalling yell which seemed to push the brute back. At the same moment he thrust away from him the glass in the animal's other paw. The monkey, loosing its hold on his throat, jumped back across the wide table with incredible quickness without losing its seated attitude, and sat clutching the tumbler close to his breast and showing his teeth whilst he manifested his rage in a hideous trumpeting.

Before that, at our first coming into the room he had nearly frightened the life out of Ellen

Terry. She had sat down on the bench along the wall. The monkey looked at her and seemed attracted by her golden hair. He came and sat by her on the bench and, turning over, laid his head in her lap, looking up at her and at the same time putting up his paw as big as a man's hand and as black and shiny as though covered with an undertaker's funeral glove. She looked down, saw his eyes, and with a scream made a jump for the doorway. The monkey laughed. He had a sense of humour—of his own kind, which was not of a high kind.

A little later he regained his good temper and forgave us all. When we went round the gardens he got on his tricycle and came with us. In the monkey house was a great cage as large as an ordinary room, and here were a large number of monkeys of a mixed kind. Our gorilla—for such he really was—started to amuse himself with them. He got a great stick and standing close to the cage hammered furiously at the bars, all the while trumpeting horribly. In the midst of it he would look round at us with a grin, as much as to say:

"See how I am frightening these inferior creatures!" They were in an agony of fear, crouching in the farthest corners of the great cage, moaning and shivering.

VIII

Irving had had an incident with a monkey some years before. On June 16, 1887, we went to Stratford-on-Avon, where he was to open a fountain the next day. We stayed with Mr. C. E. Flower, at Avonbank, his beautiful place on the river. In his conservatory was a somewhat untamed monkey; not a very large one, but with anger enough for a wilderness of monkeys. Frank Marshall, who was of our party, would irritate the monkey when we went to smoke in there after dinner. It got so angry with his puffing his smoke at it that it shook the cage to such an extent that we thought it would topple over. We persuaded Marshall to come away alone, and then Irving, who loved animals, went over to pacify the monkey. The latter, however, did not discriminate between malice and good intent, and when Irving bent down to say soothing things to it a long arm flashed out and catching him by the hair began to drag his head towards the cage, the other paw coming out towards his eyes. It was an anxious moment; but this time, as on the later occasion, a sudden screech of full lung power from the actor frightened the monkey into releasing him.

IX

Irving loved all animals, and did not, I think, realise the difference between pets and *feræ naturæ*. I remember once at Baltimore — it was the 1st January 1900—when he and I went to Hagenbach's menagerie which was then in winter quarters. The hall was a big one, the shape of one of those great panorama buildings which used to be so popular in America. There were some very fine lions; and to one of them he took a great fancy.

UNCEREMONIOUS TREATMENT

It was a fine African, young and in good condition with magnificent locks and whiskers and eyebrows, and whatsoever beauties on a hairy basis there are to the lion kind. It was sleeping calmly in its cage with its head up against the bars. The keeper recognised Irving and came up to talk and explain things very eagerly. Irving asked him about the lion; if it was good-tempered and so forth. The man said it was a very good-tempered animal, and offered to make him stand up and show himself off. His method of doing so was the most unceremonious thing of the kind I ever saw, it showed absolutely no consideration whatever for the lion's *amour-propre* or fine feelings. He caught up a broom that leaned against the cage—a birch broom with the business end not of resilient twigs but of thin branches cut off with a sharp knife. It was the sort of scrubbing broom that would take the surface off an ordinary deal flooring. This he seized and drove it with the utmost violence in his power right into the animal's face. I should have thought that no eye could have escaped from such an attack. He repeated the assault as often as there was time before the lion had risen and jumped back.

Irving was very indignant, and spoke out his mind very freely. The keeper answered him very civilly indeed I thought. His manner was genuinely respectful as he said:

"That's all very well, Mr. Irving. But it doesn't work with lions! There's only one thing that such animals respect; and that's force. Why, that treatment that you complain of will save my life some day. It wouldn't be worth a week's purchase without it!"

Irving realised the justice of his words—he was always just; and when we came away the gratuity was perhaps a little higher than usual, to compensate for any injured feelings.

X

"The Flying Dutchman" play never, I am sorry to say, materialised. *The Christian* and *The Eternal City* and *The Prodigal Son*, together with his plays, kept Hall Caine busy. As for Irving, his work and the two illnesses in 1897 and 1898 allowed no opportunity for new work other than that to which he was committed. The two men were, however, close friends and met on every possible occasion. One of the last plays—if not the very last—that Irving went to see was *The Prodigal Son* at Drury Lane. He was very pleased with George Alexander, who played the part of Oscar. He said to me, when we met after his seeing it :

"From an actor's point of view he was all-important. He kept the play together!"

He did not mean that the play was loose-knit or disjointed. It was a purely professional criticism, from the acting side. It is possible in any play for an actor or a group of them to let a play lose interest; others can keep it moving and so sustain the interest of the audience.

LVIII

IRVING AND DRAMATISTS

Difficulty of getting plays—The sources—Actor as collaborator—A startled dramatist—Plays bought but not produced—Pinero

I

ONLY those who are or have been concerned in theatrical management can have the least idea of the difficulty of obtaining plays suitable for acting. There are plenty of plays to be had. When any one goes into management—indeed from the time the fact of his intention is announced—plays begin to rain in on him. All those rejected consistently throughout a generation are tried afresh on the new victim, for the hope of the unacted dramatist never dies. There is just a sufficient percentage of ultimate success in the case of long-neglected plays to obviate despair. Every one who writes a play sends it on and on to manager after manager. When a player makes some abnormal success every aspirant to dramatic fame tries his hand at a play for him. It is all natural enough. The work is congenial, and the rewards—when there are rewards—are occasionally great. There is, I suppose, no form of literary work which seems so easy and is so difficult—which while seeming to only require the common knowledge of life, needs in reality great technical knowledge and skill. From the experience alone which we had in the Lyceum one might well have come to the conclusion that to write a play of some kind is an instinct of human nature. To Irving were sent plays from every phase and condition of life. Not only from writers whose work lay in other lines of effort; historians, lyric poets, divines from the curate to the bishop, but from professional men, merchants, manufacturers, traders, clerks. He has had them sent by domestic servants, and from as far down the social scale as a workhouse boy.

But from all these multitudinous and varied sources we had very few plays indeed which afforded even a hope or promise. Irving was always anxious for good plays, and spared neither trouble nor expense to get them. Every play that was sent was read and very many commissions were given and purchase money or advance fees paid. In such cases subjects were often suggested, scenario being the basis. In addition to the plays, in which he or Ellen Terry took part, which he produced during his own management he purchased or paid fees or options on twenty-seven plays. Not one of these, from one cause or another could he produce. One of these made success with another man. Some never got beyond the scenario stage. In one case, though the whole purchase money was paid in advance, the play was never delivered; it was finished—and then sold under a different title to another manager! One was prohibited—by request—by the Lord Chamberlain's department. Of this play, *Robert Emmett*, were some interesting memories.

II

In Ireland or by Irish people it had often been suggested to Irving that he should present Robert Emmett in a play. He bore a striking resemblance to the Irish patriot—a glance at any of the portraits would to any one familiar with Irving's identity be sufficient; and his story was full of tragic romance. From the first Irving was taken with the idea and had the character in his mind for stage use. In the first year of his management he suggested the theme to Frank A. Marshall, the dramatist; who afterwards co-operated with him in the editorship of the " Irving " Shakespeare. He was delighted with the idea, became full of it, and took the work in hand. In the shape of a scenario it was so far advanced that at the end of the second season Irving was able to announce it as one of the forthcoming plays. As we know the extraordinary success of *The Merchant of Venice* postponed the work then projected for more than a year. Marshall, therefore, took his work in a more leisurely fashion, and it was not till the autumn of 1881 that the play appeared in something like its intended shape. But by that time *Romeo and Juliet* was in hand and a full year elapsed before *Robert Emmett* could be practically considered. But when that time came the Irish question was acute. Fenianism or certain of its *sequelæ* became recrudescent. The government of the day considered that so marked and romantic a character as Robert Emmett, and with such political views portrayed so forcibly and so picturesquely as would be the case with Irving, might have a dangerous effect on a people seething in revolt. Accordingly a " request " came through the Lord Chamberlain's department that Mr. Irving would not proceed with the production which had been announced. Incidentally I may say that nothing was mentioned in the " request " regarding the cost incurred. Irving had already paid to Frank Marshall a sum of £450.

In the early stages of the building up of the play there was an interesting occurrence which illustrates the influence of the actor on the author, especially when he is a good stage manager. One night Marshall came to supper in the room which antedated the Beefsteak Room for that purpose. The occasion was to discuss the scenario which had by then been enlarged to proportions comprehensive of detail—not merely the situations but the working of them out. Only the three of us were present. We were all familiar with the work so far as it was done ; for not only used Marshall to send Irving a copy of each act and scene of the scenario as he did it, but he used very often to run in and see me and consult about it. I would then tell Irving at a convenient opportunity and when next the author came I would go over with him Irving's comments and suggestions. This night we all felt to be a crucial one. The play had gone on well through its earlier parts ; indeed it promised to be a very fine play. But at the point it had then reached it halted a little. The scene was in Dublin during a phase or wave of discontent even with the " patriotic " party as accepted in the play. Something was necessary to focus in the minds of certain of the characters the fact and cause of discontent and to emphasise it in a dramatic way. After supper we discussed it for a long time. All at once Irving got hold of an idea. I could see it in his face; and he could see that I saw he had something. He glanced at me in a way which I knew well to be to back him up. He deftly changed the conversation and began to speak of another matter in which Marshall was interested. I knew my cue and joined in, and so we drifted away from the play. Presently Irving asked Marshall to look at a play-bill which he had had framed and hung on the wall. It was one in which Macready was "starred" along with an elephant called "Rajah"—this used in later years to hang in Irving's dressing-room. Marshall stood up to look at it closely. Whilst he was doing so, with his back to us, Irving got half-a-dozen wine glasses by the stems in his right hand and hurled them at the door, making a terrific crash and a litter of falling glass. Frank Marshall, a man of the sunniest nature, was not built spiritually in a heroic mould. He gave a cry and whirled round, his face pale as ashes. He sank groaning into a chair speechless. When I had given him a mouthful of brandy he gasped out:

"What was it? I thought some one had thrown a bomb-shell in through the window!"

"That was exactly what I wanted you to think!" said Irving quietly. "That is what those in Curran's house would have felt when they recognised that the fury to which they had been listening and whose cause they could not understand was directed towards them. You are in the rare position now, my dear Marshall, of the dramatist who can write of high emotion from experience. The audience are bound to recognise the sincerity of your work. Just write your scene up to that effect. Let the audience feel even an indication of the surprise and fear that you have just felt yourself, and your play will be a success!" He said this very seriously but with a bland smile and his eyes twinkling, for through all the gravity of the issue in the shape of a good play he enjoyed the humour of the situation. Frank Marshall recovered his nerves and his buoyancy after a while, and when we broke up in the early morning he took his way home eager to get to work afresh and full of ideas.

As Irving was for the time debarred from playing the piece, when completed he let Boucicault have it to see what he could do with it. He did not, I think, improve it. Boucicault played it himself in America, but without much success.

The following list, not by any means complete, will show something of the wide range which Irving covered in his search for suitable plays. I give it because certain writers, who do not know much of the man whom they criticise so flippantly or so superciliously, have been in the habit of saying that Irving did not encourage British dramatists. To those who were on the "inside track" their utterances often meant that he did not accept, pay for, and produce *their* worthless plays or those of their friends, and he did not talk about his business to chance comers. Moreover, he held that it was not good for any one to produce an inferior play. The greatest of all needs of a theatre manager is a

UNUSED PLAYS

sufficiency of plays, and it is sheer ignorant folly for any one to assert that a manager does not accept good plays out of some crass obstinacy or lack of ability on his own part.

Author	Play
W. G. Wills	Rienzi
,,	Mephisto
,,	King Arthur
,,	Don Quixote
Frank Marshall	Robert Emmett
Richard Voss	Schuldig
J. J. C. Clarke	George Washington
,,	Don Quixote
Fergus Hume	The Vestal
Penrhyn Stanlaws	The End of the Hunting
H. T. Johnson	The Jester King
Egerton Castle and Walter Pollock	Saviolo
O. Booth and J. Dixon	Jekyll and Hyde (from Stevenson)
J. M. Barrie	The Professor's Love Story
F. C. Burnand	The Isle of St. Tropez
,,	The Count
H. Guy Carleton	The Balance of Comfort
Ludwig Fulda	The Bloody Marriage [1]
Walter Pollock	Villon

For obvious reasons I do not give what any of these authors received for play or option or advance fees; but the total was over nine thousand pounds.

Regarding one of the plays, Irving's exact reason for not playing it was that he felt it would not suit him—or rather that he would not suit it. He liked the play extremely, and when after studying the scenario very carefully he had to come to the conclusion that it was not in his own special range

---

[1] This was dramatised for Irving by W. L. Courtney, but the opportunity for its production had not come at the time of his last illness.

of work, he obtained permission from the author to submit it to two of his friends in turn, John L. Toole and John Hare. Both these players were delighted with the work, but neither had it in his vogue. Finally another actor saw his way to it, and made with it both a hit and fortune.

The play was Barrie's *The Professor's Love Story;* the actor who played it E. S. Willard. This is a good instance of delayed fortune. For my own part, knowing the peculiar excellences and strength of the three players who refused it, I cannot but think that they were all right. The play is an excellent one, but wants to be exactly fitted. Irving was naturally too strong for it; Toole was a low comedian, and it is not in the vein of Low Comedy; Hare's incisive finesse would have militated against that unconsciousness of effect which is the " note " of the Professor.

III

In addition to the above plays on which he adventured wholly or in part Irving made efforts regarding plays by other authors, amongst whom were Mrs. Steel, K. and Hesketh Pritchard, Marion Crawford, Sir Arthur Conan Doyle, Henry Arthur Jones, W. L. Courtney, Miss Mary Wilkins, Robert Barr. These included the possible dramatisation of several novels.

A. W. Pinero was always regarded by Irving as a great intellectual force, and to the last he was in hopes that some day he would have the opportunity of playing in a piece by him. He often expressed his wish to Pinero; and more than once have Pinero and I talked and corresponded on the subject. Pinero, however, would not think of giving Irving a play that would not have suited him. He had for Irving a very profound regard and a deep personal affection. They were always the best of friends and Pinero was loyalty itself. I do not think that any man understood Irving's power and the excellence of his method better than he did. I fear, however, that that very affection and regard stood in the way of a play; Pinero, I think, wanted to surpass himself on Irving's behalf.

LIX

MUSICIANS

Boito—Paderewski—Henschel—Richter—Liszt—Gounod

I

MUSICIANS always took a deep interest in Irving's work both as actor and manager. They seemed to understand in a peculiarly subtle way the significance of everything he did.

II

BOITO

Boito came to the Lyceum on June 13, 1893, when we were playing *Becket*. I talked with him in his box and in the little drawing-room of the royal box. He afterwards came round on the stage to see Irving. He was wonderfully impressed with *Becket*. He said to me that Irving was "the greatest artist he had ever seen." Two nights later, 15th June, he came to supper in the Beefsteak Room. Irving had got some musicians and others to meet him. The following were of the party: A. C. Mackenzie, Villiers Stanford, Damrosch, Jules Claretie, Renaud, Brisson, Le Clerc, Alfred Gilbert, Toole, Hare, Sir Charles Euan Smith,

Bancroft, Coquelin, Cadet—an extraordinary group of names in so small a gathering.

III

PADEREWSKI

Paderewski was greatly taken with Irving's playing and with the man himself. He came to supper one night in the Beefsteak Room. Irving met him several times and was an immense admirer of his work. He offered to write for Irving music for some play that he might be doing. I met him a good many times privately, and heard him play in the house of Mrs. Goetz in Hyde Park Terrace in 1891, 1892, and 1895. On one of these occasions he played Bach's Chromatic Fantasia, an Interlude of Mozart, and an Interlude and a waltz by Chopin. It was certainly a delightful occasion.

I remember one very peculiar incident in which Paderewski had a part. Whilst we were playing in New York, Hall Caine, who had been up in Canada trying to arrange the copyright trouble there, came to New York also. One Sunday in November 1895 he and I took a walk in the afternoon. Our destination took us down Fifth Avenue, which in those days was a great Sunday promenade. Hall Caine was soon recognised—he is, as some one said, " very like his portraits " ; and as he has an enormous vogue in America certain of the crowd began to follow after him at a little distance. It is of the nature of a crowd to increase, if merely because it *is* a crowd ; and in a short time I saw, when by some chance I looked back, a whole streetful of people close behind us and the crowd momentarily swelling. We increased our pace a little, wishing to get away; but the crowd kept equal pace. Between 42nd and 40th Street we met another crowd coming up the Avenue following Paderewski who was walking with a friend. We stopped to talk, whereupon *both* crowds pressed in on us—it was too interesting an opportunity to be missed to see two such men, and each so remarkable in appearance, together.

It was with some difficulty, and by going into a hotel on one side and leaving it by another that we managed to escape.

It is always interesting to the public to see a grouping of popular favourites. In the course of my own experience I have met with many such instances—which is natural enough considering that I lived for more than twenty-five years amongst great artists. One such occasion I remember well: a lovely Sunday afternoon in early June 1887 when Irving had a coaching party to Oatlands Park where we dined with him. The whole road out of London was thronged with people, for the chestnuts were out in Bushey Park. On the box of the coach sat Irving and Toole and General (then Colonel) Cody " Buffalo Bill " who Coriolanus-like had that spring struck London " like a planet." The grouping took the public taste and we swept along always to an accompaniment of admiring wonder, sometimes to an accompaniment of cheers.

IV

GEORG HENSCHEL

Georg Henschel was from the very first a great admirer of Irving away back from 1879, and so he used to come to the Lyceum and sometimes stay to supper in the Beefsteak Room, or in the room we used before it. I shall never forget one night when he sang to us. There were a very few others present, all friends and all lovers of music. Two items linger in my memory unfailingly; one a lullaby of Handel and the other the "Elders' Song" from Handel's *Susannah*. I had myself first heard him sing at the Handel Festival at the Crystal Palace in 1878, when I was much struck by his magnificent voice and his power of using it. We had all become great friends before he went to Boston where—I think succeeding Gerische—he took over the conductorship of the Boston Symphony Orchestra. He had wished to study practically orchestral music. One forenoon—February 28, 1884—by previous arrangement Irving and I went to the Music Hall to hear his orchestra play Schumann's *Manfred*. It was quite a private performance given entirely for Irving; the gentlemen of the orchestra, all fine musicians, were delighted to play for him. He was entranced with the music and the rendering of it. When we were driving back to the Vendôme Hotel in Commonwealth Avenue where we were both staying he talked all the time about the possibilities of producing Byron's play. He had had it in his mind for a long time as a work to be undertaken; indeed the *répétition* which we had just heard was the outcome of his having mentioned the matter to Henschel on a previous occasion. He was nearer to making up his mind to a definite production that morning than he had ever been or ever was afterwards.

It was agreed between them that later on, if he should undertake to do *Julius Cæsar*, for which he had already arranged the book, Henschel was to compose the music for it.

V

HANS RICHTER

Hans Richter was another great admirer of Irving. He too is a great master of his own art, and has the appreciative insight that only comes with greatness. Richter was not only a musician; he had had so much experience of stage production at Bayreuth and elsewhere that if he did not originate he at least understood all about it. I remember one day, 24th October 1900, after lunch with the Miss Gaskells in Manchester, when he talked with me about the new effect for *The Flying Dutchman* at the Wagner Festival on the following year. This was especially regarding lighting. They had succeeded in so arranging lights that the two ships were to approach each other one in broad sunlight, the other bathed in moonlight.

With Hans Richter I had once the felicity of another such experience in its own way as Irving's comprehensive reading of *Hamlet;* truly another delightful experience of the survey of a great work

THE COMPOSER'S PURPOSE

at the hands of a master. It was when in the house of my friend E. W. Hennell, Hans Richter amongst a few friends sat down to the piano and gave us a *résumé* of Wagner's *Meistersinger*, singing snatches of the songs as he went on, and now and again explaining some subtle purpose in the music that he played. It was an hour of breathless delight which no money could purchase. With my wife I attended the Wagner Cycle at Bayreuth that summer and heard the opera in all its magnificent perfection; but I never got so clear an insight to the great composer's purpose as when Richter pictured it for us.

VI

THE ABBÉ FRANZ LISZT

On 14th April 1886 Abbé Liszt came to the Lyceum to see *Faust* and to stay to supper in the Beefsteak Room. He was then the guest of Mr. Littleton, staying at his house at Sydenham. At that time musical London made such a rush for the old man that it was absolutely necessary to guard him when he came to the theatre. All the real music lovers of the younger generation wanted to see him, for they had not had opportunity before and were not likely to have it again. He was then seventy-five years of age and had practically given up playing inasmuch as he only played to please himself or his friends. That night he was accompanied by Mr. and Mrs. Littleton together with the sons and daughters-in-law of the latter, and by

Stavenhagen his pupil, and Madame Muncacksy. As it was necessary to keep away all who might intrude upon him—enthusiasts, interviewers, cranks, autograph-fiends, notoriety seekers who would like to be seen in his box—we arranged a sort of fortress for him. Next to the royal box on the grand tier O.P. was another box separated only by a partition, part of which could be taken down. This box was on the outside from the Proscenium. We had the door of this box screwed up so that entrance to it could only be had through the royal box. Liszt sat here with some of the others unassailable, as one of the Mr. Littletons kept the key of the other box and none could obtain entrance without permission.

There was an interesting party at supper in the Beefsteak Room, amongst them, in addition to the party at the play, the following : Ellen Terry, Professor Max-Müller, Lord and Lady Wharncliffe, Sir Alexander and Lady Mackenzie, Sir Alfred Cooper, Walter Bach and Miss Bach, Sir Morell Mackenzie, Mr. and Mrs. Alfred Littleton, Mr. and Mrs. Augustus Littleton, Mr. and Mrs. William Beatty Kingston, and the Misses Casella.

Liszt sat on the right hand of Ellen Terry who faced Irving. From where I sat at the end of the table I could not but notice the quite extraordinary resemblance in the profiles of the two men. After supper Irving went round and sat next him and the likeness became a theme of comment from all present. Irving was then forty-eight years of age ; but he looked still a young man, with raven black hair and face without a line. His neck was then without a line or mark of age. Liszt, on the other hand, looked older than his age. His stooping shoulders and long white hair made him seem of patriarchal age. Nevertheless the likeness of the two men was remarkable.

Stavenhagen played, but as it was thought by all that Liszt must be too tired after a long day no opening was made for him much as all longed to hear him. The party did not break up till four o'clock in the morning. The note in my diary runs:

> "Liszt fine face—leonine—several large pimples—prominent chin of old man—long white hair down on shoulders—all call him 'Master'—must have had great strength in youth. Very sweet and simple in manner. H. I. and he very much alike—seemed old friends as they talked animatedly though knowing but a few words of each other's language—but using much expression and gesticulation. It was most interesting."

The next day Irving and my wife and I, together with some others, lunched with the Baroness Burdett-Coutts in Stratton Street to meet Liszt. After lunch there was a considerable gathering of friends asked to meet him. Lady Burdett-Coutts very thoughtfully had the pianos removed from the drawing-rooms, lest their presence might seem as though he were expected to play. After a while he noticed the absence and said to his hostess:

"I see you have no pianos in these rooms!" She answered frankly that she had had them removed so that he would not be tempted to play unless he wished to do so.

"But I would like some music!" he said, and then went on:

"I have no doubt but there is a piano in the house, and that it could be brought here easily!"

It was not long before the servants brought into the great drawing-room a grand piano worthy of even his hands. Then Antoinette Sterling sang some ballads in her own delightful way with the contralto whose tones went straight to one's heart.

"Now I will play!" said Liszt. And he did!

It was magnificent and never to be forgotten.

VII

GOUNOD

Gounod came, as far as I know, but once to the Lyceum. That was during the first week of the season—6th September 1882—during the continuance of the run of *Romeo and Juliet*. He came round to Irving's dressing-room at the end of the third act and sat all the time of the wait chatting; Gounod was a man who seemed to speak fully-formed thoughts. It was not in any way that there was about his speech any appearance of formality or premeditation. He seemed to speak right out of his heart; but his habit or method was such that his words had a power of exact conveyance of the thoughts. One might have stenographed every sentence he spoke, and when reproduced it would require no alteration. Form and structure and choice of words were all complete.

After chatting a while Irving was loth to let him go. When the call boy announced the beginning of Act IV.—in which act Irving had no part—he asked Gounod to stay on with him. So also at the beginning of Act V., when he had to go on the stage for the Apothecary scene, he asked me to stay with Gounod till he came back—I had been in the dressing-room all the time. Whilst Irving was away Gounod and I chatted; several things he said have always remained with me.

He was saying something about some "great man" when he suddenly stopped and, after a slight pause, said:

"But after all there is no really 'great' man! There are men through whom great things are spoken!"

I asked him what in his estimation were the best words to which he had composed music. He answered almost at once, without hesitation:

"'Oh that we two were maying!' I can never think of those words without emotion! How can one help it?" He spoke some of the words—the last verse of the poem from *The Saint's Tragedy*:

> "Oh! that we two lay sleeping
> In our nest in the churchyard sod,
> With our limbs at rest on the quiet earth's breast,
> And our souls at home with God."

As he spoke, the emotion seemed to master him more and more; at the last line the tears were running down his cheeks. He spoke with an extraordinary concentration and emphasis. It was hard to believe that he was not singing, for the effect of his speaking the words of Charles Kingsley's song was the same. His speech seemed like—was music.

Later on I asked him who in his opinion was the best composer.—"Present company, of course, excepted!" I added, whereat he smiled. After a moment's thought he answered:

"Mendelssohn! Mendelssohn is the best!" Then after another but shorter pause: "But there is only one Mozart!"

LX

LUDWIG BARNAY

Meeting of Irving and Barnay—" Fluff "—A dinner on the stage—A discussion on subsidy—An honour from Saxe-Meiningen—A Grand-Ducal invasion

I

WHEN in 1881 the Meiningen Company came to London to play in Drury Lane Theatre at least one German player came with them who, though for patriotic reasons he played with the Company, had not belonged to it. This was Ludwig Barnay. The engagement began with *Julius Cæsar* on 30th May and at once created considerable interest. I was present at the first performance, and was much struck with the acting of Barnay as Mark Antony. By a happy chance I met him very soon after his arrival and we became friends. He was then able to speak but very little English. Like all Magyars, however, he was a good linguist, and before a fortnight was over he spoke the language so well that only an occasional word or phrase spoken to or by him brought out his ignorance.

At their first meeting Irving and he became friends; they "took" to each other in a really remarkable way. Barnay had come to see the play then running, *Hamlet*, and between the acts came round to Irving's dressing-room. By this time he spoke English quite well; when he lacked a word he unconsciously showed his scholarship by trying it in the Greek. Irving after a few minutes forgot that he was a foreigner and began to use words in the *argot* of his own calling. For instance, talking of the difficulty of getting some actors to study their parts properly, he said:

"The worst of it is they won't take the trouble even to learn their words, and when the time comes they begin to fluff." To "fluff" means in the language of the theatre to be uncertain, inexact, imperfect. This was too much for the poor foreigner, who up to then had understood everything perfectly. He raised his hands—palm outwards, the wrists first and then the fingers straightening—as he said in quite a piteous tone:

"Flof!—Fluoof—Fluff! Alas! I know him not!"

Thence on, Irving was very careful not to give trade vernacular without explaining it to him. Ever after that evening the two men met whenever they could; in London whilst Barnay was there, or in New York or Berlin when they were there together.

II

Barnay often came to supper in the Beefsteak Room. Edwin Booth, John McCullough and Lawrence Barrett, the three leading American tragic actors, also became friends of Barnay, and there were many gatherings of a delightful kind. Chiefest amongst them was a dinner which Irving gave to some of the Meiningen Company on the stage of the Lyceum on Sunday, 17th July 1881. There was a party of thirty, who sat at a great round table with yellow flowers. Amongst the gathering were Barnay, Cronegk—the stage manager of the Meiningers, Leopold Teller—a fine actor, George Augustus Sala, Alma - Tadema, Burdett - Coutts, Lawrence Barrett, William Terriss, Toole, F. C. Burnand. That the party was at least a pleasant one was shown by the hours it kept. We did not break up till six o'clock A.M.

III

Another delightful gathering about that time—one which became remarkable in its way—was a supper given by Toole at the Adelphi Hotel on 1st July. Amongst the guests were Irving, Barnay, McCullough, Lawrence Barrett, Wilson Barrett, Leopold Teller. After supper some one—I think it was Irving—said something on the subject of State subsidy for theatres. It was an interesting theme to such a company, and, as the gathering was by its items really international, every one wanted to hear what every one else said. So the conversational torch went round the table—like the sun, or the wine. There were all sorts and varieties of opinion, for each said what was in his heart. When it came to Barnay's turn he electrified us all. He did not say much, but it was all to the point and spoken in a way which left no doubt as to his own sincerity. He finished up :

" Yes, these are all good—to some. The subsidy in France ; the system of the Hoff and the Staadt

Theatres in Germany; the help and control in Austria which brings the chosen actors into the State service. But "—and here his eyes flashed, his nostrils quivered, and his face was lit with enthusiasm—" Your English freedom is worth them all!" Then, springing to his feet, he raised his glass and cried in a voice that rang like a trumpet:
"Freiheit!"

IV

Before the production of *Faust* in 1885 Irving took a party, including Mr. and Mrs. Comyns Carr and Ellen Terry, to Nürnberg and Rothenburg to study the ground. On the way home they went to Berlin. There Barnay gave two special performances in his own theatre, the Berliner. The bill of the play is in its way historical; the names of the honoured guests were starred. The performances were of *Julius Cæsar* and *The Merchant of Venice*.

V

The Grand Duke of Saxe-Meiningen, to whose theatre the Meiningen Company belonged, sent to Irving an Order of his own Court at the same time that he sent one to Augustus Harris, the manager of Drury Lane Theatre, where his Company had played. Later on, however, when he had seen Irving play and had met him, he said that the order sent him was not good enough for so dis-

EJECTION OF A GRAND DUKE

tinguished a man. He accordingly bestowed on him—with the consent and co-operation of the Grand Duke of Saxe-Coburg-Gotha (His Royal Highness the Duke of Edinburgh)—the Order of the Komthur Cross of the Second Class of the Ducal Saxon Ernestine House Order—a distinction, I believe, of high local order, carrying with it something in the shape of knighthood. Irving wore the Collar of the Order on the night of 25th May 1897 when the Grand Duke of Saxe-Meiningen came to supper with him in the Beefsteak Room—the only time I think when he wore the insignia of this special honour. Other guests at that supper were Colonel John Hay, the Ambassador of the United States, and his daughter Helen, whose volume of poems made such a success with the literati.

Irving's first meeting with the Grand Duke was preceded by an odd circumstance. This was on the evening of 28th May 1885.

I was passing across the stage between the acts when I saw a stranger—a tall, distinguished-looking old gentleman. I bowed and told him that no one was allowed on the stage without special permission. He bowed in return, and said:

"I thought that permission would have been accorded to me!"

"The rule," said I, "is inviolable. I fear I must ask you to come with me to the auditorium. This will put us right; and then I can take any message you wish to Mr. Irving."

"May I tell you who I am?" he asked.

"I am sorry," I said, "but I fear I cannot ask you till we are outside. You see, I am the person responsible for carrying out the rules of the theatre.

And no matter who it may be I have to do the duty which I have undertaken."

"You are quite right! ... I shall come with pleasure!" he said with very grave and sweet politeness. When we had passed through the iron door—which had chanced to be open, and so he had found his way in—I said as nicely as I could, for his fine manner and his diction and his willingness to obey orders, charmed me:

"I trust you will pardon me, sir, in case my request to leave the stage may have seemed too imperative or in any way wanting in courtesy. But duty is duty. Now will you kindly give me your name and I will go at once and ask Mr. Irving's permission to bring you on the stage, and to see him if you will!"

"I thank you, sir!" he said; "I am the Grand Duke of Saxe-Meiningen. I am very pleased with your courtesy and to see that you carry out orders so firmly and so urbanely. You are quite right! It is what I like to see. I wish my people would always do the same!"

LXI

CONSTANT COQUELIN (AINÉ)

First meeting of Coquelin and Irving—Coquelin's comments—Irving's reply—" Cyrano "

IRVING and Coquelin first met on the night of April 19, 1888. The occasion was a supper given for the purpose by M. L. Mayer, the impresario of French artists in London, at his house in Berners Street. Previous to this there had been a certain amount of friction between the two men. Coquelin had written an article in *Harper's Magazine* for May 1887 on " Acting and Actors." In his article he made certain comments on Irving which were—using the word in its etymological meaning —not impertinent, but were most decidedly wanting in delicacy of feeling towards a fellow-artist.

Irving replied to the article in an " Actor's Note " in the *Nineteenth Century* for June of the same year. His article was rather a caustic one, and in it he did not spare the player turned critic of his fellow-players.

To the " not impertinent " comments on his own method he merely alluded in a phrase of deprecation of such comments being made by one player on another. But of the theory advanced by Coquelin, in which he supported the views of

Diderot, he offered a direct negative, commenting himself freely on such old-fashioned heresies.

It is but right to mention that when, some two years later, Coquelin republished his article, with some changes and embellishments, in the *Revue Illustrée*, December 1889, under the title, "L'Art du Comédien," he left out entirely the part relating to Irving.

When the two men met at Mayer's they at once became friends. The very fact of having crossed swords brought to each a measure of respect to the other. "It is astonishing," says Colonel Damas in *The Lady of Lyons*, "how well I like a man when I have fought with him!" At first the conversation was distinctly on the militant side, the batteries being masked. The others who were present, including Toole, Coquelin fils, and Sir Squire (then Mr.) Bancroft, had each a word to say at times. Irving, secure in his intellectual position with regard to the theory of acting, was most hearty in his manner and used his rapier with sweet dexterity. Toole, who had his own grievance: that Coquelin, an artist of first-class position, late a Sociétaire of the Comédie Française should accept fee or emolument for private performances, a thing not usual to high-grade players of the British stage —limited himself to asking Coquelin in extremely bad French if it was possible that this was true. At that time Coquelin did not speak much English, though he attained quite a proficiency in it before long.

In a very short time the supper party at Mayer's subsided into gentle and complete harmony. The actors began to understand each other, and from that moment became friends. Coquelin gave imitations of certain French actors, amongst them Frédéric Le Maître and Mounet-Sully. The performance was a strange comment on his own theory that an actor in portraying a character must in the so doing divest himself of his own identity, and quite justified Irving's remark in his " note " :

> "Indeed it is strange to find an actor, with an individuality so marked as that of Mr. Coquelin, taking it for granted that his identity can be entirely lost."

To us whilst his imitations were remarkably clever, there was no possibility of forgetting for an instant that the exponent was M. Coquelin. Why should we? If an actor entirely loses his own identity the larger measure of his possible charm is gone!

I had myself first seen Coquelin in 1876 in *Les Fourchambauts*. My knowledge of French in those days was of a very inadequate kind—as I regret to say it still is; but I remember the extraordinary perfection of the *double entente*. His pronunciation of two words nearly alike in sound but quite different in idea, was of exquisite delicacy. For instance, he spoke the phrase *sans doute* so as to also mean *sans dot*. Both vowel and consonant sounds were in exact midway between the words and defendably for either meant both. I should think myself that for articulation of his own language Constant Coquelin has no peer.

I find this note in my diary regarding Coquelin on that night of Mayer's supper :

> "He is a fine actor; essentially a Comedian!"

In the course of years Irving and Coquelin met often, and the oftener they met the more their friendship ripened. For a good many years Irving took quite an affectionate interest in Coquelin and his affairs; and finally, after the latter had made his enormous success in Paris with *Cyrano de Bergerac* and was anxious to produce it in London, Irving made arrangements for playing himself for some weeks in the suburbs so that he might give up the Lyceum to his friend.

Cyrano was produced on 4th July 1898 and had a triumphant run.

Irving had purchased the English rights of the play, intending to play Cyrano himself. But on going carefully into it he came to the conclusion that the part was one hardly suitable for him; he sold the rights to Sir Charles Wyndham. It was, I think, after their last meeting that Coquelin sent Irving his picture in character as Cyrano.

There were many gatherings in the Beefsteak Room at which Coquelin was present. One I remember well as of special interest. Victor Maurel was there also and Campbell Clarke (afterwards Sir Campbell) the Paris correspondent of the *Daily Telegraph*, F. W. Hawkins, A. P. Burbank, the American actor, Major Ricarde-Seaver, and James Whitcomb Riley. The latter at Irving's request recited a few of his inimitable character sketches. Coquelin and the other actors were loud and eloquent in his praise.

LXII

SARAH BERNHARDT

Irving sees Sarah Bernhardt—First meeting—Supper in Beefsteak Room—Bastien Lepage—Tradition—Painting a serpent—Sarah's appreciation of Irving and Ellen Terry

WHEN Irving and Sarah Bernhardt met there was already that pre-disposition towards friendship which true artists must feel towards those who work greatly in their own craft. When the Comédie Française came to London in 1879 and played at the Gaiety Theatre, Irving went to one of the matinées and was immensely struck by Sarah Bernhardt's genius. He was taken round on the stage and introduced to the various members of the Company; but he did not have in that short season any opportunities of furthering friendships. That was a busy season for every one, both the London players and the foreigners. We were playing repertoire and changing the bill every few nights; the rehearsals were endless. So too with the strangers; they had a great list of plays to get through, and they also were rehearsing all day. When they could the various members of the French Company came to the Lyceum, where they were always made welcome. Indeed, all through his management Irving made it an imperative rule that his fellow-artists should when possible be made welcome at his theatre. Little people as well as great people, all were welcome. In those early days the same rule of hospitality did not hold with the Comédie Française; actors had to go in like any one else—on a "specie basis." Even Irving who had thrown his own theatre open to his French fellow-artists had to pay for his own box at the Gaiety. When, however, Jules Claretie became Director of the Théâtre Français he changed all that, absolutely.

The next year, 1880, Sarah Bernhardt was playing for a short time in London—this time her own venture—again at the Gaiety. Irving took a box for her benefit, a matinée on 16th June. Loveday and I went with him. The bill was *Jean Marie*, the fourth act of *La Rome vaincue,* and the fifth act of *Hernani*. Irving was charmed with her playing in *Jean Marie*, which is a one-act piece with the same note of sentiment in it as that of the song "Auld Robin Gray." He was also struck with her extraordinary tragic force in *La Rome vaincue*. I had myself seen that play at the Théâtre Français four years before, 9th November 1876. When in Paris I had been told that I should not miss seeing a play running at the Français in which a very young woman named Sarah Bernhardt was with extraordinary power playing a blind woman of eighty. There was such a rush to see the piece that it was being played *four times a week*—a rare thing at the Français in those days. Of course I went—I remember I had to buy my way into the parterre and then step by step down to one of the near rows from the individuals who then used to make their living by standing in line so as to get in early and then selling their places to those farther back. I was greatly struck with her acting and also, though in a lesser degree, with that of Mounet-Sully, then young on the stage. He was crude in his artistic method and somewhat rugged, but full of force and power. When I saw Sarah Bernhardt play the act of the play in London I thought that though she had gained in power and finish she had lost something of spontaneity. On that occasion the house was a poor one, but those who were there were delighted—and showed it.

On Saturday night, 3rd July of that year, 1880, Sarah Bernhardt came to supper in the Beefsteak Room. The two other guests were both friends of hers, Bastien Lepage the painter, and Libotton the violoncellist. That was a night of extraordinary interest. Irving and Sarah Bernhardt were both at their best and spoke quite freely on all subjects concerning their art which came on the *tapis*. Irving was eager to know the opinion of one so familiar with the working of the French stage and yet so daring and original in her own life and artistic method. When they touched on the subject of the value of subsidy she grew excited and spoke of the value of freedom and independence :

"What use," she said, "subsidy when a French actress cannot live on the salary, at even the Comédie Française !"

On the subject of tradition in art her manner was more pronounced. She railed against tradition on the stage—as distinguished from the guiding memory and record of great effective work. Her face lit up and her eyes blazed ; she smote her clenched hand heavily on the table, as, after a fierce diatribe against the cramping tendency of an artificial method relentlessly enforced, she hurled out:

" A bas ! la tradition ! "

Then the change to her softer moods was remarkable. She was a being of incarnate grace, with a soft undertone of voice as wooing as the cooing of pigeons. As I looked at her—this was my first opportunity of seeing her close at hand—all the wondrous charm which Bastien Lepage had embodied in his picture of her seemed at full tide. This picture of Bastien Lepage, that wherein she is seated holding a distaff, was exhibited in a silver frame at the first exhibition of the Grosvenor Gallery and met with universal admiration. With the original before one and the memory of her wonderful playing ever fresh in one's mind it was not possible not to be struck with her serpentine grace. I said to Bastien Lepage in such French as I could manage :

" In that great picture you seemed to get the true Sarah. You have painted her as a serpent with all a serpent's grace ! " He seemed much interested and asked me how I made that out. Again as well as I could I explained that all the lines of the picture were curved—there was not a single straight line in the drawing or shading. He seemed more than pleased and asked me to go on. I said that it had seemed to me that he had painted all the shadows in a scheme of yellow, shading them to represent in a subtle way the scales of the serpent skin.

He suddenly took me by both hands and shook them hard—I thought for a moment that he was going to kiss me. Then he patted me on the shoulder, and suddenly shot out the big wide white cuff then in vogue in Parisian dress, and taking a pencil from his pocket drew the picture in little, showing every line as serpentine, and suggesting the shadows with little curved and shaded lines. Then he shook hands again.

I have regretted ever since that I did not ask him to cut off that cuff and give it to me! It was an artistic treasure!

In some of the discussions on art that evening he too got excited. I remember once the violent way in which he spoke of his own dominant note:

"Je suis un ré-a-liste!" As he spoke his voice rose and quivered with that "brool" that marks strong emotion. The short hair of his bullet head actually seemed to bristle like the hair of an excited cat. He rose and brought down his raised clenched fist on the table with a mighty thump. One could realise him at that moment as a possible leader of an emeute. One seemed to see him amid a whirl of drifting powder smoke waving a red flag over the top of a barricade.

Another thing which Bastien Lepage said that night has always remained in my memory. It is so comprehensive that its meaning may be widely applied:

"In an original artist the faults are brothers to the qualities!"

We sat late that night. It was five o'clock when we broke up, and the high sun was streaming into our eyes as we left the building. Many a night after that, Sarah Bernhardt spent pleasant hours at the Lyceum—pleasant to all concerned. She grew to *love* the acting of Irving and of Ellen Terry, and whenever she had an opportunity she would hurry in by the stage door and take a seat in the wings. Several times when she arrived in London from Paris she would hurry straight from the station to the theatre and see all that was possible of the play. It was a delight and a pride to both Irving and Miss Terry when she came ; and whenever she could do so she would stop to supper. The Beefsteak Room was always ready, and a telephone message to Gunter's would insure the provision of supper. Those nights were delightful. Sometimes some of her comrades would come with her. Marius, Garnier, Darmont or Damala. The last time the latter—to whom she was then married —came he looked like a dead man. I sat next him at supper, and the idea that he was dead was strong on me. I think he had taken some mighty dose of opium, for he moved and spoke like a man in a dream. His eyes, staring out of his white waxen face, seemed hardly the eyes of the living.

One night in 1899, whilst she was playing *Hamlet* at the Adelphi, she came to supper when there were some characteristic Americans, Mark Twain, Nat Goodwin, T. I. Keenan of Pittsburg, then President of the American Press Union, Colonel Tom Ochiltree —who had a peculiar soubriquet, F. P. Dunne, I. N. Ford of the New York *Tribune*.

She was always charming and fresh and natural. Every good and fine instinct of her nature seemed to be at the full when she was amongst artistic comrades whom she liked and admired. She inspired every one else and seemed to shed a sort of intellectual sunshine around her.

LXIII

GENEVIÈVE WARD

*When and how I first saw her—Her romantic marriage—
Plays Zillah at Lyceum—" Forget me not "—Plays with
Irving : " Becket " ; " King Arthur " ; " Cymbeline " ;
" Richard III."—Argument on a " reading "—Eyes that
blazed—A lesson from Regnier*

I

ON the evening of Thursday, 20th November 1873, I strolled into the Theatre Royal, Dublin, to see what was on. I had been then for two years a dramatic critic, and was fairly well used to the routine of things. There was a very poor house indeed ; in that huge theatre the few hundreds scattered about were like the plums in a foc'sle duff. I sat down in my usual seat, which the attendants, knowing my choice, always kept for me if possible : the end seat ·O.P. or left-hand side looking towards the stage. The play was Legouve's *Adrienne Lecouvreur*, a somewhat machine-made play of the old school. The lady who played Adrienne interested me at once ; she was like a triton amongst minnows. She was very handsome ; of a rich dark beauty, with clear cut classical features, black hair, and great eyes that now and again flashed fire. I sat in growing admiration of her powers. Though there was a trace here and there of something which I thought amateurish she was so masterful, so dominating in other ways that I could not understand it. At the end of the second act I went into the lobby to ask the attendants if they could tell me anything about her as the name on the bill was entirely new to me. None of them, however, could enlighten me on any point except that she had appeared on Monday in *Lucrezia Borgia ;* and the business was very bad.

When the grand scene of the play came—that between the actress and her rival, the Princess de Bouillon—the audience was all afire. Their enthusiasm and the sound of it recalled the description of Edmund Kean's appearance at Drury Lane. I went round on the stage and saw John Harris the manager. I asked him who was the woman who was playing and where did she come from.

"She has no right to be playing to an audience like that!" I said pointing at the curtain which lay between us and the auditorium.

"I quite agree with you!" he answered. "She is fine; isn't she? I saw her play in Manchester and at once offered her the date here which was vacant." Just then she came upon the stage and he introduced me to her. When the play was over I went home and wrote my criticism, which duly appeared in the *Irish Echo* next evening.

That engagement of nine days was a series of *débuts*. In addition to *Adrienne Lecouvreur* she appeared in *Medea, Lucrezia Borgia, The Actress of Padua,* the "sleep-walking" scene of *Macbeth, The Honeymoon.* In one and all she showed great power and greater promise. It is a satisfactory memory to me to find after her career has been made and

THE ITALIAN METHOD

her retirement—all too soon—effected after more than thirty years of stage success when I find this mem. in my diary of 29th November 1873—the last night of her engagement—

" (Mem. will be a great actress)."

During the engagement, Monday, 24th November, one night behind the scenes I met a great friend of mine, the American Consul, Wilson King of Pittsburg, who was paying a visit to the actress, whom he had known since childhood, his family and hers having all been old friends. He introduced me to his countrywoman, not formally this time but as a friend. And there and then began a close friendship which has never faltered, which has been one of the delights of my life and which will I trust remain as warm as it is now till the death of either of us shall cut it short.

II

Geneviève Ward both in the choice of her plays and in her manner of playing followed at that time the " old " school. I had a good opportunity of judging the excellence of her method, for that very year 1873, after an absence of fifteen years, Madame Ristori had visited Dublin. She was then in her very prime; an actress of amazing power and finish. She had played *Medea, Mary Stuart, Queen Elizabeth* and *Marie Antoinette*. Her method was of course the " Italian " of which she was the finest living exponent—probably the finest that ever had been. Her speech was a series of cadences; the voice rose and fell in waves—sometimes ripples sometimes billows—but always modified with such exquisite precision as not to attract special attention to the rhythmic quality. Its effect was entirely unconscious. Indeed it was a method which in time could, and did, become of itself mechanical—like breathing—so that it did not in the least degree interfere even with the volcanic expression of passion. The study was of youth and at the beginning of art ; but when the method was once formed nature could express herself in it as unfettered as in any other medium. Years afterwards Miss Ward showed me one of Ristori's prompt books ; and I could not but be struck with the accentuation. Indeed the marking above the syllables ran in such unbroken line as to look like musical scoring.

Miss Ward was a friend of the great Italian and had learned most of her art from her. She was a fine linguist, speaking French, Italian, and Spanish as easily as her own tongue. At that time Ristori, who was in private life La Comtessa Campramican del Grillo, lived in her husband's ancestral home in Rome, and Miss Ward often stayed with her. Miss Ward in her private life was also a Countess, having whilst a very young girl married a Russian, Count de Gerbel of Nicolaeiff. The marriage was a romance as marked as anything that could appear upon the stage. In 1855 at Nice Count de Gerbel had met and fallen in love with her and proposed marriage. She was willing and they were duly married at the Consulate at Nice, the marriage in the Russian church was to follow in Paris. But the Count was not of chivalrous nature. In time his fancy veered round to some other quarter, and he declared that by a trick of Russian law which does not acknowledge the marriage of a Russian until the ceremony in the Russian church has been performed, the marriage which had taken place was not legal. His wife and her father and mother, however, were not those to pass such a despicable act. With her mother she appealed to the Czar, who having heard the story was furiously indignant. Being an autocrat, he took his own course. He summoned his vassal Count de Gerbel to go to Warsaw, where he was to carry out the orders which would be declared to him. There in due time he appeared. The altar was set for marriage and before it stood the injured lady, her father, Colonel Ward, and her mother. Her father was armed, for the occasion was to them one of grim import. De Gerbel yielded to the mandate of his Czar, and the marriage—with all needful safeguards this time—was duly effected. Then the injured Countess bowed to him and moved away with her own kin. At the church door husband and wife parted, never to meet again.

III

In her first youth Miss Ward was a singer and had great success in Grand Opera. But overwork in Cuba strained her voice. It was thought that this might militate against great and final success; so, bowing to the inevitable, she with her usual courage forsook the lyric for the dramatic stage. It was when she had prepared herself for the latter and was ready to make her new venture that I first saw her.

IV

During the holiday season of 1879, whilst Irving was yachting in the Mediterranean, Miss Ward rented the Lyceum for a short season commencing 2nd August. By the contract Irving had agreed to find, in addition to the theatre, the heads of departments, box-office and the usual working staff at an inclusive rent, as he wished to keep all his people together. So I had to remain in London to look after these matters. Miss Ward asked me to be manager for her also; but I said I could not do so as a matter of business as it might be possible that her interests and Irving's might clash; but that I would do all I could.

She opened in a play called *Zillah* written by her old friend Palgrave Simpson and another. It was put in preparation some time before and was carefully rehearsed. My own work kept me so busy that I did not have any time to see rehearsals till the night before the performance when the dress rehearsal was held. That rehearsal was one which I shall never forget. It was too late to say anything—there was no time then to make any radical change; and so I held my peace.

The play was of the oldest-fashioned and worst type of "Adelphi" drama! It was machine-made and heartless and tiresome to the last degree, and in addition the language was turgid beyond belief. It was an absolute failure, and was taken off after a few nights. *Lucrezia Borgia* was put up whilst a new play should be got ready. She had not made arrangements for a second new play, so we all undertook to do what we could to find a suitable play, a new one. Miss Ward gave me a great parcel of plays sent to her at various times—some two feet high of them; with a heavy heart I began to wade through them. Some five or six down the line I came on one play which at once arrested my attention. As I shortly afterwards learned it was one which had been hawked about unsuccessfully. So soon as I had read it I sent it up to Miss Ward's home by a messenger, together with a note to the effect that I thought the enclosed, with a little alteration in the first act, would make a great success. Miss Ward's judgment agreed with my own. She knew the author and wrote to him to see her. He came to the Lyceum that night. She had asked me what price she should pay, say for five years with right of renewal. I told her the price then usual for plays, so much per act, and we agreed that she should offer that price for the term of lease, to be duplicated if the option of renewal were acted on. The author came in a hurry, passing through London. Miss Ward was dressing and sent for me and asked me through her door if I could open negotiations for her and she would see the author when she was dressed. I saw him and asked the price he expected. He named that which she had decided upon, so I told him that Miss Ward would take the play; she saw him a few minutes after and the agreement was verbally made.

The play was produced on August 21—within a fortnight of the time of its discovery. It was an enormous success, and ran the whole time of her tenancy—indeed a week longer than had been decided on as Irving was loth to disturb the successful run.

The play was *Forget me not*, by Hermann Merivale and F. C. Grove. Miss Ward played it continuously for *ten years* and made a fortune with it.

V

Miss Geneviève Ward played in four of Irving's great productions, of course always as a special engagement. The first was *Becket*, in which she "created" the part of Queen Eleanor — by old custom, to "create" a stage part is to play it first in London; the second was Morgan Le Fay in *King Arthur*; the third the Queen in *Cymbeline*; and the fourth Queen Margaret in *Richard III*. In all these parts she was exceedingly good.

With regard to the last-named play, there was one of the few instances in which Irving was open to correction with regard to emphasis of a word. In Act IV. scene 3, of his acting version—Act IV. scene 4, of the original play—the last two lines of Queen Margaret's speech to Queen Elizabeth before her exit :

"Bettering thy loss makes the bad-causer worse
Revolving this will teach thee how to curse!"

When Miss Ward spoke the last line she emphasised the word *this*—"Revolving *this* will teach thee how to curse!" Irving said the emphasised word should be teach—" Revolving this will *teach* thee how to curse ! "

They each stuck to their own opinion ; but at the last rehearsal he came to her and said :

" You are quite right, Miss Ward, your reading is correct." I daresay he had not considered the reading when arranging the play. As a matter of fact in his original arrangement of the play, at his first production of it under Mrs. Bateman in 1877, Queen Margaret was not in the scene at all. In the new version he had restored her to the scene as he wished to " fatten " Miss Ward's part and so add to the strength of the play. Miss Ward was always a particularly *strong* actress, good at invective, and as the play had no part for Ellen Terry he wished to give it all the other help he could.

VI

Miss Ward has one great stage gift which is not given to many : her eyes can blaze. I can only recall two other actresses who had the same quality in good degree : Mdlle. Schneider who forty years ago played the Grand Duchess of Gerolstein in Offenbach's Opera ; and Christine Nilsson. The latter I saw in London in 1867, and from where I sat—high up in the seat just in front of the gallery—I could note the starry splendour of her blue eyes. Ten years later, in *Lohengrin* at Her Majesty's Opera House, I noticed the same—this time from the stalls. And yet once again when I sat opposite her at supper on the night of her retirement, June 20, 1888. The supper party was a small one, given by Mr. and Mrs.

Brydges-Willyams at 19 Upper Brook Street. Irving was there and Ellen Terry, Lord Burnham and Miss Matilda Levy—brother and sister of our hostess, Count Miranda to whom Nilsson was afterwards married and his daughter, my wife and myself.

Nilsson came in from her triumph at the Albert Hall, blazing with jewels. She wore that night only those that had been given to her by Kings and Queens—and other varieties of monarchs.

J. L. TOOLE AS CALEB PLUMMER

From a drawing by Fred Barnard

LXIV

JOHN LAWRENCE TOOLE

*Toole and Irving—A life-long friendship—Their jokes—
A seeming robbery—An odd Christmas present—Toole
and a sentry—A hornpipe in a landau—Moving Canterbury Cathedral—Toole and the verger—A joke to the
King—Other jokes—His grief at Irving's death—Our
last parting*

THE friendship between Henry Irving and John Lawrence Toole began in Edinburgh just fifty years ago. Toole was the elder and had already won for himself the position of a local semi-star. The chances of distinction come to the "Low" comedian quicker than to the exponent of Tragedy or "High" Comedy, and Toole had commenced his stage experience at almost as early an age as Irving—eighteen. On 20th June 1894, during a Benefit at the Lyceum for the Southwark Eye Hospital, at which he did the wonderfully droll character sketch, "Trying a Magistrate," he told me that forty-five years before, Charles Dickens had heard him do the sketch and advised him to go on the stage. Wisely he had taken the advice; from the very start he had an exceptionally prosperous career.

He, the kindliest and most genial soul on earth, became a fast friend with the proud, shy, ambitious young beginner, eight years his junior. From the first he seemed to believe in Irving and predicted for him a great career. To this end he contributed all through his life. When he toured on his own account he took Irving with him, giving him a star place in his bill, and an opportunity of exhibiting his own special tragic power in a recital of *The Dream of Eugene Aram*. I give as an illustration a bill of such a tour in 1869 which is illustrative of the method of the time.

To the last day of Irving's life the friendship of the two men each for the other never flagged or faltered. Such a thing as jealousy of the other never entered into the heart of either. Toole simply venerated his friend and enjoyed his triumph more than he did his own. He would not hear without protest any one speak of Irving except in a becoming way; and there was nothing which Toole possessed which he would not have shared with Irving. When one entertained, there was always a place for the other; whoever had the good fortune to become a friend of either found his friendship doubled at once. The two men seemed to supplement each other's natures. Each had, in his own way and of its own kind, a great sense of humour. Toole's genial, ebullient, pronounced; Irving's saturnine, keen, and suggestive. Both had—each again in his own way—a very remarkable seriousness. Those who only saw Toole in his inimitable pranks knew little how keenly the man felt emotion; how unwavering he was in his sense of duty; how earnest in his work. With Irving the humour was a fixed quantity, which all through his life kept its relative proportion to

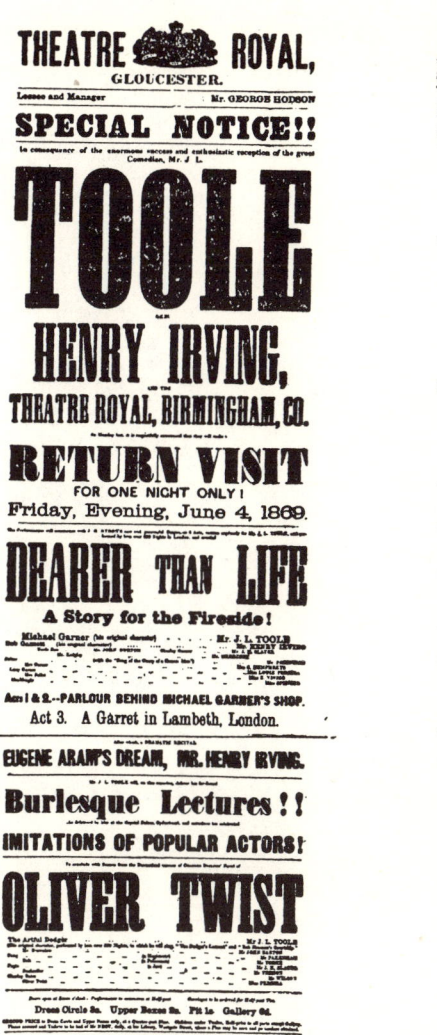

PLAY-BILL: TOOLE AND IRVING TOUR, 1869

IRVING'S JOKE ON TOOLE

Mock play-bill got up by his direction, 1883

A CLASSICAL JOKE

his seriousness; but Toole, being a low-comedian, and perhaps because of it, seemed at times vastly different in his hours of work and relaxation. For it is a strange thing that the conditions of emotion are such that what is work in one case is rest in another, and *vice versâ;* the serious man finds ease in relaxation, the humorous man seeks in quietude his rest from the stress of laughter. In their younger days and up to middle life the two men had indulged in harmless pranks. They both loved a joke and would take any pains to compass it. The tricks they played together would fill a volume. Of course from their protean powers of expressing themselves and in merging their identities actors have rare opportunities of consummating jokes. Moreover they are in the habit of working together, and two or three men who understand each other's methods can go far to sway the unwary how they will.

One of the practical jokes of Toole and Irving is almost classical: One Sunday when they both happened to be playing at Liverpool at the same time they went to dine at an old inn at Wavertree celebrated for the excellence of its hospitality. They had a good dinner and a good bottle of port and sat late. When most of the guests in the hotel had gone to bed and when the time necessary for their own departure was drawing nigh, they rang and told the waiter to get the bill. When he had gone for it they took all the silver off the table—they had fine old silver in the inn—and placed it in the garden on which the room opened. Then they turned out the gas and got under the table. Hearing no answer to his repeated knocking the waiter opened the door. When he saw the lights out, the window opened, and the guests gone he cried out :

"Done! They have bolted with the silver." Then he ran down the passage crying out : "Thieves, thieves!"

The instant he was gone the two men came from under the table, closed the door, lit the gas, and took in the silver which they replaced on the table. Presently a wild rush of persons came down the passage and burst into the room; the landlord and his family, servants of the house, guests *en deshabille*—most of them carrying pokers and other impromptu weapons. They found the two gentlemen sitting quietly smoking their cigars. As they stood amazed Irving said in his quiet, well-bred voice :

"Do you always come in like this when gentlemen are having their dinner here ?"

Toole would even play pranks on Irving, these generally taking the form of some sort of gift. For instance, he once sent Irving on his birthday what he called in his letter "a miniature which he had picked up!" It came in a furniture van, an enormous portrait of Conway the actor, painted about a hundred years ago ; it was so large that it would not fit in any room of the theatre and had to be put in a high passage. Again, when he was in Australia he sent to Irving, timed so that it would arrive at Christmas, a present of two frozen sheep and a live kangaroo. These arrived at Irving's rooms in Grafton Street. He had them housed at the Lyceum for the night, and next day sent the sheep to gladden the hearts—and anatomies—of the Costermongers' Club at Chicksand Street, Mile End, New Town. The kangaroo was sent with a donation to the Zoological Society as a contribution from "J. L. Toole and Henry Irving." A brass plate was fixed over the cage by the Society.

Toole loved to make beautiful presents to Irving. Amongst them was a splendid gilt silver claret jug; several silver cups and bowls; the trophy designed by Flaxman which was presented to Macready in 1818—a magnificent piece of jeweller's work; a "grangerised" edition of Forster's *Life of Charles Dickens*—unique in its richness of material and its fine workmanship—which he had bought in Paris for £500.

When Toole and Irving were separated they were in constant communication by letter, telegram or cable. No birthday of the other passed without a visit if near enough, or a letter or telegram if apart, and there was always a basket of flowers each to each. For a dozen years before Irving's death Toole had been in bad health, growing worse and worse as the years went on. He grew very feeble and very, very sad. But without fail Irving used to go to see him whenever he had an opportunity. At his house in Maida Vale, at Margate, or at Brighton, in which latter place he mainly lived for years past, Irving would go to him and spend all the hours he could command. Even though the width of the world separated them, the two men seemed to have, day by day, exact cognisance of the whereabouts and doings of the other, and not a week but the cables were flashing between them.

Poor Toole had one by one lost all his immediate

family—son, wife, daughter; and his tie to life was in great part the love to and from his friend. He used to think of him unceasingly. Wherever he was, Toole's wire would come unfailingly making for good luck and remembrance. He would keep the flowers that Irving sent to him till they faded and dropped away; even then the baskets and bare stalks were kept in his room.

No one appreciated more than Toole the finest of Irving's work. For instance, when he saw him play *King Lear* he was touched to his heart's core, and his artistic admiration was boundless. I supped with him that night after the play, and he said to me:

"*King Lear* is the finest thing of Irving's life—or of any one else's!"

When Toole was going to Australia there were many farewell gatherings to wish him God-speed. Some of them were great and elaborate affairs, but the last of all was reserved for Irving, when Toole, with some old friends, supped in the Beefsteak Room. When Irving proposed his old friend's health—a rare function indeed in that room—he never spoke more beautifully in his life. His little speech was packed with pathos, and so great was his own emotion that at moments he was obliged to pause to pull himself together.

Toole and I were very close friends ever since I knew him first in the early seventies. I shared with him many delightful hours. And when sorrow came to him I was able to give him sympathy and such comfort as could be from my presence. I was with him at the funeral of his son and then of his wife. When his daughter died in Edinburgh,

THE CAST OF "DEARER THAN LIFE," 1868

where he was then playing, I went up to him and stayed with him. We brought her body back to London and I went with him to her grave. With me he was always affectionate, always sympathetic, always merry when there was no cause for gloom, always grave and earnest when such were becoming. I have been with him on endless occasions when his merriment and geniality simply bubbled over. Unless some sorrow sat heavily on him he was always full of merriment which evidenced itself in the quaintest and most unexpected ways.

One evening, for instance, we were walking together along the western end of Pall Mall. When we came near Marlborough House, where on either side of the gateway stood a guardsman on sentry, he winked at me and took from his pocket a letter which he had ready for post. Then when we came up close to the nearest soldier he moved cautiously in a semi-blind manner and peering out tried to put the letter in the breast of the scarlet tunic as though mistaking the soldier for a postal pillar box. The soldier remained upright and stolid, and did not move a muscle. Toole was equally surprised and pleased when from the guardsman's moveless lips came the words:

"It's all right, Mr. Toole! I hope you're well, sir?"

Another time I was staying with him at the Granville at Ramsgate, and on the Sunday afternoon we drove out to Kingsgate. Lionel Brough was another of the party. As we passed a coastguard station we stopped opposite a very handsome, spruce, dandified coastguard. The two men greeted him, but his manner was somewhat haughty.

Whereupon the two actors without leaving their seats proceeded to dance a hornpipe. That is they seemed, from the waist up, to be dancing that lively measure. Their arms and hands took motion as though in a real dance and their bodies swayed with appropriate movement. The little holiday crowd looked on delighted, and even the haughty sailor found it too much. He unbent and, smiling, danced also in very graceful fashion.

Again at another time we found ourselves in Canterbury, where Toole amused himself for a whole afternoon by spreading a report that the Government were going to move the Cathedral from Canterbury to Margate, giving as a reason that the latter place was so much larger. Strange to say that there were some who believed it. Toole worked systematically. He went into barbers' shops—three of them in turn, and in each got shaved. As I wore a beard I had to be content with having my hair cut; it came out pretty short in the end. As he underwent the shaving operation he brought conversation round to the subject of the moving of the Cathedral. Then we went into shops without end where he bought all sorts of things—collars, braces, socks, caps, fruits and spice for making puddings, children's toys, arrowroot, ginger wine, little shawls, sewing cotton, emery paper, hair oil, goloshes, corn plasters—there was no end to the variety of his purchases, each of which was an opening for some fresh variant of the coming change.

At one other visit to Canterbury we came across in the ancient Cathedral an insolent verger. Toole, who was, for all his fun, a man of reverent nature,

REPROVING INSOLENCE

was as usual with him grave and composed in the church. The verger, taking him for some stranger of the *bourgeois* class, thought him a fit subject to impress. When Toole spoke of the new Dean who had been lately appointed the man said in a flippant way :

"We don't care much for him. We don't think we'll keep him!" This was enough for Toole. He looked over at me in a way I understood and forthwith began to ask questions :

"Did you, may I ask, sir, preach this morning?"

"No. Not this morning. I don't preach this week." We knew then that that verger was to be "had on toast." Toole went on :

"Do you preach on next Sunday, sir? I should like to hear you."

"Well, no! I don't think I'll preach on Sunday."

"Will you preach the Sunday after?"

"Perhaps."

"May I ask, sir, are you the Dean yourself?"

"No. I am not the Dean!" His manner implied that he was something more.

"Are you the Sub-Dean?"

"Not the Sub-Dean." His answers were getting short.

"Are you what they call a Canon?"

"No, I should not exactly call myself a Canon."

"Are you a minor Canon?"

"No!"

"Are you a precentor?"

"Not exactly that."

"Are you in the choir?"

"No."

"May I ask you what you are then, sir?"—this

was said with great deference. The man, cornered at last, thought it best to speak the truth, so he answered :

" I am what they call a ' verger ! ' "

" Quite so ! " said Toole gravely ; " I thought you were only a servant by the insolent way you spoke of your superiors ! "

The remainder of that personal conduction was made in silence.

On one occasion when Toole was taking the waters at Homburg, King Edward VII., then Prince of Wales, was there. He had a breakfast party to which he had asked Toole and also Sir George Lewis and Sir Squire Bancroft. In the course of conversation his Royal Highness asked Bancroft where he was going after Homburg. The answer was that he was going to Maloya in Switzerland. Then turning to Toole he asked him :

" Are you going to Maloya also, Mr. Toole ? " In reply Toole said, as he bowed and pointed to the great solicitor :

" No, sir, Ma-loya (my lawyer) is here ! "

I remember one Derby day, 1893, when we were both in the party to which Mr. Knox Darcy extended the hospitality of his own stand next to that of the Jockey Club—a hospitality which I may say was boundless and complete. When I arrived the racing was just beginning, and the course was crowded by the moving mass seeking outlets before the cordon of police with their rope. As I got close to the stand I heard a voice that I knew coming from the wicket-gate, which was surrounded with a seething mass of humanity of all kinds pushing and struggling to get close.

"Walk this way, ladies and gentlemen! Walk this way! get tickets here. Only one shilling, including lunch. Walk this way!"

A somewhat similar joke on his part was on board a steamer on Lake Lucerne, when he was there with Irving. He went quietly to one end of the steamer and cried out in a loud voice: "Cook's tourists, this way. Sandwich and glass of sherry provided free!" Then, slipping over to the other end of the boat as the crowd began to rush for the free lunch, he again made proclamation: "Gaze's party, this way. Brandy and soda, hard-boiled eggs, and butterscotch provided free!" Again he disappeared before the crowd could assemble.

A favourite joke of his when playing Paul Pry was to find out what friends of his were in the house and then to have their names put upon the blackboard at the inn with scores against them of gigantic amount. This was a never-stale source of surprise and delight to the children of his friends. He loved all children, and next to his own, the children of his friends. For each of such there was always a box of chocolates. He kept a supply in his dressing-room, and I never knew the child of a friend to go away empty-handed. With such a love in his heart was it strange that in his own bad time, when his sadness was just beginning to take hold on his very heart's core, he loved to think much of those old friends who had loved his own children who had gone?

Somehow his mirth never lessened his pathos. His acting—his whole life—has been a sort of proof that the two can co-exist. His Caleb Plummer was never a whit less moving because his audience laughed through their tears. It may be his art became typified in his life.

When Irving died I telegraphed the same night to Frank Arlton, Toole's nephew, who during all his long illness had given him the most tender care. I feared that if I did not send such warning some well-intentioned blunderer might give him a terrible shock. Arlton acted most prudently, and broke the sad news himself at a favourable opportunity the next day. When poor Toole heard it his remark was one of infinite pathos :

" Then let me die too ! "

Such a wish is in itself an epitaph of lasting honour.

Toole's belief and sympathy and help was of infinite service to the friend whom he loved. It was comfort and confidence and assistance all in one. And it is hardly too much to say that Irving could never have done what he did, and in the way he did it, without the countenance and help of his old friend. Irving always, ever since I knew him, liked to associate Toole with himself in everything, and to me who know all that was between them it is but just—as well as the carrying out of my dear friend's wishes that in this book their names shall be associated as closely as I can achieve by the Dedication. Shortly before his last illness I went down to Brighton to see him and to ask formally his permission to this end. He seemed greatly moved by it. Later on I sent the proof of the page containing it, asking Arlton to show it to him if he thought it advisable. Toole had then partially recovered from the attack and occasionally saw friends and was interested in what went on. Arlton's letter to me described the effect :

"I gave him your message last night, and I fear I did unwisely, as nurse says he has been talking all night about Sir Henry and books."

That visit to Brighton was the last time I saw Toole. He was then very low in health and spirits. He could hardly move or see; his voice was very feeble and one had to speak close and clearly that he might hear well. But his intellect was as clear as ever, and he spoke of many old friends. I spent the day with him; after lunch I walked by his bath chair to the end of the Madeira Walk. There we stayed a while, and when my time for leaving came, I told him—but not before. In his late years Toole could not bear the idea of any one whom he loved leaving him, even for a time. We used therefore to say no word of parting till the moment came. When he held out his poor, thin, trembling hand to me he said with an infinite pathos whose memory moves me still:

"Bram, we have often parted—but this time is the last. I shall never see you again! Won't you let me kiss you, dear!"

Toole died on the night of 30th July of this year and was buried in his family tomb in Kensal Green. Around his grave was a great crowd of loving and sorrowing friends.

LXV

ELLEN TERRY

First meet her—Irving's early playing with her—His criticism—How she knighted an Attorney-General—A generous player—Real flowers—Her art—Discussion on a " gag "—The New School—Last performance with Irving—The cause of separation—Their comradeship— A pet name

I

THE first time I saw Ellen Terry was on the forenoon of Monday, December 23, 1878. The place was the passage-way which led from the stage of the Lyceum to the office, a somewhat dark passage under the staircase leading to the two "star" dressing-rooms up the stage on the O.P. side. But not even the darkness of that December day could shut out the radiant beauty of the woman to whom Irving, who was walking with her, introduced me. Her face was full of colour and animation, either of which would have made her beautiful. In addition was the fine form, the easy rhythmic swing, the large, graceful, goddess-like way in which she moved. I knew of her of course—all the world did then though not so well as afterwards; and she knew of me already, so that we met as friends. I had for some years known Charles Wardell, the actor playing under the name of Charles Kelly, to

Ellen Terry, age 17.
Photograph taken by Mrs Julia Margaret Cameron,
at Freshwater in 1865.

whom she had not long before been married. Kelly had in his professional visits to Dublin been several times in my lodgings, and as I had reason to believe that he had a high opinion of me I felt from Ellen Terry's gracious and warm manner of recognition that she accepted me as a friend. That belief has been fully justified by a close friendship, unshaken to the extent of a hair's-breadth through all the work and worry—the triumphs and gloom—the sunshine and showers—storm and trial and stress of twenty-seven years of the comradeship of work together.

Irving had engaged her entirely on the strength of the reputation which she had already made in *Olivia* and the other plays which had gone before it. He had not seen her play since the days of the Queen's Theatre, Long Acre, 1867–8, when they had played together in *The Taming of the Shrew*, she being the Katherine to his Petruchio. He had not thought very much of her playing in those days. Long after she had made many great successes at the Lyceum, in speaking of the early days he said to me :

" She was always bright and lively, and full of fun. She had a distinct charm ; but as an artist was rather on the hoydenish side ! "

From the moment, however, that she began to rehearse at the Lyceum his admiration for her became unbounded. Many and many a time have I heard him descant on her power. It was a favourite theme of his. He said that her pathos was " nature helped by genius," and that she had a " gift of pathos." He knew well the value of her playing both to himself and the public, and for the early years of his management plays were put on in which she would have suitable parts. *Iolanthe* was put on for her, likewise *The Cup, The Belle's Stratagem, Romeo and Juliet, Much Ado about Nothing, Twelfth Night* and *Olivia*. Synorix was not a part for the sake of which Irving would have produced *The Cup;* neither Romeo nor Benedick is a part such as he would have chosen for himself. Neither Malvolio nor Dr. Primrose was seemingly a great rôle for a man who had been accustomed for years to "carry the play on his back."

II

I think that Ellen Terry fascinated every one who ever met her — men, women and children, it was all the same. I have heard the evidences of this fascination in many ways from all sorts of persons in all sorts of places. One of them in especial lingers in my mind: perhaps this is because I belong to a nationality to whose children "blarney" is supposed to be a heritage.

On the afternoon of Sunday, November 25, 1883, we had travelled from New York to Philadelphia, paying our first visit to the Quaker city. Irving and I were staying at the Belle Vue Hotel; there, too, Ellen Terry took up her quarters. I dined with Irving, and we were smoking after dinner when a card and a message came up. The card was that of the Hon. Benjamin H. Brewster, then Attorney-General of the United States. The message was to the effect that he had broken his journey for a few hours on his way to Washington for the purpose

KNIGHTING AN ATTORNEY-GENERAL

of meeting Mr. Irving, and begging that he would waive ceremony and see him. Of course, Irving was very pleased, and the Attorney-General came up. He was a clever-looking, powerfully-built man, but his face was badly scarred. In his boyhood he had, I believe, fallen into the fire. Until one knew him and came under the magic of his voice, and tongue, his appearance was apt to concern one over-much. He was quaint in his dress, wearing frills on shirt-front and cuffs. He was of an Irish family which had sent very prominent men to the Bar; a namesake of his was a leading counsel in my own youth. Irving and I were delighted with him. After an hour or so he asked if it were possible that he might see Miss Terry. Irving thought she would be very pleased. In compliance with the Attorney-General's request she came down to Irving's room and was most sweet and gracious to the stranger. After a while she went away; he prepared to go also, for his train was nearly due. When Ellen Terry had left the room he turned to us and said, with all that conviction of truth which makes " blarney " so effective :

"What a creature! what a Queen! She smote me with the sword of her beauty, and I arose her Knight!"

III

Ellen Terry had no sooner come into the Lyceum than all in the place were her devoted servants. Irving was only too glad to let her genius and her art have full swing; and it was a pleasure to all to carry out her wishes. As a member of a company she was always simply ideal. She encouraged the young, helped every one, and was not only a "fair" but a "generous" actor. These terms imply much on the stage, where it is possible, without breaking any rule, to gain all the advantage to the detriment of other players. To Ellen Terry such a thing was impossible; she not only gave to every one acting with her all the opportunities that their parts afforded, but made opportunities for them. For instance, it is always an advantage for an actor to stand in or near the centre of the stage and well down to the footlights. In old days such a place was the right of the most important actor; a right which was always claimed. But Ellen Terry would when occasion served stand up stage or down as might be suitable to the person speaking. And when her own words had been spoken she would devote her whole powers to helping the work of her comrades on the stage. These seemingly little things count for much in the summing up of years, and it is no wonder that Ellen Terry as an artist is, and has always been, loved. From the first, to her as an artist has always been given the supreme respect which she had justly won. No one ever cavilled, no one ever challenged, no one ever found fault. All sought her companionship, her advice, her assistance. She moved through the world of the theatre like embodied sunshine. Her personal triumphs were a source of joy to all; of envy to none.

She seems to have the happy faculty of spinning gaiety out of the very air, and adds always to the sum of human happiness.

IV

Her performance of Ophelia alone would have insured her a record for greatness; Irving never ceased expatiating on it. I well remember one night in 1879—it was after the third performance of *Hamlet*—when he took supper with my wife and me. He talked all the time of Ellen Terry's wonderful performance. One thing which he said fixed itself in my mind:

"How Shakespeare must have dreamed when he was able to write a part like Ophelia, knowing that it would have to be played by a boy! Conceive his delight and gratitude if he could but have seen Ellen Terry in it!"

Indeed it was a delight to any one even to see her. No one who had seen it can forget the picture that she made in the Fourth Act when she came in holding a great bunch—an armful—of flowers; lilies and other gracious flowers and all those that are given in the text. For my own part, every Ophelia whom I have seen since then has suffered by the comparison.

Ellen Terry loves flowers, and in her playing likes to have them on the stage with her when suitable. Irving was always most particular with regard to her having exactly what she wanted. The Property Master had strict orders to have the necessary flowers, no matter what the cost. Other players could, and had to, put up with clever imitations; but Ellen Terry always had real flowers. I have known when the rule was carried through under extreme difficulties. This was during the week after the blizzard at New York in March 1888 when such luxuries were at famine price. She had as Margaret her bunch of roses every night. I bought them one day myself for the purpose when the blooms were five dollars each.

V

Ellen Terry's art is wonderfully true. She has not only the instinct of truth but the ability to reproduce it in the different perspective of the stage. There must always be some grand artistic qualities, quite apart from personal charm, to render any actress worthy of universal recognition. To those who have seen Ellen Terry no explanation is needed. She is artist to her finger tips. The rules which Taine applies to Art in general, and to plastic art in particular, apply in especial degree to an artist of the Stage. That which he calls "selective" power, a natural force, is ever a ruling factor in the creation of character.

The finer and more evanescent evidences of individuality must to a large extent be momentary. No true artist ever plays the same part alike on different repetitions. The occasion; the variation of temperament, even of temperature; the emotional characteristic of the audience; the quickening or dulling of the ruling sentiment of the day or hour—each and all of these insensibly, if not consciously, can regulate the pressure in the temperamental barometer. When to the gift of logical power of understanding causes and effects there is added that of instinctively thinking and doing the right thing, then the great artist is revealed. It is, perhaps, this instinctive power which is the basis of creative art; the power of the poet as distinguished from that of the workman. Then comes a nicely balanced judgment of the selective faculty. There are always many ways of doing the same thing. One, of course, must be best; though others may come very close to it in merit.

Ellen Terry has the faculty of reaching the best. When one sees any other actress essay a part in which she has won applause, the actuality seems but dull beside the memory. As the object of stage work is "seeming" not "being," the effort to appear real transcends reality—with the art of stage perspective added.

VI

When Ellen Terry has taken hold of a character it becomes, whilst her thoughts are on it, a part of her own nature. In fact, her own nature

"is subdued
To what it works in, like the dyer's hand.

Her intuition, which in a woman is quicker than a man's reason, not only avoids error from the very inception of her work, but brings her unerringly by the quickest road to the best end. In the studying of her own parts and the arranging of her own business of them she had always had a free hand with Irving. At the Lyceum she was consulted about everything; and the dispositions of other persons and things were made to fit into her arrangements. I can only recall one instance when her wishes were not exactly carried out. This was at the end of the church scene of *Much Ado about Nothing* which in the Lyceum version finished the Fourth Act—the scene of the Prison which in Shakespeare ends the act having been transferred to the beginning of the last act. Here Beatrice has pledged Benedick to kill Claudio. Her newly accepted lover finishes the scene: "Go, comfort your cousin; I must say, she is dead; and so, farewell." Irving thought that the last words should be a little more operative with regard to the coming portion of the play; and so insisted in putting in the "gag" which was often in use:

Beatrice. "Benedick, kill Claudio!"
Benedick. "As sure as I'm alive I will!"

Against this Ellen Terry protested, almost to tears. She thought that every word of Shakespeare was sacred; to add to them was wrong. Still Irving was obdurate; and she finally yielded to his wishes.

To my own mind Irving was right. He too held every word of Shakespeare in reverence; but modern conditions, which require the shortening of plays, necessitate now and again the concentration of ideas—the emphasis of purposes. The words of the "tag" which he and Ellen Terry spoke, and the extraordinary forceful way they spoke them, heightened the effect. By carrying on the idea of the audience to an immediate and definite purpose they increased the "tug" of the play.

It may be interesting to note that this introduction was not, so far as I remember, commented on by any of the critics. It was not printed in the acting version, but the words were spoken—and there was no possibility of their not being heard—on every performance of our run of two hundred nights. Where there are so many Shakespeareans looking keenly for errors of text, it was odd such an addition should have passed without comment!

VII

The sincerity of Ellen Terry's nature finds expression in her art. In all my long experience of her I never knew her to strike a wrong note. Doubtless she has her faults. She is a woman; and perfection must not be expected even in the finishing work of Creation:

> " Auld Nature swears the lovely dears
> Her noblest work she classes, O;
> Her 'prentice han' she tried on man,
> And then she made the lasses, O!

But whatever faults she may have are altogether those of the individual human being, not of the artist. As the latter she had achieved perfection even when I first saw her in 1878.

The mind which balances truly each item, each evidence of character submitted to it by nature, experience or the dramatist, is the true source of art. Without it perfection must be a hazard; when there are many roads to choose from, the traveller may chance to blunder into the right one, but the doing so is the work of luck not art. But when day after day, week after week, year after year one *always* takes the right road, chance or fortune cannot be regarded as the dominating cause. The sincerity of art has many means of expression ; but even of these some are more subtle than others. Such exposition demands mind and the exercise of mind ; we may, I think, take it that intention requires intellectual effort both for its conception and execution—the wish and the attempt to turn desire into force. The carrying out of intention requires fresh mental effort. And such must be primarily based on a knowledge of the powers and facts at command. Thus it is that the actor must understand himself ; the task is even more difficult when the actor is a woman whose nature, therefore, in its manifestations is continually changing. But this very changeableness has in it the elements of force and charm. Out of the kaleidoscope come glimpses of new things which have only to be recorded and remembered in order to become knowledge. In the variety of emotions is a pauseless attractiveness which does not admit of weariness. Nature was good to Ellen Terry in the equipment for her work. Her personality enriched by the gifts showered upon her is a very treasure-house of art. No other woman of her time has shown such abounding and abiding charm ; such matchless mirthfulness ; pathos so deep.

VIII

As to the stage characters which she has made her own it would be impossible to say enough. Any one of them is worthy of an exhaustive study. In the early days of her acting, which began when her years were but few, stage art was in a poor way.

The old style of acting, eminently suitable to the age in which it had been evolved, was still in vogue, though the conditions of the great world without were changing. "The Drama's laws the Drama's patrons give" is a truth told with poetic comprehensiveness; what the public wants the actors must in reason supply. But the age when railways were still new, when telegraphs were hoped for; when such knowledge as that of the influence of worms on the outer layer of the structure of the world was being investigated, and when the existence of bacteria was becoming a conclusion rather than a guess, did not mean to be satisfied with an old-world, unnatural expression of human feeling seemingly based on a belief that passions were single and crude and that they swept aside the manifold complications of life. Ellen Terry belongs to the age of investigation. She is of those who brought in the new school of natural acting. It is true that she had learned and benefited by the teaching and experience of the old school. The lessons which Mrs. Charles Kean had so patiently taught her gave her boldness and breadth, and made for the realisation of poetic atmosphere and that perspective of the stage which is so much stronger than that of real life. But the work which she did in the new school came from herself. Here it was that her manifold gifts and charms found means of expression—of working out her purpose in relation to the characters which she undertook. If I had myself to put into a phrase the contribution to art-progress which Ellen Terry's work has been, I should say that it was the recognition of freedom of effort. She enlarged the bounds of art from those of convention to those of nature; and in doing so gave fuller scope to natural power. Since she set the way many another actress has arrived at the full success possible to the range of her gifts who otherwise would have been early strangled in the meshes of convention. The general effect of this has been to raise the art as well as widening it. The natural style does not allow of falsity or grossness; in the light which is common to all who understand, either by instinct or education, these stand out as faults or excrescences. In this "natural" method also individual force counts for its worth and the characteristic notes of sex are marked. For instance, I have heard—for unfortunately I never saw the piece—that when long ago she played *The Wandering Heir* her charm of sex was paramount; she played a girl masquerading as a boy so delightfully because she was so complete a woman. In her, womanhood is paramount. She has to the full in her nature whatever quality it is that corresponds to what we call "virility" in a man.

Her influence on her art has been so marked that one can see in the younger generation of women players how in their efforts to understand her methods they have unconsciously held her identity as their objective. In a number of them this appears as a sort of mild imitation. It was the same thing with the school of Irving. Trying to follow in his footsteps they have achieved something of his identity; generally those little personal traits or habits catching to the eye, which some call faults, others idiosyncrasies.

The advantages which both Irving and Ellen

Terry gave to dramatic art will be even more marked in the future than it is at the present; though the credit to them of its doing will be less conspicuous than it is now. Already the thoughtful work has been done; the principles have been tested and accepted, and the teaching has reached its synthetic stage.

IX

Naturally the years that went to the doing of this fine art work threw the two players together in a remarkable way, and made for an artistic comradeship which, so far as I know, has had no equal in their own branch of art. It began with Irving's management at the end of 1878 and lasted as a working reality for twenty-four years. At the Prince's Theatre, Bristol, on the last night of the Provincial Tour of 1902, December 13, she played for the last time under his management. Some months later, July 14, 1903, they played again in the same piece *The Merchant of Venice* at Drury Lane for the benefit of the Actors' Association. This occasion has become a memorable one; it was the last time when they played together.

Their cause of separation was in no wise any form of disagreement. It was simply effluxion of time. To the last hour of Irving's life the brotherly affection between them remained undimmed. Naturally when these two great players who had worked together in the public eye for nearly a quarter of a century separated Curiosity began to search for causes, and her handmaid Gossip proclaimed what she alleged to be them. Let me tell the simple truth and so set the matter right :

In the course of their long artistic co-operation Irving had produced twenty-seven plays in which they had acted together. In nineteen of these Ellen Terry had played young parts, which naturally in the course of so many years became unsuitable. Indeed the first person to find fault with them was Ellen Terry herself who, with her keen uncompromising critical faculty always awake to the purposes of her work, realised the wisdom of abandonment long before the public had ever such a thought. There remained, therefore, for their mutual use but eight plays of the repertoire—the finished work of so many years. Of these, two : *Macbeth* and *Henry VIII.*, had been destroyed by fire, and the expense of reproducing them adequately for only occasional presentation was prohibitive. Two others : *Coriolanus* and *Peter the Great*, were not popular. *Robespierre* had had its day, a long run to the full extent of its excellence. There remained, therefore, but three : *Charles I.*, *The Merchant of Venice* and *Madame sans Gêne*. The last of these had not proved a very great success in England ; in America it had been done to death. For *Charles I.*, by its very sadness and its dramatic scope, the audience could only be drawn from a limited class. So that there remained for practical purposes of continuous playing only *The Merchant of Venice*. There was one other play in which, though her part was a young one, Ellen Terry could always play, *Much Ado about Nothing*. But then Irving had grown too old for Benedick, and so for his purposes the play was past.

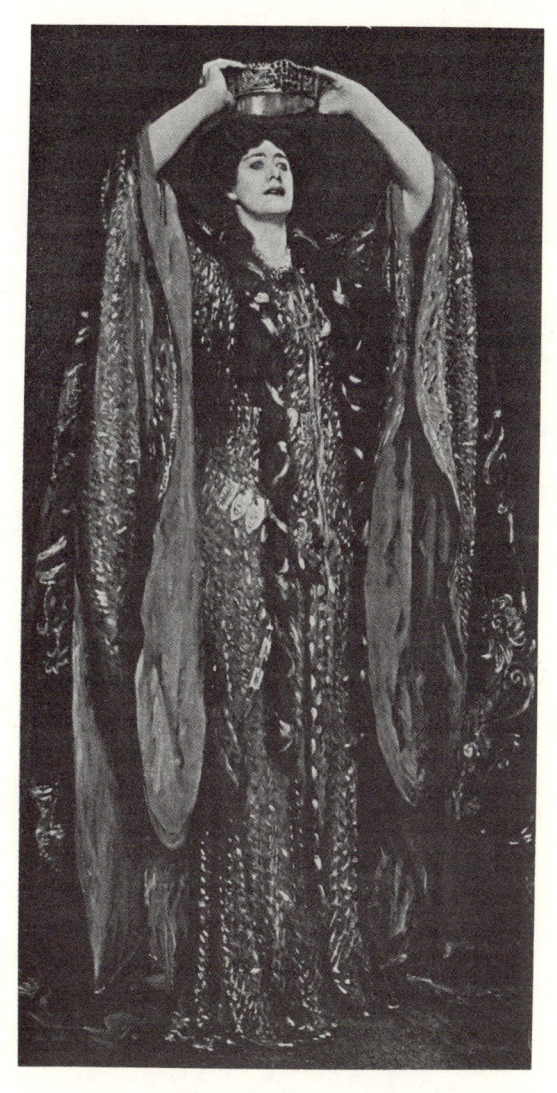

*Ellen Terry as Lady Macbeth,
from the painting by John Sargent, R.A.,
in the Tate Gallery.*

Ellen Terry did not care—and rightly enough—to play only once or twice a week as Portia—or in *Nance Oldfield,* given with *The Bells*—whilst there was so much excellent work, in all ways suitable to her personality and her years, to be done. Ordinarily one would not allude to these matters; ladies have by right no date. But when a lady's Jubilee on the Stage has been a completed fact, to whose paramount success the whole world has rung, there is no need for misleading reticence.

The mere fact of their ceasing to play together did not bring to a close the long artistic comradeship of Henry Irving and Ellen Terry. To the very last the kindly interest in each other's work and the affection between them never ceased or even slackened. Whatever one did the other followed with eager anxiety. Right up to the hour of his death Irving was interested in all that she did. On that last sad evening, even whilst anxiety for the coming changes in his own work was looming over him, he spoke to me in his dressing-room about her health and her work. He spoke feelingly and sympathetically, and with confidence and affection; just as he had always done during the long period of their working together. He had written to her himself in the same vein. In his letter he had told her what a delight it would be to him to hear her Lecture on "The Letters in Shakespeare's Plays."

X

For my own part I have no words at command adequate to tell the kindly feeling which I have always had for the delightful creature—to express my reverence and regard and love for her enchanting personality. From the very first she took me into the inner heart of her friendship; unconsciously I was given the rôle of "big brother." Nay, she found a name for me which was all her own and which one would think to be the least appropriate to a man of my inches. When I would ask her about some social duty which it was necessary for her to attend to—some important person to receive, some special entertainment to attend—she would make what nurses call a "wry face"; then she would ask:

"Bram, is this earnest?"

"Yes!" I would reply. "Honest injun!" She would smile and pout together as she would reply:

"All right, mama!" Then I knew that she was going to play that part as nicely as it could be played by any human being. Indeed it was hardly "playing a part" for she was genuinely glad to meet cordiality with equal feeling. It was only the beginning and the publicity that she disliked. The picture reproduced will show how affectionately she carried out at times her playful pet name. "Fussie" is Irving's dog; "Drummie" is her own.

I should like to write of Ellen Terry a whole volume; but after all, as this book is about Irving, I can only treat of her incidentally, woven though she was into the very texture of his artistic life.

"Drummie" "To my Ma!" — I am her dutiful child "Fussie"
Ellen Terry = Feb. 88.

MISS ELLEN TERRY, 1906

Moreover, she is some day to produce a volume of her own.

It is hard to believe that half a century has elapsed since Ellen Terry went timidly through her first part on the stage. The slim child dragging the odd-looking go-cart, which the early daguerreotype recorded as Mamilius in Charles Kean's production of *A Winter's Tale*, has been so long a force of womanly charm and radiant beauty—an actress of such incomparable excellence that in her art as in our memories she almost stands alone—great amongst the great.

Ellen Terry is a great actress, the greatest of her time; and she will have her niche in history. She is loved by every one who ever knew her. Her presence is a charm, her friendship a delight; her memory will be a national as well as a personal possession.

LXVI

FRESH HONOURS IN DUBLIN

A public reception—Above politics—A lesson in handshaking—A remarkable address—A generous gift

WHEN we visited Dublin in the tour of 1894 there were some memorable experiences. Ever since 1876 my native city had a warm place in Irving's heart. And very justly so, for it had showered upon him love and honour. This time there were two occasions which should not be forgotten.

The first was a public Reception at the Mansion-House given by the then Lord Mayor, Valentine Dillon, a friend of my own boyhood. This took place on Thursday, November 29, and was in truth an affair of national importance. At that time the long-continued feuds between Conservatives and Liberals, Home Rulers and Unionists, Catholics and Protestants, which had marked with extra virulence —for they had been long existent—the past decades, were still operative. Still, improvement was in the air; only opportunity was wanting to give it expression.

The beneficent occasion came in that Reception. Irving and Ellen Terry were delightfully popular personalities. They had no politics, and what religion either professed was not even considered; their artistic excellence shadowed all else. Lord

Mayor Dillon was a man with broad views of life and of the dignity of the position which he held for, I think, the third time. He cast very wide the net of his hospitable intent. He asked every one who was of account in any way; and all came. Some three thousand persons had been bidden and there was a full tally of guests. When once they had actually met in a common cause, one and all seemed to take the opportunity of showing that the hatchet had been buried. Men who had not spoken for years—who had not looked at each other save with the eyes of animosity, seemed glad to mingle on something of the old terms—to renew old friendships and long-severed acquaintanceship.

Irving and Ellen Terry, with some of us lesser lights supporting them, stood on the daïs beside the Lord Mayor and the Lady Mayoress; and I can bear witness that not one who passed went without a handshake from both. It was a serious physical effort. To shake hands with some thousands of persons would tax the strongest. Irving went through it with all the direct simplicity of his nature. Ellen Terry, having to supplement nature with art, rested at times her right hand and shook with the left with such cunning dexterity that no one was a whit the wiser. One and all went away from that hospitable and friendly gathering in a happy frame of mind. Dublin was a gainer by that wave of beneficent sympathy.

Two days later, on the last night of the engagement, Saturday, December 1, there was another and even more remarkable function. This was the presentation of a Public Address on the stage after the play. This Address was no ordinary one. It was signed by all the great public officials, both of the city and of the country :

> The Lord Mayor,
> The High Sheriff,
> The Lord Chancellor,
> The Commander of the Forces,
> The Lord Chief Justices,
> All the Judges,
> All the City Members of Parliament,
> The Provost of Dublin University,
> The President of the College of Surgeons,
> The President of the College of Physicians,
> All the Public Officials,
> And by a host of Leading Citizens.

The Lord-Lieutenant, Lord Crewe, was unable to take a part in it as, being representative of the Queen, he could not engage in such an honour to a private person ; but he made a point of remaining in his box so that he might be seen to be present.

When the curtain drew up the great body of the Committee, numbering about sixty, stood behind the Lord Mayor on one side of the stage. On the other Irving, with close behind him Ellen Terry, whom I had the honour of escorting, and all the other members of the Company. The Lord Mayor read the Address, which was conceived in love and honour and born in noble and touching words. In replying for himself and Miss Terry, Irving was much touched, and had to make an effort to speak at all. There was a lofty look in his eyes which spoke for the sincerity of the words which he used in his reply :

" Now when your great University has accepted me to the brotherhood of her sons, and when your city and your nation have taken me to your hearts, I feel that the cup of a player's honour is full to the brim."

THE POOR TO BENEFIT

I have not often seen him moved so much as he was that night. His speech and movement were only controlled by his strong will and the habit of self-repression.

Within and without the theatre was a scene of wild enthusiasm not to be forgotten. I have been witness of many scenes of wild generosity but none to surpass that night.

Irving was always anxious that others should rejoice in some form with his own rejoicing. Before leaving Dublin he placed in the hands of the Lord Mayor a cheque for a hundred guineas for his disposal to the use of the poor.

LXVII

PERFORMANCES AT SANDRINGHAM AND WINDSOR

Sandringham, 1889—First appearance before the Queen—A quick change—Souvenirs—Windsor, 1893—A blunder in old days—Royal hospitality—The Queen and the Press—Sandringham, 1902—The Kaiser's visit—A record journey—An amateur conductor

I

SANDRINGHAM, 1889

IN April 1889 the Prince of Wales had the honour of entertaining the Queen at Sandringham. He wished that she should see Irving and Ellen Terry, neither of whom she had seen play. Accordingly it was arranged that on April 26 the Lyceum would be closed for the evening and that a performance should be given in Sandringham in a little theatre specially built in the great drawing-room in which were placed the exquisite trophies of arms presented by Indian Rajahs during the Prince's visit. For this theatre Irving had got Walter Hann to paint an act drop; scenery of a suitable size was prepared by Hawes Craven—an exceedingly fine piece of miniature stage work. The Bill fixed was: *The Bells*, and the Trial Scene from *The Merchant of Venice*, the combination of which pieces would, the Prince thought, show both the players at their best.

On the day fixed, April 26, Irving and Miss Terry went down to Sandringham by the regular train between two and three o'clock. The special with the Company left St. Pancras at 3.55, arriving at Wolferton at a quarter to seven, whence they were driven to the house.

The drawing-room looked very beautiful, the white walls showing up the many stands of magnificent weapons and armour; greenery and flowers were everywhere. At one end was the little theatre with a proscenium opening of some twenty feet wide, the arch painted in a pleasant colour between pink and maroon. Mr. Loveday and a staff of men had been down for several days as it was found necessary to have all in order before the Queen's arrival. Sandringham is not a very vast house, and much space was required for the reception of a great Queen who always travelled with a host of servants of all degrees. There was a large gathering in the drawing-room of not only the house guests but local personages; the big music gallery at the back was full of tenants and servants. The Queen had kindly expressed her wish that the audience should do just as they wished as to applauding, and I must say that I have never seen or heard a more enthusiastic audience within the bounds of decorum.

The Queen sat in the centre in front with the Prince of Wales on her right and the Princess on her left, and others of the family beside them. Next came the guests in their degrees. The doorway was crowded with the servants—the Queen's all in black and the Prince's in Royal scarlet liveries.

Her Majesty seemed greatly pleased. It had been arranged that Irving and Ellen Terry were to join the Prince and Princess at supper. The Queen would not wait up, but was to retire at once. However, just as the players were removing their warpaint, Her Majesty sent word by Sir Henry Ponsonby that she would like to speak to Mr. Irving and Miss Terry. Irving was in the act of removing his " make-up " as Shylock, which was a job requiring some little time. He was extraordinarily quick both as to dressing and undressing; but the " priming " of earth on which stage paint is laid, grease, paint, and lampblack and spirit-gum take some little time to remove, even before the stage of soap-and-water is reached. Portia, however, is a part which does not soil, and as to mere dressing, Ellen Terry can simply fly. She knew that Irving would be at least a few minutes, and it is not good form to keep a Queen waiting. Within a minute she was tearing down the passage, with her dresser running close behind her and fastening up the back of her frock as she went. At the doorway she threw over her shoulders the scarf which was a part of her dress and sailed into the room with a grand courtesy. Within a very few minutes Irving in immaculate evening dress followed.

The Queen presented Irving with a souvenir of the occasion in the shape of a pair of sleeve links, with her monogram V. R. in diamonds in red enamel. To Ellen Terry she gave a brooch of pearls and diamonds.

Irving and Ellen Terry supped with the Royal guests. For the rest of the Company supper was prepared in the Conservatory. The heads of de-

MATHIAS AND SHYLOCK PRESENTED TO HER MAJESTY AT SANDRINGHAM, 1889

partments and workmen were entertained in the Housekeeper's room or the Servants' Hall according to their degrees. Irving had with his usual wish to save trouble arranged for supper for all the party on the train home. But the Prince of Wales would not hear of such a thing. He said that the players were his guests and that they must eat in his house. Some of the Equerries and high officials of the court supped in the Conservatory with the actors. It had been understood that there was to be no suggestion of payment of even expenses. Irving was only too proud and happy to serve his Queen and future King in all ways of his own art to the best of his power. This arrangement was held to on every occasion on which he had the honour to give a special performance before Royalty.

At half-past two o'clock the whole Company and workmen were driven to Wolferton station where the special train was waiting. It arrived at St. Pancras at a few minutes past six in the morning.

II

WINDSOR, 1893

The performance at Windsor was in its way quite a remarkable thing. In the earlier years of her reign Queen Victoria was accustomed to have from time to time theatrical performances at Windsor Castle. These were generally held in the Waterloo Chamber, where a moveable stage was erected on each occasion. In old days this stage was so low that once Mr. Henry Howe, who had to come up through a trap according to the action of the piece, had to crawl on his stomach under the stage to get to the appointed place. Howe was nearly eighty years of age when he told me this incident, but the memory was so strong on him that he laughed like a boy. When the Prince Consort died in 1861 all such gaieties were stopped, and for thirty-two years no play was given at Windsor. But when in 1889 the Queen did begin to resume something like the old life at Court her first effort in that direction was to command a performance by those players of the later day whom she had seen at Sandringham, whose merit was widely recognised and who had already won official recognition of another kind—the previous year the University of Dublin had given Irving a degree *Honoris Causa*. Moreover, the Queen wanted to see *Becket*, the work of her own Poet Laureate, which had created so much interest and thought.

Sir Henry Ponsonby, the Queen's Private Secretary, came from Windsor to see Irving at Her Majesty's wish. Irving was, of course, delighted to hold himself at the Queen's will. The only stipulation which he made was that he was to be allowed to bear the expenses of all kinds and was not to be offered fee or pay of any kind, even though such was a usual formality. For this he had a special reason; not to set himself up as an individual against the custom of the Court, but to avoid the possibility of such a *bêtise* as had in earlier years stopped the Windsor theatrical performances for a time. The way of it was this: At the commencement of the system of having such performances the Queen had left the matter in the hands of Charles Kean, then manager of the Princess's Theatre, and acknowledged head of the theatrical calling. He and his assistants made all the necessary arrangements, taking care that the gift of the Court patronage was, as fairly as was possible, divided amongst actors both in London and throughout the provinces. This worked excellently; and there were few, if any, jealousies. Kean made all the financial arrangements and paid salaries on the scale fixed on his suggestion by the Privy Purse. Matters went along smoothly so long as Kean had control. Later on, however, this was handed over to Mr. Mitchell of Bond Street, the agent who acted for the Queen with regard to her visits to London theatres and other places of amusement. At last came trouble. The scale of salary fixed was, I believe—for I can only speak from hearsay — at the rate of twice the actors' earnings in the previous year. On one occasion an actor of some repute was through some incredible stupidity paid at this rate, strictly applied though the case was exceptional. He had been for years receiving a large salary, but during nearly the whole of the previous year had been ill and of course "out of work." His total earnings therefore when divided by fifty-two amounted to but a meagre weekly wage. At a nightly standard it was ridiculous. Kean would of course, as an actor, have understood this and have carried out the spirit of Her Majesty's wishes. But the man of business went "by the card," and when the comedian received the dole sent to him he was highly indignant, and determined to taste some form of satisfaction, if only of revenge for his injured feelings. Of course the Queen knew nothing of all this, and be sure she was incensed when she heard of it. The actor's form of revenge was to send the amount of salary paid to him to the police court poor box as a contribution from himself and Queen Victoria.

I may be wrong in details of the story, for it is one of fifty years ago, but in the main it is correct. I had it from Irving and I have often heard it spoken about by old actors of the time. With such a catastrophe in his memory Irving naturally wished to be careful. He had to consider not only himself but his whole Company, hundreds of persons of all degrees. Some of them might look on the affair as an Eldorado whence should come wealth beyond the dreams of avarice and be " disgruntled " at any failure to that end. When he was himself the paymaster and shared as an individual the conditions attaching to his comrades, there could be no complaint. Henry Irving was a most loyal subject; he wished at all times to render love and honour to the Monarch, and as he was in his own way a conspicuous individual it was necessary to be careful lest his good intentions should stray.

Sir Henry Ponsonby quite understood Irving's feelings and wishes, and acceded to them. Train arrangements were to be at the expense of the Queen, who was particular that this should be the rule with all her guests. Of course Irving acquiesced. When the day—March 18, which the Queen wished—had been arranged the matter of accomplishment was left entirely in his hands. Forthwith the work of preparation began.

On the 2nd March I had taken with me to

MINIATURE SCENERY

Windsor the heads of our various stage departments and the scene painter; a week later Irving went himself, taking Loveday with him.

New scenery, exactly the same as that in use but on a smaller scale and better suited in its mechanism to the limited space, was painted; and with it a beautiful proscenium for the miniature theatre built up in the Waterloo Chamber. As there would not be room for the usual number of supers or chorus, most of these were taken by the minor members of the Company, and all were carefully rehearsed. As it was, however, the first contingent which went to Windsor on the morning of the day of performance numbered one hundred and seventy-eight persons.

We had a full rehearsal on the day of performance, lasting up to half-past four o'clock.

The day was a lovely one, cold and bright, and except when rehearsing the Lyceum Company found endless pleasure in wandering in the gardens or on the Terrace from which the view was superb; the river winding its quiet way through fields and woods; the whole fair landscape softened in misty distance. The ceaseless cawing of the rooks overhead enhanced the effect. Within doors the players examined the endless art treasures of the Castle.

At nine o'clock the Queen arrived, walking slowly through the long corridor. She sat, of course, in the centre of the daïs, with the Empress Frederick of Germany on her right and the Prince of Wales on her left. The room was exquisitely decorated with plants and flowers, and as it was filled with ladies and gentlemen in court dress and uniform, the effect was very fine. The play went well. The

Queen had with graceful and kindly forethought given orders that all present might applaud as they would—it not having been etiquette to applaud on such occasions without Royal permission. Another piece of thoughtful kindness of Her Majesty was to have amongst the guests staying for the week-end at Windsor Lord and Lady Tennyson. The adaptation of the play to the lesser space than the Lyceum was so judiciously done that one did not notice any difference.

At the close of the performance the Queen sent for Irving and Ellen Terry and complimented them on the perfection and beauty of their playing. To Irving she said:

" It is a very noble play! What a pity that old Tennyson did not live to see it. It would have delighted him as it has delighted Us!"

She also received Geneviève Ward and William Terriss.

The Queen always wished that her guests of all degrees should be made welcome, and Sir Henry Ponsonby said that she had arranged that all the Company, players and workmen of all kinds, should dine and take supper in the Castle. The dinner was less formal, but the supper was in its way a function. Four different rooms were arranged for the purpose. In the first were the acting Company and higher officials to the number of about fifty. The gentlemen of the orchestra and the heads of departments in the second and third; the workmen, &c., in the fourth. At the end all drank the Queen's health loyally.

There was an immense amount of public interest in this performance. So high it ran that all the

MARKING AN EPOCH

great newspapers asked permission to be represented. This request could not be acceded to as it was a purely private affair; the utmost that could by usage be allowed was that press representatives should during the afternoon be allowed to see the Waterloo Chamber prepared for the performance in the evening.

Late in the afternoon I received a request from a lot of the chief papers that I should myself ask permission to send a short despatch, say some five hundred words, at the close of the performance. I took the message to Sir Henry Ponsonby, who seemed very much struck with it, as though the public importance of the event had suddenly dawned on him. He said:

"I must take this to the Queen at once and learn her wishes respecting it. The matter seems to be of much more importance than I had thought!" He came back shortly, seemingly very pleased, and said to me, speaking as he approached:

"The Queen says that she is very pleased to give permission. Mr. Bram Stoker may write whatever he pleases about the event. But he must say nothing till after the performance is all over." Then he added, "The Queen also told me to explain that she was sending orders to have the telegraph office in the Castle kept open for your convenience till you have quite done with it. I had better explain that the telegraph office here is a private one and that the Queen pays for all telegrams. This she insists on."

Altogether the performance was a very memorable one. It marked an epoch in the life of the Great Queen—that in which she broke the long gloom of more than thirty years and began the restoration to something like the old happy life of the earlier years of her reign.

III

SANDRINGHAM, 1902

The second visit to Sandringham came thirteen years after the first, being in 1902 after the King's accession. The occasion was that of the Kaiser's visit. The King wished to have a surprise for him; and at the time he had his " Command " conveyed to Irving his wish was intimated that the matter should be kept absolutely secret till the event came off. This we could see was to be a difficult task; but the promise was given and kept. At the date fixed—November 14—we would be playing in Belfast, so that the task to get there and return with the loss of only one night to the audience was really a stupendous one. It would involve special arrangements with at least one shipping company and several railways. This would necessitate the fact of the journey being known to so many people that really secrecy seemed impossible of achievement. However the matter was undertaken and had to be done. Not a soul other than the actively engaged knew of the affair beforehand. Even Ellen Terry was purposely kept in the dark. As the only play to be given by Irving was *Waterloo* the cast was small, there being only four people in it. These with three others would comprise the party. One man had been sent to London to bring down the scene specially painted for the occasion and to see to arrangements. Mr. Ben Webster, who was to play his original part of Colonel Midwinter, was to come from London, where he was then playing. Let me say here that not the slightest whisper went forth on our side; and we were surprised to see an account of what was to be done, which evidently came from another branch of the entertainment being made ready for the King's Imperial guest.

When we began to consider the practicability of the journey my heart sank. There seemed no way by which the out and return journeys could be done. I was for a time seriously considering the advisability of asking for a torpedo boat to run us over from Belfast to Stranraer, Barrow, Fleetwood, or Liverpool. At last Mr. James Wright, the representative of Mr. Turnbull, Traffic Superintendent of the London and North-Western Railway, and James McDowell, Manager of the Belfast and Liverpool Steamship Company, came up to Glasgow, and after a good deal of consideration arranged a journey which could only have been done by placing the whole resources of shipping and railway companies at our disposal. The *Magic*, the fastest boat of the Belfast line, was to be taken off her regular service two days before; loaded up with the best Welsh coal, and held ready at the wharf with full steam up on the evening of the journey. The railroading would be arranged from Euston.

Faust was played in Belfast on the night of November 13. As each one of the little party finished on the stage they got dressed and were driven down to the wharf. The moment the last call was given at the end of the play Irving hurried into his travelling clothes, and he and I and Walter were whirled off to the *Magic*. The instant we passed on deck the gangway plank was drawn and the ship started off full speed. Such was contrary to law, as ships can only go part speed in the Loch. But no one made objections; we were on the King's service. Mr. McDowell came with us. Supper was ready.

We got to Liverpool at eight in the morning and found alongside the dock the special carriage, one of the Royal saloons used on the London and North-Western Railway; got on board, and were whirled off to Crewe, where we caught the fast express to Rugby. There we took on a dining-car and went on to Peterborough. Here our carriage was handed over to the Great Eastern Company, which took us on the fast train to Lynn, and thence on a special to Wolferton.

At the station we found a whole row of reporters. They were not allowed to go to Sandringham. I promised to ask for leave to send them word as soon as the performance should be over. The permission was graciously acceded, and when all was over I sent the line agreed on, " Programme adhered to." It was extended to a column next morning in some of the papers.

The King had sent a brougham for Sir Henry. In it he, Miss Hackney and I were driven at once to Sandringham. The others came on almost immediately by one of the King's motor buses. Incidentally I may say that there was some concern in the official world and certain private reprimanding because even that brougham was allowed to pass in unchallenged. The police arrangements were—very properly—carried out with the most extraordinary exactitude.

After tea Irving went to lie down for a while in the room provided for him, and let me say that it was no joke providing a room at Sandringham at that time. The Kaiser had with him a vast and important *entourage*, and all the English guests had to put up with such accommodation as was possible, which of course they were loyally glad to do.

At ten o'clock precisely, Sandringham time—which is half-an-hour ahead of standard time—the Kaiser and the Queen moved into the great drawing-room where the stage was fixed. Then followed the King and family, and guests. There were altogether some three hundred and fifty in the room.

As the movement to the theatre began there was a—to us—amusing episode. After our arrival, when things were being put in order for the performance, it had been discovered that kettle drums were missing. Either they had not been sent at all or they had gone astray. At first we took it for granted that in such a scene of pomp and splendour as was around us drums and drummers would be easy to find. But it was not so. Drums were obtainable but no drummer, and there was not time to get one from the nearest town. Now the military music is necessary for the performance of *Waterloo;* the quicksteps are not only required for the Prelude but are in the structure of the piece. For the occasion of the Imperial visit, there had been brought from Vienna a celebrated string band, the conductor of high status in his art and all the components of the band fine players. But there was no drummer; and there could be even no proper rehearsal of the incidental music of the play without the drums. We were beginning to despair, when the head constable of the county who was present said that there was one man in the police of the division who was the drummer of the Police Band of the district, and undertook to try and find him. After much telegraphing and telephoning it was found that he was out on his beat about the farthest point of his district. However, when he was located a trap with a fresh horse was sent for him. He arrived tired and foodless just before the time fixed for beginning. He was a fine performer fortunately, a master of his work, and with the score before him needed no preparation.

When the signal was given of the movement of the Royalties the Conductor took his baton, but when he looked at the score of the Prelude, which is continually changing time with the medley of the various regimental quicksteps, he said:

"I cannot play it."

"Go on, man! Go on!" said Belmore, who was acting as stage manager.

"I cannot!" he answered; "I cannot!" and stood unmoving. Things were serious, for already the procession was formed and the Kaiser and the Queen were entering the room. It had been arranged that the Prelude was to play them to their seats. "Give me the stick!" said Belmore suddenly, and took the fiddle bow with which he conducted from the unresisting hand of the stranger. Of course all this was behind the scenes and amongst ourselves only. Then he began to conduct. He had never done so, but he had some knowledge of music.

AN AMATEUR CONDUCTOR

But the gentlemen of the band did not hesitate. They were all fine musicians and well accustomed to playing together. Probably they were not averse from showing that they could play perfectly without a conductor at all! They certainly did seem to play with especial verve. Belmore was a sight to behold. He seemed to know all the tricks of leadership, modifying or increasing tone with one hand whilst he beat time with the other; pausing dramatically with uplifted baton or beating with sudden forcefulness; screwing round with his left hand as though to twist the music into a continued unity. Anyhow it—or something—told. The music went excellently and without a hitch.

Waterloo went splendidly, and we heard afterwards that the Kaiser was delighted with it. It was followed by *Dr. Johnson*, in which Mr. and Mrs. Arthur Bourchier took the principal parts. Irving was asked to supper with the Royal party; so too were Mr. and Mrs. Bourchier. The rest of us supped in the Conservatory with the Equerries and others.

At one o'clock—half-past one Sandringham time—we drove to Wolferton, where two trains stood ready to start. One, a long one for London—the other a special consisting of engine and brake-van and the two sleeping saloons. The row of reporters were again on the platform and went back on the London train.

Our party got to sleep as soon as we could. At a quarter to seven in the morning we got to the dock at Liverpool and went aboard the *Magic* which stood ready with steam up. The tide was low, but as there was much fog in the river Mr.

McDowell arranged that the dock-gates should be opened before the usual hour. We actually stirred up the mud with the screw as we passed out into the Mersey. The river was dark with thick fog and we had to find our way, inch by inch, to beyond New Brighton. We were beginning to despair of arriving at Belfast in time when we cleared the belt of fog. We came out seemingly all at once into bright sunshine which lasted all the way home. It was a delightful day and a delightful run. The sun was bright, the air fresh and bracing and the water of sapphire blue so calm that passing to the south'ard of the Isle of Man we ran between the Calf and the Hen and Chickens—the dangerous cluster of rocks lying just outside it.

We ran full tilt up Belfast Lough and arrived at the wharf at five o'clock in good time for a wash and dress for the theatre.

When Irving stepped on the stage that night he got a right hearty cheer.

That journey was in many ways a record.

LXVIII

PRESIDENTS OF THE UNITED STATES

Chester Arthur—Grover Cleveland—A judgment on taste—McKinley—The " War Room "—Reception after a Cabinet Council—McKinley's memory—Theodore Roosevelt—His justice as Police Commissioner—Irving at his New Year Reception

I

HENRY IRVING had the honour of calling four Presidents of the United States by the name of friend.

The first was General Chester A. Arthur, who was in his high office in 1884 when Irving first visited Washington. The President sent to him a most kindly invitation to a Reception through Clayton McMichael, then Marshal of the district of Columbia. This was on the night of Saturday, 8th March. They had already met on Wednesday, 5th. Irving had called at the White House and had the honour of an interview. On the occasion of the Reception he had asked Irving to remain with a very few intimate friends after the rest had gone. They sat till a late—or rather an early hour.

II

Irving's first meeting with Mr. Grover Cleveland was when the latter was President-Elect. The occasion was the matinée for the benefit of the Actors' Fund at the Academy of Music in New York, December 4, 1887. Mr. Cleveland was in a box, and when Irving had with Ellen Terry played the fourth act of *The Merchant of Venice* he sent to ask if he would come to see him in his box. The occasion seemed rather peculiar as Irving thus described it to me that evening :

" When I came into the box Mr. Cleveland turned round and, seeing me, stood up and greeted me warmly. As I was thus facing the stage I could not help noticing that a man dressed exactly as I dressed Shylock, and with a wig and make up counterparts of my own, was playing some droll antics with a pump and milk cans. The President-Elect saw, I suppose, the surprise on my face, for he turned to the stage for a moment and then, turning back to me again, said in a grave way :

" ' That doesn't seem very good taste, does it ! ' Then leaning against the side of the box with his face to me and his back to the stage, he went on speaking about Shylock."

III

Major McKinley was a friend before he was nominated for President. The first meeting was at New York on November 16, 1893. He came to the play with Melville Stone, a great friend of Irving's—who introduced Irving to him. The following week we all met again at supper with John Sergeant Wise. This time Joseph Jefferson was of the party. Afterwards in Cleveland Mark Hanna brought him round

THE "WAR ROOM"

to see Irving in his dressing-room. This was after his election. Amongst other things we spoke of the possibility of Mark Hanna coming as United States Ambassador to London. "Ah! if he only would!" said McKinley.

In 1899, during our visit to Washington, Irving and I called at the White House to pay our respects to the President then in his second term of office. The officials of course recognised Sir Henry, and said that they knew the President would wish to see him. A Cabinet meeting was on, but when word was sent the President graciously sent a message asking Irving to wait as the Cabinet was nearly over and he wished to see him. We waited in the "War Room," a small — by comparison — room off the Council Chamber. Here we were taken charge of by Colonel Montgomery, who explained to us the mechanism by which the President was made aware of and could control all that was then going on in the Philippines where the war was being pursued with grim determination on both sides. All round the room were land maps and sea charts, and on either was marked as news came the position of each body of soldiers or each ship. The room was full of telegraph instruments and telephones some one of which was nearly always at work. Whilst we were waiting a message came that a certain advanced party of United States troops were surrounded and in great danger, and a message was sent by the President to hold their position at any cost, relief was coming. Irving was immensely struck with all this, and said it was the most wonderful piece of organisation he had ever known.

Presently word was brought that the Cabinet

Council was over and would we go in. It was a really impressive sight—all the more as there was no pomp or parade of any sort. In the middle of the great room with its row of arched windows stood the President, the baldness of his domed forehead making more apparent than ever his likeness to Napoleon. Grouped round him were the various chiefs of State departments, amongst them John Hay, Secretary of State; Elihu Root, Secretary for War; Charles Emory Smith, Postmaster-General, all of whom were by that time old friends. We had known them intimately since 1883-4. The President was sweetly gracious. We thought that he did not seem well in health; there was a waxen hue in his face which we did not like. The terrible labour of the Presidency—increased in his time by two wars—was undoubtedly telling on his strength. We were with him quite half-an-hour, a long while for such a place and time, and then came away.

That night we supped with the Secretary for War in his house in Rhode Island Avenue; he had a great gathering of officials—nearly all the Cabinet, the Paymaster-General, General Bates and his wife, and Mr. and Mrs. Thomas Nelson Page, friends whom Irving held dear—as I have the pleasure of so doing myself.

Indeed that was a long week in Washington. I do not know that in all my experience of Irving he ever went out so many times in a week. Sunday night, 24th December, reception and supper at the house of Wayne Macveigh, formerly Federal Attorney-General and late United States Ambassador to Italy; Tuesday as I have said; Wednesday to lunch with the British Ambassador, Lord Pauncefote — Ellen Terry being of the party; Thursday to lunch with the Postmaster-General—here were all the Cabinet except the Attorney-General, who was ill; Friday to lunch with the Secretary of State, and to supper with the Nelson Pages. This last was one of the most delightful parties which Irving—or any one else—ever had the privilege of attending. Four o'clock found us still unbroken.

At that visit to the White House we saw President McKinley for the last time. His assassination was attempted on 6th September 1901; he died on 14th.

On the 18th September Irving gave his Reading of *Becket* at Winchester for the King Alfred Millenary. He was called on to speak, and after speaking of King Alfred and what he had done for the making of England, he said:

> "All that race which looks on King Alfred's memory as a common heritage is in bitter grief for one whom to-morrow a mourning nation is to lay to rest. President McKinley was at once avatar and emblem of noble purpose, high thought and patriotism. He, like his predecessor of a thousand years ago, though he worked immediately for his own country, worked for all the world; and his memory shall be green for ever in the hearts of a loyal and expansive race—in the hearts of all English-speaking people."

IV

Irving's first meeting with Theodore Roosevelt was on 27th November 1895. The occasion was a luncheon party given by Seth Low, ex-Mayor of Brooklyn and then President of Columbia College, where a week before Irving had lectured on "The Character of Macbeth." The party numbered sixteen all told and included Charles Dudley Warner, W. D. Howells, Joseph Choate, Professors Morse, Price, and Brander Matthews. At that time Mr. Roosevelt was Commissioner of Police for the City of New York, with absolute power over the whole force. He had been appointed for a term of years irremovably. After the Lexow Commission it was necessary that the force should be re-organised. To do so required brains, energy, integrity, and an iron hand. Irving and I used often to talk of him and the task which he had undertaken, and we were both delighted to meet him. He and Irving had a chat together before lunch and again after it. For myself he was a person of extraordinary interest. Mr. Low, whom I had met a few years before at dinner in the house of the Baroness Burdett-Coutts, introduced me, and before lunch we had a chat.

Before he left he came to me and said:

"I am holding a sort of Court of justice the day after to-morrow—a trial of the charges made against policemen during the last fortnight. Would you like to come with me; you seem to be interested in the subject?"

Of course I jumped at the chance; it was exceedingly kind of him to give me such a unique opportunity. I went down at the hour appointed. The place was an immense hall where were gathered all the complainants with their witnesses, and the police with their witnesses. I estimated the number of persons present at not less than a thousand. The place of judgment was a raised table at the end of the room. The Commissioner sat behind it, and I beside him. Everything was done in perfect order. The Commissioner had the list of cases before him, and when one was over a lusty officer with a stentorian voice called out the next. Those interested in each case had been already grouped, so that when the case was announced the whole body thus segregated moved up in front of the table. The method was simple. The case was stated as briefly as possible—the Commissioner saw to that; the witnesses for the prosecution gave their evidence and were now and again asked a question from the Bench. Then the defendant had his say and produced his witnesses, if any; and again came an occasional searching question from the Commissioner, who when he had satisfied himself as to the justice of the case would smite the table with his hand and order on the next case. While the little crowd was changing places he would write a few words on the paper before him—judgment and perhaps sentence in one. The Commissioner was incarnate justice, and his judgments were given with a direct simplicity and brevity which were very remarkable. Each one would take only a few minutes; sometimes as few as two or three, never more than about twelve or fifteen. As there were very many cases brevity was a necessity.

Now and then in a case very difficult of conclusion Mr. Roosevelt, when he had written his decision, would turn to me and say:

" What do you think of that ? " I would answer

to the best of my own opinion : " I think the man's innocent ! " or " I think he is guilty ! " Then he would turn up the paper, lying face down, and show me what had been his own decision. As in every such case it was exactly what I had said, I thought—naturally—that he was very just.

I came away from the Court with a very profound belief in Mr. Roosevelt. I wrote afterwards in my diary :

> " Must be President some day. A man you can't cajole, can't frighten, can't buy."

On December 28, 1903, Irving commenced a week's engagement at Washington. On the morning of Friday, January 1, 1904, he received a letter from the President saying that he was that day holding his New Year's Reception and that he would be very pleased if he would come. Sir Henry would be expected to come by the private entrance with the Ambassadors. It was such a letter as to make its recipient feel proud—so courteous, so full of fine feeling and genuine hospitality—so significant of his liking and respect. The night before we had kept Irving up rather late. After the play and supper some of his comrades stopping in the hotel went up to bid him God-speed—to usher out the Old Year and to usher in the New—to keep the " First Foot " in Scotch fashion.

Irving did not rise next morning till a little later than usual and so did not receive the kind letter of the President in time to take full advantage of it. When he was dressed we went off to the White House and went in by the private entrance at the back. The Ambassadorial functions were over, but we were brought up at once and met him just as the section of " Veterans of the War " were beginning to pay their respects. He stood a little inside the doorway on the right and shook hands with every one who came—no light task in itself as there were on the queue for the reception a good many thousands of persons, male and female. The long line four deep extended far into the neighbouring streets, winding round the corners like a huge black snake, and disappearing in the distance. The serpentine appearance was increased by the slow movement as the crowd advanced inch by inch.

Beside the President stood Mrs. Roosevelt and beyond him all the ministers of his Cabinet with their wives in line—all the ladies were in full dress. The room was in form of a segment of a circle and the crowd passed between red cords stretched across the base of the arc, the President's party being behind either cord. The President gave Irving a really cordial greeting and held him for a minute or two speaking—a long time with such a crowd waiting. He did not know that I was with Irving, but when he saw me he addressed me by name. He certainly has a royal memory! He asked us to go behind the ropes and join his family and friends. This we did. We remained there a full hour, and Irving was made much of by all.

LXIX

KNIGHTHOOD

Irving's intimations of the honour—First State recognition in any country—William I. and Haase—A deluge of congratulations—The Queen's pleasure—A wonderful Address—Former suggestion of knighthood

I

LATE in the afternoon of Friday, May 24, 1895, I got from Irving the following telegram:

"Could you look in at quarter to six. Something important."

When I saw him he showed me two letters which he had received. One was from the Prime Minister, the Earl of Rosebery, telling him that the Queen had conferred on him the honour of knighthood in personal recognition and for his services to art.

The other was from the Prince of Wales congratulating him on the event.

The announcement had given him very much pleasure, and even when I saw him he was much moved. Together we drove to Ellen Terry's home in Longridge Road to tell her the news.

The next day was the Queen's Birthday on which the "Honour List" was promulgated, and when it was known that Irving was so honoured the telegrams, letters and cables began to pour in from all parts of the world. For it was in its way a remarkable event. It was the first time that in any country an actor had been, *quâ* actor, honoured by the State. When Got had been given the Legion of Honour by the French Government it had been specially intimated that it was as a Professor that he was its recipient. In Germany where the theatre is largely a State undertaking, recognition is not given to actors. Irving used to tell a story of Haase, the German actor, who was a great favourite with the Kaiser, William I. During a performance the Kaiser sent for Haase, who put on his dress coat with all the decorations given to him by various States and Bodies. The Emperor noticed them and said :

" Why, Haase, what a lot of orders you have ! "
To which the actor ventured to reply :

" Your Majesty, there is only one which could make me happy."

" And what is that, Haase, what is that ? "

" One given at the hand of your Majesty ! "

" No ! no ! Haase," he replied quickly, " you must not think of that ! That can never be ! An actor can neither give nor receive a challenge ! "

It really seemed as if the whole world rejoiced at the honour to Irving. The letters and telegrams kept coming literally in hundreds during the next two days, and cables constantly arrived from America, Australia, Canada, India, and from nearly all the nations in Europe. They were bewildering. Late in the afternoon of Saturday Irving sat at his desk in the Lyceum before piles of them opened by one of the clerks. Presently he turned to me with his hand to his head and said :

"I really can't read any more of these at present. I must leave them to you, old chap. They make my head swim." Of course he did in time read them all; and sent answers too. For three days several men were at work copying out the answers as he sorted them out into heaps, each heap having a similar wording. It was quite impossible to send a distinctly different answer to each—and it was not necessary.

The actual knighting took place at Windsor Castle on July 18. The account of it was told by Arthur Arnold, who was knighted in the same batch, and who came very soon after Irving. He said that the Queen, who usually did not make any remark to the recipient of the honour as she laid the sword on his shoulder, said on this occasion:

"I am very, very pleased."

II

The corollary of the honour came the next day when on the Lyceum stage a presentation was made to Irving by his fellow-players. This was unique of its kind. It was an Address of Congratulation signed by every actor in the kingdom. The Address was read by Sir (then Mr.) Squire Bancroft. Irving was greatly touched by it; few things were so essentially dear to him as the approval of his fellows. The unanimity was in itself a wonder. The Address was in the shape of a volume and was contained in a beautiful casket of gold and crystal designed by Johnston Forbes-Robertson—a painter as well as a player.

HENRY IRVING

Reproduced by permission of Mrs. Aria (from her Irving collection)

Johnston Forbes-Robertson was a devoted friend of Henry Irving, and at his death he took a prominent part in securing that the dead player should be laid to rest in Westminster Abbey.

III

The idea of knighthood for Irving was not new in that year, 1895. I mention this now because after his death a statement was made that he had by a lecture at the Royal Institution compelled the Government to give him knighthood. The statement was, of course, more than ridiculous. Here is what happened to my own knowledge :

In 1883, before Irving's visit to America, I was consulted, I understood on behalf of a very exalted person, by the late Sir James Mackenzie, as to whether the conferring of knighthood would be pleasing to Mr. Irving. It has never been usual to confer the honour on an unwilling recipient any more than it has been to allow any " forcing " to be effective. I asked for a day to find out. Then I conveyed the result of my veiled inquiry into the matter. At that time Irving thought it was better that an actor, whilst actively pursuing his calling, should not be so singled out from his fellows. On my showing the matter was not proceeded with at that time. From the very beginning of his management of the Lyceum he had been scrupulously particular that all the names given on the cast of the play should be printed in the same type. That rule was never altered even after his knighthood. But as he was no longer " Mr." and would not be called by his title he thenceforth appeared as " Henry Irving." Advertisement was, of course, different as to type, but he did not use the title.

IV

But in the twelve years that had elapsed since 1883 many things had changed. Other Arts had benefited by the large measures of official recognition extended to them, and the very fact of the art of Acting not having any official recognition was being used as an argument that it was not an art at all. Indeed his lecture at the Royal Institution, whilst it was in no way intended to " force " recognition or had no power of so doing, was taken as a manifest proof that the conferring of the honour would be regarded in a favourable light. Thus it was that in 1895 no " judicious " opinion was asked; none was necessary. The Prime Minister was assured that there could not be any *contretemps*, and even the Prince of Wales felt secure in his most gracious letter of congratulation.

I feel it too bad that one who in his days tried to live up to the ideal of discretion, and has regarded reticence as a duty rather than a motive, should have to speak openly, even after a lapse of years, on so private a matter, and I can only trust that I may be forgiven should any one with the power of forgiveness see the need of it. But such statements as those to which I have alluded are calculated to destroy all the claim of gracious courtesy—of the spontaneous kindness from which high favour springs; and it is, I think, better that

I should be deemed to err than that such a misconception should be allowed to pass.

V

The King was always a most gracious and generous friend to Irving. Throughout the whole management of the Lyceum and to the time of Irving's death, King Edward, both as Prince and King, extended to him the largest measure of his approval. He gave him a position by his very courtesy and by the hospitalities which he graciously gave and accepted. When players dined with him the post of honour on his right hand was always given to Irving. He showed his own immediate surroundings in private as well as the world in public that he respected Irving as well as liked and admired him. He showed that he considered the Player in his own way to have brought some measure of honour to the great nation that he rules and whose countless hearts he sways.

He often honoured the player by being his guest in the theatre. At the marriage of the present Prince of Wales he was given a place in St. James's Palace; at the Queen's funeral he was bidden to a seat in St. George's Chapel at Windsor. At the King's coronation he was amongst the guests invited to Westminster Abbey.

And, whether as Prince or King, his Most Gracious Majesty Edward VII. R. et I. had no more loyal, no more respectful, no more believing, no more loving subject than Henry Irving.

LXX

HENRY IRVING AND UNIVERSITIES

*Dublin—Cambridge—Glasgow—Oxford—Manchester—
Harvard—Columbia—Chicago — Princeton — Learned
Bodies and Institutions*

I

DUBLIN

THE first University to recognise Irving's great position was that of Dublin. In 1876 it gave him an informal Address. In 1892 it conferred on him the degree of Doctor of Literature—" Litt.D." As this was the first occasion on which a University degree was given *Honoris Causa* to an actor, *quâ* actor, it may be allowable to say something of it.

It had for a long time been the intention of the Senate to confer on him a suitable degree. The occasion came in the celebration of the Tercentenary of the University, which was founded by Queen Elizabeth.

In order to be present Irving had to go out of the bill at the Lyceum, where we were then playing *Henry VIII*. He and I travelled to Dublin by the mail of Tuesday, 5th July. We had heard that the Dublin folk and the Irish generally were very pleased that he was to receive the honour, but the first evidence we saw of it was the attitude of the chief steward on the mail boat. He could not make enough of Irving, and in his excitement confused his honours and invented new ones. He was at a loss what to call him. He tried " Docthor," but it did not seem to satisfy him. Then he tried " Sir Henry "—this was three years before he was knighted ; but this also seemed inadequate. Then he tried " Docthor Sir Henry " ; this seemed to meet his ideas and to it he stuck.

The function of the conferring of degrees was a most interesting one, the mere pageant of it was fine. There were representatives of nearly all the Universities of the world, each in its proper robes. As Irving passed to his place in the Examination Hall he was loudly cheered. I was, of course, not close to him ; I sat with the Senate, of which I am a member. He looked noble and distinguished, and the robes seemed to suit him. His height and bearing and lean figure carried off the peculiarly strong mass of colour. The robes of the Dublin Doctor of Letters are scarlet robes with broad facing of deep blue, and scarlet hood with blue lining. The cap is the usual Academic " mortarboard" with long tassel. When Irving was present at the formal opening of the Royal College of Music, where all who were entitled to do so wore Academic dress, his robes stood out in startling prominence.

Of course, each recipient of a degree received an ovation, but there was none so marked as that to Irving. He went up with the President of the Royal Academy, Sir Frederick (afterwards Lord) Leighton and Mr. (now Sir) Lawrence Alma-Tadema, R.A., these three being bracketed in the agenda of the function. When the conferring of degrees was over and the assembly in the Examination Hall poured out into the quadrangle, Irving was seized by a great body of some hundreds of students and carried to the steps of the dining-hall opposite, where he was compelled to make a speech.

At the banquet that night there was something of a *faux pas*, which was later much commented on. The whole toast list was as follows:

I. The Queen.
II. The Prince of Wales.
III. The Universities.
IV. Trinity College, Dublin.
V. Science, Literature and Art.

The last toast was proposed by the Marquis of Dufferin and Ava, and was responded to for Science by Lord Kelvin; for Literature by the Bishop of Derry; and for Art by Sir Frederick Leighton. The latter was, of course, quite correct, for the President of the Royal Academy is naturally the official mouthpiece for the voice of Art in this country. The mistake was that, in speaking for Art, Sir Frederick limited himself to Painting. He spoke in reality for himself and Alma-Tadema, but ignored completely the sister Art of Acting, the chief exponent of which was a fellow-recipient of the honour which he himself had received that day and who was present as a guest at the banquet. The comments of the press on the omission were marked, and the authorities of the University did not like the mistake. Leighton evidently heard some comment on it, for a few days afterwards he wrote to Irving to explain that he did not think he was intended to reply, except for his own Art.

It was this circumstance that made up Irving's mind to put forward on some suitable occasion the claims of his own Art to a place in the general category. The opportunity came a little more than two years afterwards at the Royal Institution. On that occasion he selected for his subject, " Acting : an Art"—the truth of which he proved logically and conclusively. I mention the circumstance here as his silence has been misconstrued. I have since his death seen it stated that he gave the lecture for the purpose of forcing the Crown to give him a knighthood—a statement silly beyond belief.

II

CAMBRIDGE

The second University to honour the Player was Cambridge. The occasion was this :

He was asked by the Vice-Chancellor, Mr. Hill, to give the " Rede " Lecture for 1898. This request is, from the antiquity and record of the function, in itself an honour.

The Rede Lecture was delivered at noon in the Senate-House of the University on Wednesday, 15th June 1898, for the night of which day he had closed the Lyceum. Irving had chosen as his subject, " The Theatre in its relation to the State." Throughout his life he always selected some subject connected with his work. His art with him was the Alpha and Omega of his endeavour. In this case he showed that, though some might regard the theatre as a mere pleasure-house, it had in truth a much more important use as a place of education.

> "I claim for the theatre that it may be, and is, a potent means of teaching great truths and furthering the spread of education of the higher kind—the knowledge of the scope and working of human character."

The lecture was beautifully and earnestly delivered and was received with very great enthusiasm. Very picturesque the lecturer looked in the rostrum in his Dublin robes. These he exchanged later in the day, when he received his Cambridge degree, D.Litt. This dress, all scarlet and red with velvet hat, looked even more picturesque than that of Dublin University.

That was an exhausting day. A journey from St. Pancras at 8.15 A.M. A visit to the Vice-Chancellor at Downing Lodge, Cambridge. The Public Lecture. Luncheon with the Vice-Chancellor in Downing Hall, with speech. The Conferring of Degree. A Garden Party at King's College. A Dinner Party in Hall given by the Master and Fellows of Trinity College to the Recipients of degrees. A Reception in the house of the Master of Trinity. And finishing up with a quiet smoke among a few friends at the rooms of Dr. Jackson.

The next morning there was a delightful breakfast in the house of Frederick Myers—Mrs. Myers, formerly Miss Tennant, was an old friend of Irving. Lord Dufferin was the youngest of the party, despite his seventy-two years. I think the Marquis

A GLIMPSE OF THE PAST

of Dufferin and Ava had the most winning manner of any man I ever met. There was a natural sweetness of the heart and an infinite humour from the head whose combination was simply irresistible. His humour was of enormous and wide-embracing range, and touched with illumination whatever subject he talked of. He and Irving had much to say to each other. The rest who were present wished to hear them both; and so there was silence when either spoke. Irving seemed quite charmed with Lord Dufferin and gave way to him altogether. The picture rises before me of the scene in the study of Frederick Myers after breakfast, well shown by the wide window opening out on the beautiful garden behind the house. Seated on the high fender with padded top, with his back to the fireplace, sat Lord Dufferin, and round him in a close circle—the young girls being the closest and looking with admiring eyes—the whole of the rest of the party. His clear, sweet, exquisitely-modulated voice seemed to suit the sunshine and the universal brightness of the place. Lord Dufferin's voice seemed to rise and fall, to quicken or come slowly by a sort of selective instinct. It struck me as being naturally one of the most expressive voices I had ever heard.

That night Irving played *The Medicine Man* at the Lyceum, and I thought I detected here and there a trace of the influence of Lord Dufferin in the more winning passages of the play.

III
GLASGOW

Irving now held University degrees from Ireland and England. The Scottish degree came in another year. For a long time Professor Herbert Story, D.D., LL.D., the Professor of Ecclesiastical History of the University of Glasgow, had a very high opinion of Henry Irving and of the good work which he had done for education and for humanity. I remember well a talk which Dr. Story had with me in his study after I had lunched with him on 26th June 1896. Incidentally he mentioned that he thought his University should give Irving a degree. Two years after, 22nd October 1898, he told me that it was in contemplation to carry this out in the following year. In that year Professor Story was presented by the Queen to the Principalship of the University on the resignation of Dr. Caird from that high position. On the 20th July 1899, the honour was actually completed when Irving was invested with his degree of LL.D.

That was, I think, the only honourable occasion of Irving's life since 1878 at which I was not present. But it was quite impossible; I was then in bed with a bad attack of pneumonia. I had been looking forward to the occasion, for Principal Story and his wife and daughters were friends of mine as well as of Irving. It was the only occasion at which in twenty-seven years I was not present when honour was done to him. I read, however, of the heartiness of his reception, both in the Bute Hall, where the degrees were conferred, and by the great mass of the students without. In his speech introducing him Professor Glaister said :—

"Sir Henry Irving's name stands as a synonym for the best and highest in dramatic art. . . . He has acquired an unrivalled fame in this country and in America. His fidelity to the best traditions of the stage, and his exclusion from his repertory of all that is vulgar or prurient, have been recognised as influences which elevate and purify dramatic art, and which have made the Theatre a powerful agent in promoting the general taste and culture of the people. His consummate stage management, his constant interest in the cause of charity and in the progress of education, his high character, his writings upon and his supremacy in his own profession have been already acknowledged by many marks of royal, academic, and popular favour. . . . This University desires that you will confer upon him in this degree its mark of appreciation of his valuable services."

In his reply, amongst other things Irving said :

"Nearly forty years ago I played in Glasgow. An ambitious lad I was then. Most young players have their heads in the clouds, but upon no cloud did my aspiring eye ever in its finest frenzy perceive the Senate of Glasgow University sitting for the purpose of crowning my career with academic honours. Had such a vision been vouchsafed to me I should have felt that my opportunities of scholarship in early life made a University degree an ironical chimera. . . . Standing up before you to-day I am most keenly conscious of the honour you have done to the art which has had the faithful service of my life. . . . To-day's incidents, so far as they concern myself as a representative of the stage in your midst, are luminous with more liberal ideas; for this reason above all I am grateful to Professor Story for his eloquent acknowledgment that the drama and its interpreters have their share of the humanities which it is the aim of the highest culture to sustain."

IV

OXFORD

On Sunday, 7th March 1886, Irving and I went to Oxford to stay with W. L. Courtney, then a Don of New College. For some years the two men had been close friends and Courtney whenever he was in London, would come to supper in the Beefsteak Room. This Oxford visit was arranged for some time, for Courtney was anxious to have Irvine meet some of the Heads of Colleges. The dinner was naturally a formal one, for in Oxford a very strict order of procedure rules. The Vice-Chancellor of the University—Dr. Jowett, Master of Balliol College —was there; also the Master of University, the President of Magdalen, and the Warden of Merton, the last three with their wives. Professor Max Müller was also a guest, his wife and daughter completed the party of fourteen. Jowett was in great form that evening. He was always a good and original talker, but he seemed on that evening to be on his mettle. During dinner one of the ladies sounded to Irving the praises of the *Ober-Ammergau* play, its fine effects, its deep moral teaching, and so forth. Irving listened attentively, and presently said quietly :

"It is so good they ought to bring it to the Crystal Palace." The lady was quite shocked, and turning to the Vice-Chancellor said :

"Oh, Mr. Vice-Chancellor, do you hear what Mr. Irving says, 'That the *Ober-Ammergau* play should be brought to the Crystal Palace!'" The pause round the table was marked. All wanted eagerly to hear what the Vice-Chancellor, who in those days ruled Oxford, would say to such a startling proposition. His answer startled them afresh when it came :

"Why not!"

The result of the *rapprochement* which Courtney had so kindly effected was that Irving was asked to give an Address at the University. He, of course, assented to the honourable request, and the date was fixed for Saturday, 26th June. The subject which he chose for the discourse was, "English Actors : their Characteristics and their Methods."

Irving and I with a couple of friends left Paddington on that day at six o'clock. On arriving at Oxford he and I went at once with W. L. Courtney, who had met us at the station, to the New Examination Hall, where the Address was to be given. Irving always liked to see beforehand the place in which he was to act or to speak ; a very valuable precaution, for experience enabled him when he knew something of the dimensions and conditions of the place to pitch his voice from the very start in the proper key. From there we drove to Balliol, where we were staying with the Master. At half-past nine o'clock we went to the hall with the Master. In the party were the Earl and Countess of Dalhousie and the Bishop of Ripon and Mrs. Boyd-

Carpenter, who with others were guests at his house. The great hall was crowded to suffocation with an immense audience, and the reception was warm in the extreme. Had I not known it before I could have told that the undergraduate lungs were in excellent condition. The discourse was received with rapt attention pointed with applause; and the conclusion was followed by a salvo of cheers. Then came the presentation of an Address, made by the Vice-Chancellor in a delightful, carefully worded speech. Amongst other things Dr. Jowett said:

> "I express . . . our admiration of him for the great services which he has rendered to the world and to society by improving and elevating the stage. . . . The life of the great actor is not so bright and pleasant as some of us imagine. . . . He has his times of depression too, and more than ordinary share of the troubles of human life. There is the fierce light of criticism which is always beating upon him; he has to be above his audience, yet he must also feel with them."

Then after explaining the views of Plato on whose work he was so supreme an authority, regarding the rhapsodist, and of Socrates on the same subject, he went on, following up the views of the latter with regard to the good company he kept:

> "And so of a great English actor we too might say that he lives in the best society, the society of Shakespeare and Goethe, and is a far better interpreter of them than a thousand commentators, for he thinks and feels with them and studies them not out of a book only; they are his personal friends, and his highest ambition is to render back to the world as a living fire the thoughts which they long

ago conceived. For things which we hear with our ears and see with our eyes make a far deeper impression on us than what we read. And the drama is the only form of literature which is not dead, but alive, and is always being brought to life again and again by the genius of the actor. . . . The indirect influence of the theatre is very great, and tends to permeate all classes of society, so that the condition of the stage is not a bad index or test of a nation's character. We in England are in part what we have been made by the plays of Shakespeare. Our literature, our manners, our religion, our taste have to a very great extent been affected by them. And those who, regardless of their own pecuniary loss or gain, have brought back Shakespeare to the English stage, who have restored his plays to their original form, who have quickened in the English people the love of his writings and the feelings of his greatness may be truly considered national benefactors."

Surely a noble tribute this from a man of such personal and official distinction to the worth of the drama, the stage, and the great actor to whom his praise was given.

That night we supped with Courtney in the Common Room of New College. Alfred Austin, afterwards the Poet Laureate, was amongst those present. He and Irving had much conversation about a play, *Savonarola*, which the former had written some time before.

The next day, Commemoration Sunday, we all attended with the Vice-Chancellor at St. Mary's Church, where the Bishop of Ripon preached a remarkable sermon on the theme of Moses and the Burning Bush, which he applied with extraordinary dexterity to the political position.

The dinner party that night at the Vice-Chancellor's was a large one, and its arrangement the supreme of topsy-turveydom with regard to precedence. As the chief guest had no official rank in a community where all was governed by hard-and-fast rules of procedure, all law of precedence was foregone. The only bishop of the party was assigned to the woman in the room of no official status. The only royal guest of the party, a grandson of the Queen, was not given a lady at all. And so throughout. Irving sat next to Lady Dalhousie, then in the full tide of her magnificent beauty. I shall never forget the appearance which those two presented. She in a dress of rich silk of the colour then in vogue which was known as *sang-de-bœuf*; this with splendid old *Point de Vénise* made a fitting shrine for so much loveliness. He so handsome and so dignified looking, with grave, intellectual, refined features and mobile grace of expression. That dinner was in every way delightful; after it we all went over to a concert in the hall. The Vice-Chancellor had originated Sunday night concerts, which were immensely popular.

Breakfast next morning was another pleasant function, at which all the house-party were present. The "Master," as Dr. Jowett was called, was in great form. I remember his quoting a remark of Tennyson's :—

"I would rather get six months than put two S'S together in verse!"

Irving and I, and my wife, who had been staying with the Courtneys for Commemoration, and who had with them attended all the functions of the

Vice-Chancellor, went up to town with the Dalhousies. We little thought that we should never see either of them again. About a year afterwards she died of fever, and he who loved her to distraction could not bear his great loss and shot himself.

V

VICTORIA UNIVERSITY OF MANCHESTER

In 1894 Manchester had no University exclusively its own. Its College, Owens College, was chartered by the Queen in 1880 and it was afterwards grouped with the Colleges of Liverpool and Leeds in the Victoria University. It was not till 1904 that it became a University by itself.

Before the time of visiting Manchester, on his tour of 1894, Irving was asked to give a lecture to the Owens College Literary Society. To this he acceded, and chose as his subject "The Character of Macbeth."

His reason for the choice was that he had wished to make, under important conditions, a reply to some of the criticisms with which he had been assailed on his re-production of Shakespeare's play in 1888, but a suitable opportunity had not up to now appeared. Some of these criticisms had been ridiculous, some puerile, some even infantile. I remember Irving telling me that one ingenuous gentleman had gone so far as to suggest that the Messenger who in Scene 5, Act I. announces to Lady Macbeth the coming of the King, should have a bad cold, his contention having been that Lady Macbeth says in her soliloquy :

> "The raven himself is hoarse
> That croaks the fatal entrance of Duncan
> Under my battlements."

The delay in his answer to the various feeble or foolish things spoken of his work did not detract from its power. His reasoning on the character from the text and from a study of the authorities which Shakespeare had evidently had before him when he wrote, was absolutely masterly. I venture to say that no student of the play can form any kind of correct estimate of Macbeth's character without reading it.

The lecture was given on the afternoon of Tuesday, 11th December, in the Chemical Theatre, the largest hall then appertaining to the College and holding some eight hundred persons. That the student element manifested itself in no uncertain way is shown by the note in my diary :

> "H. I. got enormous reception. Cheers were startling! On leaving, students wanted to take out horses and draw carriage, but wiser counsels prevailed."

Ellen Terry and Geneviève Ward were both of our little party on the occasion.

VI

HARVARD

I

Irving gave addresses at Harvard on two separate occasions.

The first was on 30th March 1885, on which

occasion he took as his subject "The Art of Acting."

We were then playing in New York, but as Irving had promised to come to Boston for the occasion, we left on Sunday afternoon. Several friends came with us, amongst whom were William Winter, of the New York *Tribune,* and Mr. Dorsheimer, ex-Governor of New York State. The train, on which we had a special carriage, was met at Worcester by a deputation of Harvard students, who travelled back with us to Boston. The address was given on the Monday evening, 30th, in the Sanders Theatre, a beautifully proportioned hall of octagon shape, which though looking not large yet held on that occasion over two thousand people. The crowd was so great at the doors both inside and outside that when we arrived at half-past seven we could not get in. Finally we had to be taken in through the trap-door to the coal cellar, from which by devious ways we were escorted to the platform. The Address went well. My note says:

"Went well. H. I. looked very distinguished."

That was in reality a mild putting of the fact. Distinguished was hardly an adequate adjective. Even from that sea of fine intellectual heads his noble face shone out like a star.

We were all to sup with the President of the College, Mr. Elliot; but when the time of departure came we could not find Winter. We searched for him high and low, but without avail. As a large party was waiting at the President's house we had to make up our minds to go without him. I had, however, one more last look and found him. He was in the coal cellar, which was about the only quiet place in the building. He sat on a heap of coal; on the ground beside him was a lighted candle stuck in the neck of a bottle which he had somehow requisitioned. When I came upon him he was writing furiously—if so rude a word may be applied to an art so gentle. He glanced up when I spoke with an appealing look and, with raised hand, said with passionate entreaty :

"Bram, for God's sake!"—I understood, and left him, having secured from a local fireman the promise of unfaltering obedience to my instructions to wait and take him to the carriage which we left for him. I also left a telegraph messenger on guard, for I saw that he was writing on telegraph "flimsy."

Any one who will take the trouble to look up the file of the New York *Tribune* of the following day—March 31, 1885—will read as fine a piece of descriptive criticism as can well be. I hope that such an one when he finishes the article will spare time for a glance, from the eye of imagination, at the silent figure phrasing it in the gloom of the coal cellar.

II

Irving's second Address at Harvard was nine years later. On that occasion his subject was: "The Value of Individuality," and the Address was given in the afternoon, the place being the same, the Sanders Theatre. There was again a great audience and a repetition of the old enthusiasm.

That night the Tremont Theatre in Boston, where we were playing, saw an occasion unique to the place, though not to the actor. The University had proclaimed a "Harvard Night," and the house was packed with College men, from President to jib. At the end of the performance—*Nance Oldfield* and *The Bells*—the students presented to Irving a gold medal commemorative of the occasion.

I may perhaps, before leaving the subject of Harvard University, mention a somewhat startling circumstance. It had become a custom during our visit to Boston for a lot of Harvard students to act as "supers" in our plays. There seemed to be a brisk demand for opportunities and the local super master grew rich on options. When we played *King Arthur* in 1895 there were many of these gentlemen who wore armour—the beautiful armour designed by Burne-Jones. The biggest of the men available were chosen for this service, and there were certainly some splendidly stalwart young men amongst them. A few of them got "skylarking" amongst themselves on the stage before the curtain went up. Sky-larking in full armour is a hazardous thing both to oneself and to others, and a blow struck in fun with the unaccustomed weight of plate armour behind it had an unexpected result, for the stricken man was knocked head over heels senseless just as Irving had come on to the stage to see that all was correct for the coming scene—" The Great Hall of Camelot." He reprimanded the super shortly and told him that if he undertook duties he should respect them, and himself, in performing them gravely. Imagine his surprise when in the morning he received a bellicose cartel from the offended young man challenging him to mortal combat. Irving, who took all things as they were meant, understood that the man was a gentleman who considered himself wronged and wrote him a pleasant letter in which he explained the necessity of taking gravely the work which others considered grave. The young man *was* a gentleman—in my intercourse with them I have always found Americans to be so—and wrote a handsome letter of apology for his misconduct on the stage and explained that he had had no intention of either breaking rules or hurting any one else.

And so on that occasion no blood was shed.

VII

COLUMBIA UNIVERSITY

Owens College, Manchester, blossoming into Manchester University, had a parallel in the growth of Columbia University, New York. In 1895 when, at the request of its President, Seth Low, Irving delivered the address on " Macbeth," which he had delivered in Manchester, it was still merely a College though the matter of its coming development was then at hand. Before our next visit to America in 1899 the whole new University of Columbia had been built and equipped. On 14th November 1899 I was taken all over it by President Low, and was amazed to see what had been done within the four years. The great Library, which the President had himself built and presented, was a magnificent centre for so fine and thoughtfully-conceived a piece of work.

Irving's address was given in the Library, the

largest hall in the old building, which had been somewhat dismantled for the purpose. It held some fifteen hundred persons. The occasion was Irving's first experience of the New York College cry, which has a startling effect when enunciated in unison by a thousand lusty throats. When he entered the Library with the President, who took in Ellen Terry, the cheering began and soon formulated itself into this special concourse of sounds. At the close of the address, which went extremely well, the enthusiastic cheering was repeated. And again Ellen Terry had her special share of it.

VIII

CHICAGO UNIVERSITY

Irving addressed the University of Chicago twice. The first was on 17th March 1896, when he repeated his lecture on " Macbeth." The second on April 25, 1900, when he repeated the lecture which he had given in 1895 at the Royal Institution : " Acting : an Art." Both addresses were given in the Kent Hall which was on each occasion crowded to excess.

The University of Chicago might well be taken as an illustration of the rapid growth possible in America. In the fall of 1893 the ground on which it stands was a section of the World's Fair, what was called " The Midway Pleasaunce." In the spring of 1896, less than two years and a half, the University was built, organised and furnished with students to its full capacity.

IX

PRINCETON UNIVERSITY

The last address which Irving gave in America was at Princeton University, where on March 19, 1902, he read a paper on the subject of "Shakespeare and Bacon," an eloquent and logical defence of Shakespeare against his detractors.

X

LEARNED BODIES AND INSTITUTIONS

The following is a list of various addresses given by Irving at Institutions and before learned Bodies other than Universities :—

"The Stage." Perry Bar Institute, near Birmingham, 6th March 1878.

"The Stage as it is." Philosophical Institute, Edinburgh, 8th November 1881.

"Shakespeare and Goethe." Goethe Society, New York, 15th March 1888. (*Given at Madison Square Theatre.*)

"Hamlet." Literary and Scientific Institute, Wolverhampton, 19th February 1890. (*This was given at the Agricultural Hall.*)

"The Art of Acting." Philosophical Institute, Edinburgh, 9th November 1891. (*This was given in the Music Hall.*)

"Shakespeare as a Playwright." Twentieth Century Club, Chicago, 2nd November 1893. (*Given in the private theatre in the house of Mr. George Pullman.*)

"Municipal Theatres." Literary Institute, Walsall, 26th September, 1894. (*Given in the Grand Theatre.*)

VARIOUS ADDRESSES

"Acting: an Art." Royal Institution, London, 1st February 1895.

"Macbeth." Contemporary Club, Philadelphia, 17th April 1896 (*given at the New Art Gallery*). Also at the Catholic Social Union, London, 17th May 1898 (*given at the house of Cardinal Vaughan*).

"Actors and Acting." Liberal Club, Buffalo, 4th February 1902.

LXXI

ADVENTURES

Over a mine-bed—Fires : Edinburgh Hotel; Alhambra, London; Star Theatre, New York; Lyceum—How theatre fires are put out—Union Square Theatre, New York—"Fussy" safe—Floods—Bayou Pierre—How to get supper—On the Pan Handle—Train Accidents : Explosions; "Frosted" wheel; A lost driver—Storms at sea—A reason for laughter—Falling scenery—No fear of death—Master of himself

I

OVER A MINE BED

ON 9th August 1880 Irving and I went for a short holiday together. The heat in London was very great. We began at Southsea, where we stopped at the Pier Hotel; that evening after dinner in the afternoon we got a lug-sail boat and went over to Ryde, returning by moonlight. The next day we walked on the Esplanade. Southsea was very full, and along the sea front a vast crowd of people moved in endless procession. Every one seemed to know my companion, and he became surrounded with a crowd which, though the composing individuals changed, never left him. At last he got tired of shaking hands and answering endless commonplace questions. In a momentary pause he said to me :

"I can't stand any more of this. Let's get a boat and have a sail. We can get quiet that way anyhow!"

We went down on the beach and picked out a likely looking boat that was ready launched. The boatman was very deaf, but as he seemed also dumb we regarded him as a find. He hoisted his sail and we began to steal away from shore. Behind us was a lot of shouting, and many people ran down on the beach gesticulating and calling out. We could not distinguish what they said; but we were both so accustomed to hear people shouting at Irving that we took it that the present was but another instance of clamorous goodwill.

We had got away from shore about half a mile when suddenly there was a terrific sound close to us, and the boat was thrown about just as a rat is shaken by a dog. A column of water rose some thirty yards from us and for quite half a minute the sea round us seemed to boil. The old boatman seemed very much frightened and found his voice to the extent of ejaculations of a prayerful kind, mingled with blasphemy. There seemed some excuse for him, for it was certainly very terrifying. To us, who did not understand, it seemed like an earthquake, or a volcanic eruption of some kind. Irving, however, was quite calm; he did not seem put out at all. The only motion he made was to put on his pince-nez which had been shaken off. I am not as a rule very timorous myself.

As the sea began to resume its normal calm it presented a strange appearance. All around us were strewn floating fish, mostly belly up, the white catching the eye everywhere. There were scores—hundreds of them, all seemingly dead. We lifted a lot of them into the boat. A few did not move at all, but after a while most of them began to wriggle and flop about. These had only been stunned.

We had after the first surprise taken it for granted that the shock had been from some sub-marine explosion; but we were content to await developments. When the boatman began to get over his agitation he enlightened us:

"'Tis they torpedoes; they've fired 'em by wire from Fort Monckton. 'Tis silly I am not to have thought on 'em an' kept out of the way!" Then he explained that the event of the day was to be an attack on Fort Monckton—the low-lying fort which guards the mouth of the harbour of Portsmouth—by the *Glatton*, then the most up-to-date of our scientifically equipped ships. We appeared to have come right over the mine-bed. The prudent fisherman had by this time put his boat's head against such wind as there was and began to gather up the unforeseen harvest of the sea. He was intent on this, though his hands shook and he kept looking around him apprehensively. We drifted with the tide. Presently a little distance in front of us another mine went off, and our friend got agitated afresh. He implored us to come away, and began to slack the sheet which he had drawn tight. Irving had lit a cigar and was calmly smoking. He had evidently taken a common-sense view of the situation.

"Why should we come away? We are, I take it, in about as safe a place as can be. The mines here have been fired and we don't know where the others are. If we go on, no matter in what direction, we shall probably come across another explosion. Let us stay where we are—and enjoy ourselves!" And stay we did and enjoyed—to a certain extent—the thunder of the cannon which later on, when the attack developed, rolled over the water and was brought to our ears, we being so close to the surface, in a way to make us feel as if each fresh explosion was close at hand.

I think, however, that we both enjoyed the attack more that night when the actual sham battle was fought. In those days search-lights were new and rare. Both the *Glatton* and Fort Monckton were well equipped with them, and during the attack the whole sea and sky and shore were perpetually swept with the powerful rays. It was in its way a noble fight, and as then most people were ignorant of the practical working of the new scientific appliances of war, it was instructive as well as fascinating. We, who had been out in the middle of it during the day, could perhaps appreciate its possibilities better than ordinary civil folk unused to the forces and horrors of war!

II

FIRES

a

The first fire of which Irving and I were spectators together was in November 1881. We were playing at Edinburgh and stayed in the old Edinburgh

Hotel opposite the Scott Memorial. The house was pulled down long since. The hotel was made up of several houses thrown into one, and was of the ramshackle order. It would have been easily set on fire; and had it got well alight nothing could have saved it.

Loveday and I supped with Irving in his sitting-room on the second storey, and after supper were enjoying our smoke. It was then late for Edinburgh, nearly one o'clock. As we sat we heard a queer kind of roaring and crackling sound in the passage outside.

"That sounds like a fire!" I said, and ran out to see if I could help. In the passage a curious scene presented itself. A sort of housemaid's closet in the back wall was well alight; the flames were roaring. The night porter, when collecting the boots, had seen it and was now trying to put it out. He was in a really dangerous position, and was behaving very bravely. I ran up to my room just overhead and brought down two great jugs of water which were on my wash-hand stand. When I got down a tall man was standing near the closet and talking very angrily to the porter. He was attired in a long white night shirt under which his bare feet and legs displayed themselves. He was not making the least effort to help, but kept on abusing the man who was working. Considering that the chances were that in a few minutes the whole hotel would be on fire, with what awful result none could foresee, it was strange conduct. In the midst of the hurry, for by this time we were all doing what we could, I had to laugh at the absurd situation and his out-of-place blaming:

SELF-CONCEIT AND BARE LEGS

"This is a pretty nice sort of thing for a gentleman staying in your damned hotel to have to endure! Do you always do this sort of thing, sir? Nice thing indeed! A gentleman to be waked up out of his bed by your infernal stupidity in setting the house on fire. Are we all to be burned in our beds? Nice sort of conduct indeed! Edinburgh should be ashamed of itself!" Irving and Loveday and I were all hard at work but were doing little good. The porter who knew the place was trying to get at the water tap within. He succeeded at last, and when a jet of water could be used in that narrow space the fire was soon held in check. We stood for a while to admire the angry stranger, still "jawing" away at the porter, who took not the least notice of him. By this time the other guests were alarmed and came running out of their rooms in various stages of night gear and partial dressing, till the passage was thronged with frightened women and men full of inquiries.

When we went back to the room to finish our smoke we left them all there. The unclad stranger was in the midst, still in a sublime state of indifference to decorum, haranguing—at what or whom he did not seem to know, for the porter had gone. In the room Irving said, as he cut the end of a fresh cigar:

"I wish I had that fellow's self-conceit—or even a bit of it. With it I could do anything!"

b

The next fire we were at was on 6th December 1882. We had supped together in the Lyceum after the play and were leaving tolerably early. We were going out by the private door in Burleigh

Street, when there came a sudden red glare in front of us a little to the right, or north, just as we were crossing the side-walk to the cab. In those days he always used a four-wheeler; he did not have a brougham till twelve or thirteen years later—and then it was a hired one.

"Hullo!" said Irving, "there is a fire! It seems pretty close too. I suppose you're off!" It was a standing joke with him against me that whenever there was a fire within range I was off to it hot-foot. I ran back to my office to put on a heavier pair of shoes—attending a fire is wet work and evening shoes are not fit for it. I was just putting them on when a vehicle stopped hurriedly at the door and there was a loud rapping. I ran out—Irving was back.

"Come quick," he said, "don't wait to change. It's the Alhambra." We jumped into the cab and the man drove for all he was worth. We got into Leicester Square just as the police were clearing the place and forming a cordon. All the Bow Street men knew us both and they hurried us into a doorway just where the Empire Music Hall is now. From there we had a splendid view, the place all to ourselves.

The fire had made quick headway and as we got to our place the whole theatre seemed alight within, and the flames burst out of the windows. The Fire Brigade got to work quick; but when a building of that size and with so large an interior gets alight there is no checking it. The only thing that can be done with any prospect of success is to try to prevent it spreading. Within a time which seemed incredibly short the roof began to send up sparks and flames, and then all at once it seemed to be lifted and to send up a fiery column of flames and sparks and smoke and burning ashes, which a few seconds later began to fall round us like rain. There was a terrific crash, and more leaping and towering flames. And then the roof fell in.

It was a magnificent, if costly, sight. Fortunately no one was killed or even injured. One of the firemen had his wife and baby at the top of the theatre, I was told; and that it was the delay in saving them that made the warning to the Brigade later than it might have been.

After the fall of the roof, the rest was detail. We waited an hour or so and then came away.

c

At the next fire we were not together. Irving was on the stage of the Star Theatre, New York, and I happened to be standing at the back of the parquet near the aisle which in all American theatres runs straight back from the orchestra rail. The occasion was the first night of Irving's playing *Hamlet* in New York, and the house was crowded to excess in every part. The play went well; incidentally I may say that it was an enormous success. All went well till the " play scene." The light for the mimic stage was supposed to be given from the attendants ranged on each side carrying torches. These torches were of spirit, as such give leaping flames which are picturesque and appear to give good light, though in truth their illuminating quality is small. Early in the scene one of these torches got overheated, and the flaming spirit running over set fire to one of the stage draperies. The super-master, Marion, who was "on" in the scene, at once ran over and tore down the curtain and tramped it out.

Through it all Irving never hesitated or faltered for an instant. He went on with his speech; no one could take it from movement, expression or intonation that there was any cause for concern.

Still a fire in a theatre has very dreadful possibilities; and at the first sign of flame a number of people rose hurriedly in their seats as if preparatory to rushing out. There was all over the house a quick, quiet whisper:

"Sit down!" As if in obedience, the standers sat.

There was but one exception. A lanky, tallow-faced, herring-shouldered, young man, with fear in his white face, dashed up the aisle. It is such persons who cause death in such circumstances. There is a moment when panic can be averted; but once it starts *nothing* can stop it. The idea of "*Sauve qui peut!*" comes from the most selfish as well as the most weak of human instincts. I feared that this man might cause a panic, and as he dashed up I stepped out and caught him by the throat and hurled him back on the ground. At such a time one must not think of consequences, except one, which is to prevent a holocaust. The rude, elementary method was effective. No one else stirred. I caught the fallen man and dragged him to his feet.

"Go back to your seat, sir!" I said sternly. "It is cowards like you who cause death to helpless women!" He was so stunned or frightened

HENRY IRVING

Painted at special sittings, in the year 1902, for Henry W. Lucy's collection, by Edwin A. Ward

that he did not make the least remonstrance, but went sheepishly back to his seat.

On the way he had to pass a man who stood a little in front of me—a tall, powerful, black-bearded, masterful-looking man. As the other was passing he put out his hand, and with finger and thumb caught the lappet of the young man's coat and drew him close. Then he said in a low voice, full of personal indignation as at a wrong to himself:

"Do you know that you rushed past me like a flash of lightning!" Then he suddenly released him and turned his eyes to the stage. I think it was the most contemptuous expression I ever saw. The rest of those present moved no more. It left me with a very firm impression that no one need fear for the courage and self-restraint of an American audience.

d

Two years after we had at the Lyceum a somewhat similar experience of a stage fire. This was during *Faust*. A curtain caught fire, and was promptly put out by the nearest person. Another such fire occurred in 1891 in *The Corsican Brothers*.

Stage fires generally have very small beginnings, and if they are taken in time are hardly dangerous. At a Theatres Parliamentary Commission the Hon. Sir Spencer Ponsonby-Fane, then and for a great number of years the permanent official in the Lord Chamberlain's department, to whom was entrusted the supervision of London theatres, was asked by a Committee man:

"How are fires in theatres usually put out?" His answer was sufficiently explanatory:

"With the carpenter's cap!" When a flame is small it can be smothered in an instant.

It is a reassuring fact that during the last century hardly a life was lost by fire in a London theatre. Indeed there were even very few injuries. I remember one exception which occurred at a panic—arising, as it turned out, without cause—at the Grecian Theatre some twenty years ago. On this occasion the audience did not lose their heads, but they began to move out quickly. There was one old gentleman who would not join in the movement. He said he had always heard that in case of a fire in the theatre the best thing any one of the audience could do was to remain quietly in his seat, and that he did not intend to stir. As it turned out he was the only person injured. He was sitting at the end of a row in the Pit close to the doorway; and as he would not stir, the rest of the audience simply walked over him!

Coolness and theory are most excellent qualities in life. But even they can be exaggerated or out of place!

e

There was one other fire which had a bearing on Irving's interests though he was not in it or near it. This was the burning of the Union Square Theatre, New York, on the 28th February 1888. This theatre backed on to the side of the Star Theatre where we were playing. The Morton House beside it, at the corner of Broadway and Union Square, caught fire. The theatre was quite burned out. When I saw it, which was quite by chance, it was well alight. I had been paying visits with my wife, and was in orthodox frock coat and silk hat. There was a great crowd held back by the cordon of police. I managed to pass the guard, as I was concerned in the Star Theatre, and inside saw the Fire Chief of that section—the Thirteenth Street. He and I had become great friends in the process of years. The American firemen are born to their work and they are all splendid fellows. If they like you they drop the " Mr." at once ; and when they call you by your Christian name that is, in their own way, the highest honour they can pay you. I was " Bram " to Chief Bresnin and his men. He said to me :

" Would you like to come into the theatre ? It may be of use to you some day to know what a theatre is like inside when it is burning ! " I acquiesced eagerly, and we hurried to the stage entrance. A policeman stood there, and when I went to pass in barred the way. The Fire Chief was surprised. " He is with me ! " he said. The other answered gruffly :

" You can go in, of course ; but I won't let him ! It's murder to let him go in there ! " The chief was speechless with indignation. From his point of view it was a gross affront to question any direction of his. By New York rules the Fire Chief takes absolute command, and the police have to obey his orders. Bresnin threw back the lappel of his uniform coat and showed his badge as Fire Chief.

" Do you see that ? " he asked. The other answered surlily :

" I see it ! "

" Then if you say one word—even to apologise for your insolence—I shall have you broke ! Stand back ! Come on, Bram ! "

I wanted to go on. But even if I had wished to hang back, I could not do so then. In we went.

The place was a veritable hell. It seemed to be alight in every part; the roaring of the flames was terrific. The streams of water from some twenty fire-engines seemed to be having no effect at all, they did not make even steam, but seemed to simply dry up. The heat was of course very great, but as the draught was coming behind us we did not feel it much. It seemed to be all overhead. I was made aware of it by my silk hat collapsing over my eyes, like a big tam-o'-shanter. The whole place seemed moving and tumbling about; great beams were falling, and brick work rattled down like gigantic hail. We stood on the stage. Here my own special knowledge of the safest place supplemented the fireman's general experience. It was by no means safe. Within a minute a huge beam, all ablaze, came thundering down not far from us and drove end on right through the stage like a bullet through a sheet of paper. We kept an eye on the door close to us, and when things got perilous we came away.

I went back to the Brunswick Hotel where Irving and I were both staying. I sent for his man, Walter, to tell him if the "Governor" had been alarmed he had better go into his room where he was having his regular afternoon nap and tell him that as yet the Star Theatre was all right, and would probably escape as the ruins of the other theatre were falling and the firemen would be able to deal with them. I had just come from it. He answered me:

"It's all right, sir! The Governor knows about

the fire. Some one here went up and woke him and told him that the Star was on fire! So he sent for me."

"What did he say?" I asked. He grinned as he replied:

"He said: 'Is Fussy safe, Walter?' So when I told him the dog had been with me all the time, he said 'All right!' and went to sleep again!"

III

FLOODS

a

On Saturday night, 1st February 1896, we played in New Orleans, and as we were to play in Memphis on Monday, arranged that our "special" should leave as soon as possible after the play. We had all ready for a quick start, and so far as our part was concerned had loaded up and were ready to start at the time fixed, one o'clock. We did not start, however; something was wrong on the line. It was two o'clock when we heard that we should have to go by a different route, the Valley section, as there had been a "wash out" on the course destined for us. In New Orleans the heat had been intense, almost unendurable, and higher up the Mississippi valley there had been terrific rainstorms. It was three o'clock before we started. All went well till the forenoon of next day when we came to a creek called Bayou Pierre. This was a wide valley seemingly miles across—it was really between one and two miles. Here the line was carried on a long tressel bridge. But the flood was out and the whole great valley was a turgid river whose yellow, muddy water rushing past swirled in places like little whirlpools. It had risen some four feet over the top of the bridge, so that no one could say whether the track remained or had been swept away. There was a short and hurried conference between our train master and the local engineer and they determined to "take the chances." And so we started.

It was necessary to go very slowly, for in that alluvial soil the running water weakens any support; the motion and vibration of a heavy train might shake down the structure. Moreover, the water level was almost up to the level of the floor of the carriages. Any wave, however little, might drown out the fires. It was a most remarkable journey; the whole broad surface of the stream was starred with wreckage of all sorts; hayricks, logs, fences, trees with parts of the roots sticking up in the air; now and again the roof of a barn or wooden shanty of some kind. Several times the floating masses carried snakes!

Our own little group—Irving, Ellen Terry, Loveday and myself—took the experience calmly. Indeed we enjoyed its novelty. Of course things might have turned out very badly. It was on the cards that any moment we might find that the bridge had been swept away—there could be no possible indication to warn us; or the passage of our long train might cause a collapse. In either case our engine would dive head foremost and the shock of its blowing up would throw the rest of the train into the flooded bayou. Irving sat quietly smoking all the time and looking out of the windows on either side as some interesting matter " swam into his ken."

In the other cars the same calm did not reign. There were a good many of the company who were quite filled with fear. So fearful were they that, as I was told later, they got reckless and in their panic *confessed their sins*. I never heard the details of these confessions, and I did not want to. But from the light manner in which they were held by the more sturdy members I take it that either the calendar of their sins was of attenuated or mean proportions ; or else that the expression of them was curtailed by a proper sense of prudence or decorum. Anyhow, we never heard of any serious breach or unhappiness resulting from them.

We crossed Bayou Pierre at last in safety, and kept on our way. Ours by the way was the last train that crossed the bayou till the flood was over. We heard next day that one section of the bridge close to the bank had gone down ten minutes after we had crossed. It had been an anxious time for the officials of the line. We could see them from both banks perpetually signalling to our driver, who was signalling in reply. It made the wide waste of water seem wider and more dangerous still. The only really bad result to us was that we arrived in Memphis too late to get anything to eat. In those days the rules governing hours in the South-Western Hotels were very fixed, especially on Sundays. Up to nine o'clock you could get what you wanted. But after nine the kitchen was closed and money would not induce them to open it. Irving and Ellen Terry had of course ordered each their own dinner, and these, cold, waited them in their rooms; but the rest of us were hungry and wanted food of some kind. So I tried strategy with the "boy" who attended me, a huge, burly nigger with a good-humoured face and a twelve-inch smile. I said:

"What is your name?"

"George, sah! George Washington."

"George!" I said, as I handed him half a dollar—"George, you are an uncommonly good-looking fellow!"

"Yah! Yah! Yah!" pealed George's homeric laughter. Then he said:

"What can I do for you, sah!"

"George, your cook is a very stout lady, is she not?"

"Yes, sah, almighty stout, wide as a barrel. Yah! Yah! Yah!"

"Exactly, George. Now I want you to go right up to her, put your arms round her—tight, and give her a kiss—a big one!"

"'Fore Gad, sah, if I did, she'd open my head wid de cleaver!"

"Not so, George! Not with a good-looking fellow like you."

"An' what then, sah?"

"Then, George, you tell her that there is a stranger here who is perishing for some food. He is sorry to disturb so pretty a woman, who he is told is the belle of Memphis; but *necessitas non habet leges*. Explain that to her, won't you, like a good fellow? Make me out tall and thin and aristocratic-looking, with a white thin face and a hectic spot on each cheek bone, a black, melting and yearning eye, and a large black moustache—don't forget the moustache. Ask her if she will of her gracious kindness break the iron rule of discipline that governs the house, and send me some food, *anything* that is least troublesome. A slice of cold meat, some bread and a pitcher of milk, and if she has any cold vegetables of any sort, and the cruet, I can make a salad!"

George laughed wildly and hurried out. I could hear his cachinnation dying away down the long passage. Presently I heard it swelling up again as he drew near. The heavy footfall drew closer, and the door was kicked in after the manner of negro waiters—in hotels there is an iron or brass plate at the base of the dining-room door for the purpose. George Washington bore an enormous tray, resting on an open palm spread back over his shoulder. When he laid it down its weight made the table shake.

On it was food of all sorts enough for a dozen people—beef, ham, tongue, turkey, bread and butter, pies of several kinds, milk, a salad bowl, and a lot of different cold vegetables, and the cruet. Such of my companions who were staying at our hotel came to my room and shared the banquet.

That episode was worth a whole silver dollar to George. It was divided, I presume, with the adipose cook; for there was no external appearance of his head having been " opened wid de cleaver." For the remaining days of our stay he followed me when opportunity served like a shadow. A very substantial shadow; quite a Demogorgon of a shadow!

b

We had had a somewhat similar experience of a flood some years before, though of nothing like so dangerous a nature. This was on 3rd February 1884, on our journey from Cincinnati to Columbus. The thaw had come on suddenly on the southern watershed of the northern hills when the ground through a long rigorous winter was frozen to a depth of several feet. Of course, the water, unable to sink into the ground, ran into the streams, and the Ohio River was flooded. As we left we could see that it was up to the top of the levée. Later on it rose some *forty feet* higher. It was a record flood. We went by the Pan Handle route of the Pennsylvanian Railway. As we went, whole tracks of country were flooded; in places we ran where the roads were under water, and a mighty splash our engine sent ahead of her. We went very fast, "rushing" all the bridges, especially the small ones of which there were many. In a stopping time I had a chat with the driver—one whom the depôt-master of Cincinnati had told me he had put on specially because he was a bold driver who did not mind taking a risk. I asked him why he went so fast over the bridges, as I had heard it was much safer to go slow.

"Not in a flood like this!" he answered. "You see, the water has been out some time and the brick work is all sapped and sodden with wet. Mayhap we may shake a bridge down now and then, but I like them to fall *behind* me, and not whilst we're crossing. The depôt-master told me I was to get you folks in; and, by the Almighty,

I mean to do it if I shake down all the bridges in the Pan Handle. Anyhow, this is the last train that will run over the section till the floods are over."

IV

TRAIN ACCIDENTS

At a rough computation the railroad journeys of Irving's tours ran over fifty thousand miles—more than twice round the Equator. The journeys were nearly always taken in special trains running at all sorts of hours, and almost invariably in the bad seasons of the year. It is not to be wondered at, therefore, that we had a certain percentage of accidents. That some of these accidents did not entail loss of life is the source of wonder. Several times we have had the train on fire; once so badly that the danger was very great. It was only by the chance of it being discovered just as we were coming into a station that the whole train was not lost. As it was, the Insurance Company had to liquidate damages to our goods to the extent of £500.

Three times the bolt head of the engine has been blown out, once entailing a delay of six hours, until not only another engine but another driver who knew the road as well as the engine, could be found.

Once in February 1900 when on our way from Indianapolis to Louisville some accident or explosion took place which seemed to shatter the whole engine into scrap iron. But no one was hurt.

On 17th January 1904 we went from Pittsburg to Buffalo. The cold was intense. There were ten feet of snow lying on the hills, and down the serpentine valley our driving wheel got "frosted" and flew to pieces. Fortunately we were on a stretch of level ground. Down the valley are here and there the remains of train wrecks on the bank of the river. Our engine was a very powerful one, a great Pennsylvanian fast hauler ; the great wheel was so thick that I could not lift a seemingly small fragment of it from the ground.

The very next week, Sunday, 24th January, when going from Albany to Montreal, we met with another accident. I had been most careful about a good engine, and the agent of the New York Central had given us the spare engine used in case of need for the New York and Chicago " Flyer." The cold was again intense and the snow thicker than ever. Up high amongst the Andirondack Mountains, where the wind roared over hill and through valley, the snowdrifts piled up in places to great heights. That was an exceptionally severe winter and railroading was hard. We climbed all right to the top of a pass amongst the hills and were going along steadily when there was a sharp explosion. Then in a few seconds the train drew up with a jerk. Our saloon was at the end of the train, so it took me some little time to reach the engine, as I had gone outside instead of passing through the train. The road just there was running on an embankment, and the snow-plough had swept the track, only leaving the snow piled at the sides so that to pass the carriages was difficult leg-deep in the snow. On the sloping embankment the snow lay many feet deep; and as the whole place was intersected with storm rivulets there were great holes like caverns in the snowdrift. The other men had also tumbled out of their carriages in much concern. We came across the train crew working in frantic haste. They told us that both the driver and the fireman were missing, and they feared that they had been blown off into one of the watercourse cavities. In such case either or both might die before we could find them, for these cavities were secret—they were honeycombed out beneath the blanket of snow. Very shortly we found the fireman. He had been on the outside of the engine when the explosion had occurred and was blown into the snowdrift head down. He was nearly choked when he was taken out.

But there was no sign of the driver, and the search went on. Immediately after the accident the brakesman had run back on the track to flag " Danger " lest any other train should come down upon us. This is the imperative rule in such cases. When he had done this duty he was to run along the track to the last station we had passed about a mile back, and bring help.

I was back on the line about a quarter of a mile when an engine piled with men came up at a furious pace. As it drew near the men began to call.

" Has he been found ? " I shook my head.

Close to our train they stopped and the men leaping from the engine spread themselves along the slopes of the embankment beginning a systematic search. Presently one of the crew of our train came along leaping through the deep snow calling out that the driver was found and was on the engine. We rushed back and found him there smearing his burns, which were pretty bad, with oil. The explosion had set his clothes on fire, but he had not lost his head. He had waited to turn the steam off, and then had taken a header into the deep snow wherein he had rolled himself till he had put the fire out. When he had managed to crawl out of his burrow the others of the crew, seeing the engine empty, had gone back to make search for him. He, not knowing that he was missed, had climbed quietly back into his cab.

When Irving heard of the man's gallantry in stopping whilst all on fire to turn off steam before thinking of himself he said it was a thing that should be rewarded in a marked way. He was quite willing to give the reward himself, but he thought that the company would like to, and ought to, join in it. So we got up a subscription which he headed. We handed to the injured men a little purse of sixty-one dollars. They declared that they would like to take their injuries over again any time for half the money or a quarter of the kindness.

The occasions when we were delayed by minor accidents to the train—hot-boxes, breaking steam-pipes, freezing steam brakes, snows-up, washes-out, broken bridges—were never ending. Many of them were not matters for much concern, but they were all causes of delay; and in touring, delay is often disastrous.

V

STORMS AT SEA

a

Irving was across the Atlantic eighteen times, of which one, in 1886, was for a summer holiday trip. Of course there were many times when there was bad weather; but on one crossing in 1899 we encountered a terrific storm. The waves were greater by far than any I had ever seen when I crossed in the *Germanic* in the February of the same year during the week of the worst weather ever recorded. On the occasion we were on the Atlantic transport S.S. *Marquette*. The weather had been nice for three days from our leaving London. But in the afternoon of the fourth day, 18th October, we ran into the track of a hurricane. As we went on the seas got bigger and bigger till at last they were mountainous. When we were down in the trough the waves seemed to stand up higher than our masts. The wind was blowing furiously something like a hundred miles an hour, but there was no rain. The moon came out early, a splendid bright moon still in its second quarter, so that when night fell the scene was sublimely grand. We forged on as long as we could, but the screw raced so furiously as the waves swept past us that we had perforce to lie by for six hours; it was not safe to go on as we might lose our screw-head. The tossing in that frightful sea was awful. Most of those on board were dreadfully frightened. Irving came out for a while and stood on the bridge holding on like grim death, for the shaking was like an earthquake. He seemed to really enjoy it. He stayed as long as he could and only went in when he began to feel the chill. Ellen Terry came out with me and was so enraptured with the scene that she stayed there for hours. I had to hold her against the rail for at times we rolled so that our feet shot off the deck. I showed her how to look into the wind without feeling it; to hold the eyes just above the bulwark—or the " dodger " if you are on the bridge—and a few inches away from it. The wind strikes below you and makes a clear section of a circle right over and round your head, you remaining in the calm. To test the force of the wind I asked her to put out her hand, palm out so as to make a fair resistance; but she could not hold it for an instant. Neither could I; my hand was driven back as though struck with a hammer.

In the companion-way of the *Marquette* several trunks too large for the adjacent cabin had been placed. They had been carefully lashed to the hand-rail, but in that wild sea they strained at their lashings rising right off the ground the way a chained dog does when he raises himself on his hind legs. One of the trunks, belonging to Irving, a great leather one, full of books and papers, was lashed by its own straps. In the companion-way had gathered nearly all the passengers, huddled together for comfort—especially the women, who were mostly in a panic. In such cases the only real comfort a poor woman can have is to hold on to a man. I happen to be a big one, and therefore of extra desirability in such cases of stress. I was sitting on a trunk on the other side of the companion-way from Irving's trunk, surrounded by as many of the womenkind as could catch hold of me, when in a roll of extra magnitude the leather straps gave way and the trunk seemed to hurl itself at us. I shoved the women away right and left, but missed the clearing its course myself by the fraction of a second. The corner of it caught me on the calf sideways, fortunately just clearing the bone. Another half-inch and I should certainly have lost my leg. I was lifted into the music saloon which was close at hand and my trouser leg cut open. We had three American footballers on board and these at once began to rub and knead the injured muscle, quite the best thing to do. Then it seemed as if every soul on board, man, woman, and child, had each a separate bottle of embrocation or liniment. These were all produced at once—and used.

Before a minute was over the skin of the wounded spot and for inches around it was completely rubbed off! The pain was excruciating—like an acre of toothache; but I suppose it did me good. In the morning my foot was quite black, but by degrees this passed away. I limped for a week or two and then got all right.

The women had a sore time of it that night. They nearly all refused absolutely to go to their cabins, and, producing rugs and pillows, camped in the music saloon which was on deck.

One young man, who spent most of his time leaning on the counter of the bar, gained instant notoriety by christening the saloon: *"the Geeser's Doss-house!"*

b

On Saturday, 5th October 1901, we left the Thames for New York on the Atlantic transport S.S. *Minnehaha*. In the river the wind began to blow, and by the time we rounded the South Foreland a whole gale was on. Our boat was a large one, so that we on board did not mind, but it was a bad time for the pilot whom we had to shed at Dover. The row boat to take him off had come out to us in the comparative shelter of the Goodwins and had trailed beside us on the starboard quarter, nearly swamped in the rough sea. When we slowed down off Dover the sea seemed to get worse than ever. To look at it in the darkness of the night, each black slope crested with white as the lighthouse lit up its savage power, one could not believe that a little boat could live in it. It took the men on board all their time to keep her baled. A number of us men had gone down on the afterdeck to see the pilot depart. He was a huge man; tall as he was, the breadth of his shoulders seemed prodigious. When he descended the rope-ladder and debarked, which was a deed requiring skill and nerve, he seemed to overweight the little boat, he so towered over the two men in it. When a few strokes took them out of the shelter of our good ship, the boat, as she caught the gale, lurched sideways so much that it looked as though she were heeling over. My own heart was in my mouth. I heard a sudden loud laugh behind me, and turning round, saw one of the passengers, a stranger to me. I cried out with angry indignation :

" What the devil are you laughing at ? Is it to

see splendid fellows like that in danger of their lives? You ought to be ashamed of yourself. The men could actually hear you!" For a few seconds he continued laughing wildly; then turning to me said quite heartily:

"Sorry! It's a shame I know; but I could not help laughing!" Despite myself and my indignation I could not help smiling.

"What at?" I said again. "There's nothing to laugh at there!"

"Well, my dear fellow," he gasped out, "I was laughing to think that I'm not a pilot!" And once again his wild laughter pealed out.

VI

FALLING SCENERY

In the great mass of scenery in a theatre and its many appliances, some of considerable weight, resting overhead there are certain elements of danger to those on the stage. Things have to be shifted so often and so hastily that there is always room for accident, no matter what care may be exercised. For instance, in Abbey's theatre in New York—afterwards "The Knickerbocker"—on the first night of Irving's playing *Macbeth*, one of the limelight men, who was perched on a high platform behind the proscenium and O.P., fell on the stage together with the heavy gas cylinder beside him. The play was then over and Irving was making a speech in front of the curtain. Happily the cylinder did not explode. The man did not seem at the moment to be much injured, but he died on his way to hospital. Had any one been waiting underneath in the wing, as is nearly always the case all through a play, that falling weight must have brought certain death.

I have myself seen Irving lifted from the stage by the Act drop catching his clothing. I have seen him thrown into the "cut" in the stage with the possibility of a fall to the mezzanine floor below. On another occasion something went wrong with the bracing up of the framed cloths and the whole scene fell about the stage. This happened between the acts whilst Irving was showing the stage to some American friends, Mr. and Mrs. Francis of Troy, N.Y. Happily no one was hurt. Such accidents, veritable bolts from the blue, are, however, both disconcerting and alarming. During *Faust* the great platforms which made the sloping stage on which some hundreds of people danced wildly at the Witches' Sabbath on the Brokken had to be suspended over the acting portion of the stage. The slightest thing going wrong would have meant death to all underneath. In such cases there must always be great apprehension.

VII

I have mentioned all these matters under the heading of "adventures"—torpedoes, fires, floods, train accidents, storms at sea, mishaps of the stage —for a special reason. Not once in the twenty-seven years of our working together did I ever see a sign of fear on Henry Irving. Whether danger came in an instant unexpectedly, or slowly to expecting eyes, it never disturbed him. Danger of any kind, so far as I ever had the opportunity of judging, always found him ready.

When he was lying ill at Wolverhampton in the spring of 1905 Ellen Terry ran down from London, where she was then playing, to see him. She had known from me and others how dangerously ill he had been and was concerned as to how fear of death might act on his strength. She had asked him if he had such fear; her description of the occasion as she gave it to me after his death left nothing open to doubt:

"He looked at me steadily for a minute, and then putting his third finger against his thumb—like that—held his hand fixedly for a few seconds. Then with a quick movement he snapped his fingers and let his hand fall. How could I not understand!"

As the great actress spoke, her face through some mysterious power grew like Irving's. The raised hand, with the fingers interlaced, was rigid till with a sudden movement the fingers snapped, the hand going down as propelled from the wrist. It conveyed in a wonderful way the absence of a sense of fear, even on such a subject as Death. Even at second hand it was not possible not to understand. It said as plainly as if in words: "Not *that!*" There was no room for doubt!

I have often heard him relate an incident from which he said he learned much. It referred to a certain habit of mind: an experience learned and carried so far as to become a part of one's nature —a veritable second nature. There used to be a Superintendent at Bow Street, who in the early days of the Vaudeville and the Lyceum was a friend of his. Mr. Thompson was a very capable officer who had in his years of experience learned the value of self-control. One evening Irving and David James coming along the Strand saw the Superintendent before them, and determined to try an experiment on him. They crept softly up behind him and clapped sudden and violent hands on his shoulders. He did not turn or draw away suddenly, as an ordinary individual acting instinctively would have done. He stayed very still and turned his head slowly round till he saw who and what it was that disturbed him. As Irving said, he was a master of himself—of his face. No one could have gathered from either expression or action what his emotions were. The lesson which he thus learned he applied twice at least to the practice of his art. Once was negatively—that is, the negative side of the lesson, when in his departure from the Court in *The Merchant of Venice* he dropped his shoulder and shrank from the touch of Gratiano; the other was his eternal consciousness of danger and preparation to meet it instinctively in *Eugene Aram*.

This is indeed part of that " Dual Consciousness " to which Irving so often alluded and which had in his estimation so basic a part in the Philosophy of his Art. We shall have to consider it when we reach that portion of the subject of this book: the summing up of the guiding principles of his art.

LXXII

BURNING OF THE LYCEUM STORAGE

Difficulty of storing scenery—New storage—A clever fraud—The fire—Forty-four plays burned—Checkmate to repertoire

AT ten minutes past five on the morning of Friday, 18th February 1898, I was wakened by a continuous knock at a door somewhere near my house in Chelsea. I soon discovered that it was at my own house. I went downstairs and opened the door, when a muffled up cab-driver gave me a letter. It was from the police station at Bow Street telling me that the Lyceum Storage, Bear Lane, Southwark, was on fire. The four-wheeler was waiting, and I was soon on the way there as fast as the horse could go. It was a dim, dank morning, bitterly cold. I found Bear Lane a chaos. The narrow way was blocked with fire-engines panting and thumping away for dear life. The heat was terrific. There was so much stuff in the storage that nothing could possibly be done till the fire had burnt itself out; all that the firemen could do was to prevent the fire spreading.

These premises deserve some special mention, for they played an important part in many ways, as shall be seen.

One of the really great difficulties in the management of a London theatre is that of storage. A "going" theatre has to be always producing new plays and occasionally repeating the old. In fact, to a theatrical manager his productions form the major part of his stock-in-trade. Now, no one outside theatrical management—and very few who are inside—can have any idea of the bulk of a lot of plays. In Irving's case it was really vast; the bulk was almost as big as the whole Lyceum theatre. To get housing for such is a very serious matter. In the first place, the rental is, on account of the space—no matter where the locality, great. In the second, it does not do to have it too far away from the theatre, for in such case the cartage to and from, together with the workmen's time, makes an enormous item of expense. In the third place, storage for scenery has to be of a kind where it can easily be got at. Scenery is long, unhandy stuff to handle. That of the Lyceum was forty-two feet long when the cloths were rolled up round their battens; the framed cloths were thirty feet high and six feet wide in the folding plaques. In the first ten years of Irving's management we had to keep the scenery stored in all sorts of places and the space available in the theatre was packed solid. We were always on the look out for a really fine storage; and at last we heard of one. This consisted of two great, high railway arches under the Chatham and Dover Railway, then leased to the South-Eastern. It was a part of Southwark where the ground lies low and the railway line very high, so that there was full height for our scenes. In front was a large yard. We took the premises on a good long lease and set to work to make them complete for our work. The backs of the arches were bricked up. Great scaffold poles were firmly fixed for the piling of scenery against them. It is hard to believe what lateral pressure a great pack of scenery can exercise. Before we had occupied this storage a year one of the poles gave way and the scenery sinking against the new wall at the back of the arch carried it entirely away. We had to pay expenses of restoration to the injured neighbour and to compensate him. We had the entire yard in front roofed over, brought in gas, which was carefully protected, and water, and made the storage the best of its kind that was known. The experience of a good many years went to the making of it.

We had had to put in a clause when making the agreement to take the lease for a reason not devoid of humour to any one not a sufferer by it. When I went to look at the arches I found them full almost to the top with mud—old mud that had been put in wet and had dried in time to something like the consistency of that to be found at Herculaneum. The manager of the estate office of the railway told me the history of it.

Some years before, the arches were placarded as to let, and in due course came an applicant. He said he was satisfied with the rent and took out his lease. The railway people were pleased to get such a big place off their hands and took no more trouble about it till the half-year's rental became due. They applied to the lessee, but could get no reply. So they sent to the premises to make inquiries. There was no one there; and they could not hear any tidings of the lessee. They did find, however, that the arches were filled with mud, and discovered on inquiry that the lessee had taken a contract for the removal of road sweepings. This is a serious item in municipal accounts, for the conveyance of such out of London is costly, whether by road or barge or rail. Into the arches he had for half a year dumped all the stuff; thousands and thousands of loads of it. He had drawn his money as earned from the municipal authorities. Rent day drew near, and as he feared discovery he had bolted, leaving every one, including the contractors for carting, unpaid.

It took the railway company months of continuous work with a large staff of men and carts and horses to remove the accumulation.

As the premises were secure in every way we could devise, we looked upon them as comparatively immune from fire risk. No one lived in them. They were all brick, stone, and slate—as the insurance policies put it. They were completely isolated front and back; at the sides were blocks of solid brickwork like bastions. I had at first, with Irving's consent, insured the contents for £10,000, but only that year when the policies were to be renewed he said it was wasting money as the place was so secure, and would not let me put on more than £6000.

In these premises were the scenes for the following plays, forty-four in all, of which in only ten Irving himself did not play. Twenty-two were great productions:

Hamlet.   *Much Ado about Nothing.*
The Merchant of Venice.   *Twelfth Night.*
Othello.   *Macbeth.*

AN IRREPARABLE LOSS

Henry VIII.	*Louis XI.*
King Lear.	*Charles I.*
Cymbeline.	*The Lyons Mail.*
Richard III.	*The Bells.*
The Corsican Brothers.	*The Iron Chest.*
The Cup.	*Iolanthe.*
The Belle's Stratagem.	*The Amber Heart.*
Two Roses.	*Robert Macaire.*
Olivia.	*Don Quixote.*
Faust.	*Raising the Wind.*
Werner.	*Daisy's Escape.*
The Dead Heart.	*Bygones.*
Ravenswood.	*High Life Below Stairs.*
Becket.	*The Boarding School.*
King Arthur.	*The King and the Miller.*
Richelieu.	*The Captain of the Watch.*
The Lady of Lyons.	*The Balance of Comfort.*
Eugene Aram.	*Book III. Chapter V.*
Jingle.	*Cool as a Cucumber.*

For the plays there were over *two hundred and sixty* scenes, many of them of great elaboration. In fact, each scene, even if only a single cloth at back with wings and borders, took up quite a space. There were in all more than *two thousand* pieces of scenery, and bulky properties without end. The armour and "hand" properties were stored in the theatre. And the prime cost of the property destroyed was over thirty thousand pounds sterling.

But the cost price was the least part of the loss. Nothing could repay the time and labour and artistic experience spent on them. All the scene painters in England working for a whole year could not have restored the scenery alone.

As to Irving, it was checkmate to the "repertoire" side of his management. Given a theatre equipped with such productions, the plays to which they belong being already studied and rehearsed, it is easy to put on any of them for a few nights. There is only the cost of carting and hanging the scenes and generally getting ready—small matters in the vast enterprise of putting on a big play. They had had their long runs, and though they were good for occasional repetitions, few of them could be relied on for great business over any considerable period. Several of them were held over for a second run, of which good things might have been fairly expected. For instance, *Macbeth* was good for another season. It was taken off because of the summer vacation when it was still doing enormous business. *Ravenswood*, too, had only gone a part of its course when the Baring failure, as I have shown, necessitated its temporary withdrawal. *Henry VIII.* and *King Arthur* and *Becket* and *Faust* were certain draws. When for repertoire purposes in later years several were required, *Louis XI.*, *Charles I.*, *The Bells*, *The Lyons Mail*, *Olivia*, *Faust*, and *Becket* were all reproduced at an aggregate cost of over eleven thousand pounds.

The effect of the fire on Irving was not only this great cost, but the deprivation of all that he had built up. Had it not occurred he could have gone on playing his repertoire for many years, and would never have had to produce a new play.

The fire was so fierce that it actually burned the building of the railway arches three bricks deep and calcined the coping stones to powder. The Railway Company, therefore, not only made a rule that in no case was theatrical scenery ever to be stored on their premises, but actually refused to

NO NEED FOR STORAGE

allow us to reinstate or to have use for the term of their lease. They were prepared to fight an action over it, but the scenery having all been burned, we had no more present use for so large a storage, and we compromised the matter.

LXXIII

FINANCE

*The protection of reticence—Beginning without capital—
An overdraft—A loan—A legacy—Expenses at commencement of management—Great running expenses—
Sale to the Lyceum Company—Irving's position with them*

I

So much that is erroneous regarding Irving's financial matters has been said at any time from the beginning of his success on to the day of his death—and after, that I think it well to speak frankly of the matter now. Indeed there is no reason that I know of why it should not be made public. During his lifetime, ever since his business affairs were conducted on a big scale, we observed for purely protective reasons a very strict reticence. It must be remembered that a theatre, and especially a popular one, is a centre of great curiosity. Every one wants to know all about it, and curiosity-mongers if they cannot discover facts invent them. The only possible safeguard that I know of is strict reticence at headquarters, and the formulation of such a system of accounts as makes it impossible for lesser officials to know any more than their own branch of work entails. To this end all our books at the Lyceum were designed and kept. Not one official of the theatre outside myself knew the whole of the incomings and the outgoings. Some knew part of one, some knew part of the other; not even that official who was designated "treasurer" knew anything of the high finance of the undertaking. The box-office keeper made entry of daily receipts and checked over the nightly booking-sheet so as to secure accuracy in his own work; but he had no knowledge whatever of the cash receipts at pit or gallery, where all is ready money. The treasurer made to the bank such lodgments as I gave him; he paid treasury to the actors and staff on each Friday according to the list which I gave him, and on every Tuesday he paid such accounts as were settled in cash and such of my own cheques as I gave to his keeping for the purpose to be paid according to my list. But he did not pay all the salaries—did not know them. Certain of them I myself paid, and these were not of the smaller amounts. He did not pay all the trade accounts; not the larger of them in any case. The weekly accounts of the heads of departments—carpenters, property, wardrobe, gas, electric, supers, chorus, orchestra, &c.—having been thoroughly checked in the office and vouched for by the stage manager, were paid in bulk to the heads of the departments, who distributed the amounts, and returned to me the receipted accounts with vouchers. In fact, the minor books kept by the various departments of both receipts and expenditure had practically only one side. Such officials either received money for handing in to me or paid out money given to them for the purpose. None of them did both. Thus it was that we kept our business to ourselves. Even in such a matter as free admissions none except those in the " office " knew of them. They did not go through the box-office at all, but were sent out under my own instruction in each individual case. Even the " bill orders "—the equivalent given in kind to those small traders who exhibit in their windows bills of the play of " double crown " or " folio " size, were not distributed in the usual way through the " bill inspector," but sent out in properly directed envelopes by the clerical staff. The account-books of the theatre were kept by myself and rigidly preserved in a great safe of which I alone had the key. The safe stood in the room which Irving and I and Loveday used in common, so that the books were always available for Irving's purposes when he required them. The accounts were very carefully audited by chartered accountants whose clerks made monthly check of details. Then at the end of each season the audit was completed by the accountants themselves, who made return to Irving direct in sealed envelopes.

Thus I can say that all through Irving's management from the time of my joining him in 1878 till the time of my handing over such matters as were in my care to his executors—by their own desire, after his will had been found, and before his funeral—no one, except Irving himself, myself, and the chartered accountants (who made audit and whose profession is one sworn to individual secrecy) knew Irving's affairs. I am thus particular because the very reticence which we adopted as a policy and pursued as a system was a wise protection, with of course such attendant possibilities as belong to a custom of strict reticence. Not once, in all our long connection of friendship and business, have I given to any one without Irving's special permission a single detail of his business. It was not until 1904, when I was writing an article by request of the Editor of the *Manchester Guardian*, apropos of his return to Sunderland after an absence of nearly fifty years, that we made known even approximately the vast total of his takings during his management. I quoted figures in that article—which in modern form the paper designated as " an appreciation "—with Irving's consent, and ran up to London from Derby, where we were then playing, to verify them. When we were arranging the matter I reminded him that I had never in all the years given a figure unless he had asked me to. Whereupon he said :

" But you are always free to use what figures and anything else of mine you will. You know, my dear fellow, what confidence I have in your discretion. You are quite free in the matter, now and always ! "

With this permission I feel at ease in now dealing publicly with matters regarding which I have been silent for so many years. I deal with them now because I regard them as good for Irving—for that memory which he valued more than life.

When Irving took over the Lyceum from Mrs. Bateman he had then accumulated no fortune. He received only a salary up to the time of Colonel Bateman's death. He then had salary—an extraordinarily mild one considering all things—and a prospective share of profits, which under the circumstances did not amount to much. Practically such little as he had in the autumn of 1878 was rather in the nature of a treasury balance than of capital. Of course, in his tour he was earning good money, and this came in a "ready" form; but the expenses which he was incurring in the reorganising and beautifying the Lyceum were vastly in excess of his present earning. When I came to London and took over his financial matters his bankers, the London and County Bank, had already arranged with him a large overdraft, some £12,000, for which he had given bills. This debt and all others incurred in preparation of his long campaign at the Lyceum were duly paid. Throughout his whole managerial life his payment was twenty shillings in the pound, with added interest whenever such was due or possible.

When he was undertaking the provincial tour in the autumn of 1878—the first under his own management, his friend, Mrs. Hannah Brown, the life-long friend and companion of the Baroness Burdett-Coutts, pressed on him a loan of fifteen hundred pounds. She had wished him to accept a larger sum, but he limited the amount to this. Indeed he took it at all to please her; such a sum went but a small way in the vast enterprise on which he had entered. Unhappily she died before he began to play in his own theatre. The sum which she had lent was repaid to her executor in due season.

When he first knew her, Mrs. Brown was a very old lady. She had been immensely struck with his power, and had recognised before most others the probable destiny that lay before him. When she was almost if not entirely blind he used to often go to see her and the Baroness, in the house in

Stratton Street or elsewhere as they resided. Of course, all this I only know from being told it, for Mrs. Brown had died just before I came to live in London. Lady Burdett-Coutts told me of the great affection which Mrs. Brown had for the clever man whose genius she so much admired, and whose friendship was such a delight in her old age. Not long after Irving's death, when I was dining with her and Mr. Burdett-Coutts, she said :

" I don't think he ever passed the house in her later years without coming in to see her, if only for a moment ! " Others, too, of the old friends have spoken to me of Mrs. Brown without stint; and of her Irving often spoke to me himself. She used to go to the Lyceum time after time. During the long run of *Hamlet* she went some thirty times. For her pleasure the Baroness rented from the management a box at the Lyceum. This was not in itself unique for she had already a box at Drury Lane Theatre and another at Her Majesty's Opera House. I was told that when the old lady was dying —she was then I believe about or over eighty— that she spoke of Irving and his future, mentioning him as : " My poor brave boy ! " Irving was then forty, but he was still a " boy " to a woman of her great age.

Mrs. Brown had very considerable means of her own, and a bequest paid by her executor to Irving was five thousand pounds. This was handed to him at the final settlement of her affairs in, strange to say, bank notes. That evening he told me of it when he arrived at the theatre. When he did so I opened the door of the safe thinking that he intended to place it there in safety until the next morning, when it could be lodged in bank. I was mightily surprised when he told me that he had not got it with him. He smiled at me as he said:

"I was afraid to carry it with me. I never in my life had so much money close to me!"

"What have you done with it?" I asked.

"I left it in my room at home!"

"Is it put by safely?" I asked again.

"Oh yes!" he added quickly, as though justifying himself. I had an idea that it was *not* quite safe and went on with my queries:

"Where is it?" He smiled, I thought superiorly, as he answered:

"In my hat-box!"

"You locked it, I hope?" Again the smile:

"What would be the use of that? If I had locked away anything it would only have called attention to it. The hat-box is simply lying there as usual with the lid half off. No one would dream of suspecting it—not in a thousand years!"

This illustrates, I think, in a remarkable way the subtlety of his own character, and the method by which he judged others. He had passed the possibilities "through his mind," and was so content with his knowledge that he backed it with a fortune. Later on there was a boy who *did* take things from his rooms. He was, however, found out and the property recovered, all except Edwin Forrest's watch of which a part had been probably melted down.

That legacy of five thousand pounds was, so far as I know, and had there been other I should certainly have known, the only money which Irving received for which he did not work, through all the long course of his years of much toil. I mention it now specifically because one of the unkindly, presuming that his ignorance of fact was the ignorance of others also, made after the actor's death a statement that he had been "subsidised." It ought not to be necessary to contradict such reckless statements — they ought never to have been made; but having been made it is best to let the exact facts be known. The best of all bucklers, for the living or the dead, is simple, honest truth.

The needs of the theatre were very great; at the beginning almost overwhelming. On my first taking over the responsibility of business affairs I acquired a wide experience of what is known as "pulling the devil by the tail." When Irving took the Lyceum its entire holding capacity was £228. Sometimes under extraordinary pressure, when every inch of standing room was occupied, we got in a little more; but only once in the first two seasons did we cover £250. That was on Irving's "Benefit," as it was then called.

The autumn of 1881 was devoted to enlarging and improving the house. At a cost of over £12,000 it was made to hold another £100. Thence on, various improvements and certain dispositions of the seating were effected, which brought up the holding power to a maximum of about £420, though on very special occasions we managed to squeeze in a little more. Some idea may be formed of the vast expense of working such a theatre as the Lyceum, and in the way which Irving worked it, when I say that on that theatre he spent in what we called "Expenses on the House" a sum of £60,000. During my time the "Production account" amounted to nearly £200,000.

The takings for his own playing between the time of beginning management, 30th December 1878, and the day of his death, 13th October 1905, amounted to the amazing total of over two million pounds sterling.

II

Only those who have experience of the working of a great theatre can have any idea of the vast expenditure necessary to hold success. A play may be a success or a failure, and its life must have a natural termination; but a theatre has to go on at almost equal pressure and expense through bad times and good alike. It is necessary for the management to have a large reserve of strength ready to be used if need arises. This implies ceaseless expenditure; a portion of which never can be repaid because the plays which involve it have to be abandoned. It is really too much work for one man to have to think of the policy of the future, and of carrying it into effect, whilst at the same time he has to work as an artist in the running play. No monetary reward would atone for such labour; only ambition can give the spur. Things, therefore, are so constituted in the theatrical world that the ambitious artist *must* be his own manager. And only those strong enough to be both artist and man of business can win through. The strain of ceaseless debt must always be the portion of any one who endeavours to uphold serious drama in a country where subsidy is not a custom. In the future, the State or the Municipality may find it a duty to support such effort, on the ground of public good. Otherwise the artist must pay with shortened life the price of his high endeavour. Light performances may and generally do succeed, but good plays seriously undertaken must always be at great risk to the venturer. For more than twenty-five years Irving did for England that which in other nations is furthered by the State; and his theatre was known and respected all over the world. This entailed not only hospitality in all forms to foreign artists, but to many, many strangers attracted by the fame of his undertaking, and anxious to meet so famous a man in person. This duty Irving never shirked; he had ever a ready hand for any stranger, and in the long career of his ministration of the duties of hospitality he actually aided, so far as one man could do, the popularity of his own country amongst the nations of the world. Such men are the true Ambassadors of Peace, as well as National benefactors. Reputation for hospitality and charity is a factor in the enlargement of the demands made on these. When duty called Irving was never found wanting, in this or any other form.

But still through all it must be remembered that the more he had to spend the harder he had to work to earn the wherewithal to do it. When I came to him first, six performances each week in heavy plays was deemed sufficient work for the strongest; but as time went on a matinée was added. And for some twenty years seven performances a week was the working rule. In light, amusing, or unemotional plays this is not too much; for when a run is on, the ordinary work of rehearsal is suspended. But for heavy plays it is too much. Still what is one to do who is playing for the big stakes of life. Brain and body, nerve and soul have to be ground up in the effort to hold the place already won. Irving was determined from the very first to strain every nerve for the honour of his art; for the perfecting of stage work; for his own fame. To these ends he gave himself, his work, his fortune. He forewent very many of the ordinary pleasures of life, and laboured unceasingly and without swerving from his undertaken course. He gave freely in its cause all the fortune that came to him as quickly as it accrued. It was only when through shocks of misfortune and the stress of coming age he was unable to put by the large sums necessary for further developments, that he had to forestall the future temporarily. Bankers are of necessity stern folk and unless one can give *quid pro quo* in some shape they are pretty obdurate as to advances. Therefore it was that now and again, despite the enormous sums that he earned, he had occasionally to get an advance. Fortunately, there were friends who were proud and happy to aid him. Such never lost by their kindness; every advance was punctiliously met, and the attachment between him and such friends grew ever and ripened. It would be invidious to mention who those friends were. Some perhaps would not like their names mentioned, and so "the rest is silence."

There were not many occasions when such measures were necessary. I only mention them now lest any of those friends should deem me wanting, in even such a partial record as this, did I not mention that Henry Irving had constant and loving friends who held any power in their hands at his disposal, and were alike glad and proud to help him in the splendid work which he was doing. Let me, as the only mouthpiece that he now can ever have, since I alone know all those friends, say that to the last hour of his life he was grateful to them for their sympathy, and belief, and timely help ; and for all the self-confidence which their trust gave to him.

III

When after his long illness in 1898–1899 the proposition of selling his interest in the Lyceum was made to Irving by the Lyceum Theatre Company—the parent Company—the terms suggested were these :

He was to convey to the Company his lease—of which some eighteen years were still to run, and all his furniture and fittings in the theatre. He was for five years—the duration of the contract—to play an annual engagement of at least a hundred performances at the Lyceum on terms which were mentioned and which were between 10 per cent. and 25 per cent. less than he was in the habit of receiving in any other theatre. He was to hand over to the Company one-fourth of all his profits made by acting elsewhere, he guaranteeing to play on tour at least four months in each year. He was to give the Company free use of such of his scenery and properties as were not in his own use.

He was to pay all the expenses of production of plays in the first year, and in the other years 60 per cent. of the same. For the first season he was to guarantee the Company a minimum of £100 for their share of each performance. He was to pay all the stage expenses, and half of the advertisements.

For this the Company were to pay him down £26,500 in cash and £12,500 in fully paid shares in proportion of the two classes, viz., £100,000 6 per cent. preference shares and £70,000 ordinary shares.

I protested to Irving against the terms. I had already worked out the figures of results, according to such data as were available, of this scheme and also of an alternative one, in case he wished to abandon or alter the one on which we had already decided. The difference was that, according to the alternative scheme, he would at the end of five years, in addition to the total of profits realisable by the Company scheme, be still in possession of his theatre, scenery, and property of all kinds.

That I was correct has been shown by the unhappy result of the Company enterprise. The Company lost almost persistently except in the seasons when Irving played. The one exception was, I believe, when William Gillette played *Sherlock Holmes*, a piece which Irving recommended the directors to accept. I was present at its first night in New York, and saw at once its London possibilities.

The Company lasted from the beginning of 1899 till the end of the season of 1902. During this period of less than four years the total amount in cash accruing to the Company from Irving's acting was roughly £29,000.

In estimating this amount I took as the basis of the Company's expenses the cost of running the theatre in our own time for the number of weeks covering the time of Irving's seasons with the Company. This allowed as liberal an amount as our own management, which was carried out on a much more generous scale. I excluded only the item of rental, which, as the Company was its own landlord, would be represented by the productiveness of the capital. The above amount would, roughly, have paid during each of the whole four years in which the contract lasted the preference shareholders their whole 6 per cent. and the ordinary shares over $1\frac{1}{2}$ per cent. in each entire year, leaving seven whole months of each year, exclusive of summer holidays, for earning the 4 per cent. dividend on the £120,000 mortgage debentures, and increasing the dividend on the ordinary shares.

It will from the above figures be seen that the contract which Irving made with the Lyceum Company was not in any way a beneficial one for him, but an excellent one for them.

I am particular about giving these figures in detail, for at some of the meetings of the Company there was the usual angry " heckling " of the directorate regarding losses; and there were not lacking those who alleged that Irving was in some way to blame for the result. But I am bound to say that when, at the meeting in 1903, I thought it necessary to put a stop to such misconception and gave the rough figures showing the results of his playing during the time the contract existed, my statement was received even by the disappointed shareholders with loud and continuous cheers—the only cheers which I ever heard at a meeting of the Company. I honestly believe that there was not one person in the room who was not genuinely and heartily glad to be reassured from such an authoritative source as myself as to Irving's position with regard to the Company.

The cancellation of the contract between Irving and the Lyceum Theatre Company was in no way due to any fault or default of his. It became necessary solely because the Company was unable to fulfil its part. The London County Council, in accordance with some new regulations, called on the Company to make certain structural alterations in the theatre. The directors said they could not afford to make them as their funds were exhausted; and so the theatre had to remain closed. At that time Irving had already undertaken vast responsibilities with regard to the play of *Dante*, for which he had made contracts with painters and costumiers, and had engaged artists. It was vitally necessary that he should have a theatre wherein to play; and so there was no alternative but to annul the contract. Even as it was, he had to take upon his own shoulders the whole of the vast cost of the production upon which he had entered as a joint concern.

In fine, Irving's dealings with the Company may be thus summed up. He received in all for his property, lease, goodwill, fixtures, furniture, the use of his stock of scenery and properties, and a fourth of his profits elsewhere, £39,000 paid as

RESULT OF THE CONTRACT

follows: cash, £26,500; shares, £12,500. He repaid by his work £29,000 in cash. The shares he received proved valueless.[1] He gave, in fact, his property and £2500 for nothing ;—and he lost about two years of his working life.

I should like to say, on my own account, and for my own protection, inasmuch as I was Sir Henry Irving's business manager, that from first to last I had absolutely no act or part in the formation of the Lyceum Theatre Company—in its promotion, flotation, or working. Even my knowledge of it was confined to matters touched on in the contract with Irving. From the first I had no information as to its purposes, scope or methods, outside the above. I did not take a single share till it began to look queer with regard to its future; I then bought from a friend five shares for which I paid par value. This I did in order that I might have a right to attend the meetings. Later, in 1903, when shares were selling at all sorts of prices I bought some in the open market. This was simply as a speculation, as I regarded the freehold of the Lyceum as a valuable property which might eventually realise a price which would make my investment at the prevailing figures a good one. These shares I protected on the winding-up and re-construction of the Company with an assessment of 25 per cent. of their face value. But finally, seeing the conditions under which the new Company was

[1] The preference shares at the break up sold for, as well as I remember, *seven pence* for each fully paid share of one pound sterling. He would never sell his shares lest his doing so might injure the property of the Company. They were only parted with at the winding up, when the Receiver sold, on his own authority, all unapplied-for shares.

about to work, I sold them in the usual way through my broker.

As a matter of fact I was on the Atlantic or in America at the time the parent company or syndicate—to whom it was that Irving had sold his property—was formed. When I arrived home this association had become merged in the Lyceum Theatre Company which had been floated, and of which the whole capital had been subscribed. Not for nearly a year afterwards did I even see a copy of the prospectus of the Company.

Bram Stoker
1906

LXXIV

THE TURN OF THE TIDE

High-water mark—A succession of disasters—Pleurisy and pneumonia—"Like Gregory Brewster"—Future arrangements decided on—Offer from the Lyceum Company—Health failing—True heroism—Work and pressure—His splendid example—The last seven years—Time of Retirement fixed—Singing at Swansea—Farewell at Sunderland—Illness at Wolverhampton—Last performances in London—Last illness—Death—A city in tears—Lying in state—Public Funeral.

I

"THERE is a tide in the affairs of men." For twenty-five years it flowed for Henry Irving without let or lull. From the production of *The Bells* in November 1871 he became famous; and thence on he bore himself so well that with the exception of the disgruntled few who grudge success to any one, he was accorded by all an unquestioned supremacy in his chosen art. For a full quarter of a century there was nothing but ever-increasing esteem and honour and position; an undeviating prosperity which made all things possible to the ambitious actor. True, the success was accompanied throughout by endless labour and self-sacrifice, and by grinding responsibility. His life was more strenuous than the lives of most successful men. For an actor's work is altogether personal, and when in addition to the practice of his art he undertakes the added stress and risk of management such, too, is altogether personal. But, after all, labour and responsibility are the noblest roads by which a man may travel towards honour. By any other way success is merely the outcome of hazard.

But the tide must turn some time—otherwise the force would be not a tide but a current. The turning came on the night of 19th December 1896 —the night of the production of *Richard III*. A night of unqualified success—as should be when high-water mark is reached. A night which seemed to crown the personal triumph of the years. After the performance and when the cheering crowd had taken their reluctant way, Irving had a large gathering on the stage. Such had become a custom on first and last nights of the season, and now and again on marked occasions. They were very delightful opportunities for large and comprehensive hospitality, enjoyed, I think, by all. So soon as the curtain fell the scenery would be put rapidly into the " scene docks " and the stage left clear. Then the caterers, Gunter's, who had everything ready, would place long tables round three sides of the stage and prepare a cold " standing " supper for all who were expected. During this time Irving would have rapidly changed his costume for evening dress; so that by the time the waiting guests in the auditorium were beginning to file in on the stage through the iron door in the proscenium O. P., he would meet them coming from his dressing-room. I used to stand at the door myself so as to see that

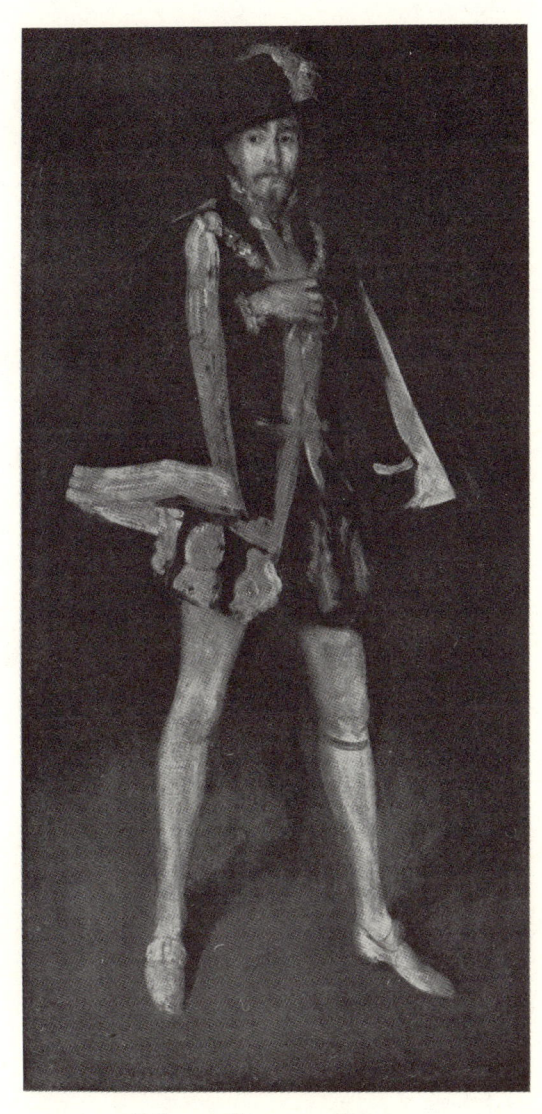

*Henry Irving as Philip II.
in Tennyson's Queen Mary,
painted by James McNeill Whistler.*

A GATHERING ON THE STAGE

no chance guests whose presence was welcome were denied. For very often there were in the house some whom Irving would like to welcome, and of whose presence we were ignorant to the last. The whole proceeding was an informal one. There were no invitations except such verbal ones as I conveyed myself. On such occasions there would be from three to six hundred guests on the stage, an enormous number of whom were persons whose names were at least widely known; representatives of art and letters, of statesmanship and the various forms of public life; of the great social world, of the professions, of commerce—of the whole great world of personal endeavour.

On this particular occasion there was a large gathering. When the curtain went up on the empty proscenium, the big stage seemed a solid mass of men and women. One could tell Irving's whereabouts by the press of friends thronging round to congratulate him on the renewal of his success in *Richard III.* of twenty years before.

Little by little as time wore away the crowd thinned. When the last had gone Irving and a very dear friend of his, Professor (afterwards Sir James) Dewar, went for a while to the Garrick Club. After the strain of such a night sleep was shy and the kindest thing that any friend could do was to keep with him and talk over matters old and new, so as to make a break between strain and rest. That night was a strangely exciting one to Irving. On it he had reproduced after a lapse of just twenty years one of the greatest and most surprising successes of his earlier life. For *Richard III.* when he played it in 1877 was a new thing to all who saw it. Clement Scott, writing of it in the *Daily Telegraph*, had said :

> " The enjoyment derived from the performance was undoubtedly heightened by the pleasurable astonishment with which the playgoer made the unexpected discovery of a new source of dramatic delight. It is not often that a frequenter of theatres can recall in the course of a long experience one particular night when the channels of thought seemed to be flushed by a tide of new sensations."

On the night of its revival all the old triumph came back afresh. No wonder that the player was too high-strung to rest. From the Garrick the two friends walked to Albemarle Street where Dewar had his rooms in the Royal Institution. There they sat and smoked for a while and discussed the philosophy of Acting and the form of education which would be most beneficial for Irving's sons. When Irving rose to go home—he lived literally " round the corner " in 15A Grafton Street, Dewar went with him. Irving insisted on his going in for a few minutes. This he acceded to, anxious that the super-wearied man should not feel lonely at such a time. After a cigar Dewar left. It was then coming daylight, and Irving announced his intention of taking a bath before turning in. Dewar left him tranquil and now ready for his needed rest.

The stairs in the Grafton Street " upper part " were steep and narrow, and Irving in the dim light of morning stealing to the internal staircase slipped a foot on the top stair. Unfortunately on the narrow landing stood an old oak chest. His knee as he slipped struck this, and the blow and the strain of recovery ruptured the ligatures under the knee-cap. When in the morning the surgeon who had been sent for saw him he declared that it would be utterly impossible for him to play for some time. Further advice was even more pessimistic, placing the period at months.

The disaster of that morning was the beginning of many which struck, and struck, and struck again as though to even up his long prosperity to the normal measure allotted to mankind.

It was ten weeks before he was able to play again. Ellen Terry had gone to Homburg—whither she had been recommended—the day after *Cymbeline*—which had preceded *Richard III*.—had been taken off. It was the end of January before she could give up her "cure" and return to London. She played *Olivia* for three weeks with good effect. We had tried *Cymbeline* for a week after Christmas; but with Irving and Ellen Terry out of the cast the receipts were such that though the salaries rent and such running expenses had to be paid in any case, it was cheaper to close than go on. The entire income did not nearly pay the expenses of keeping the theatre open instead of shut.

That accident of a foot-slip cost Irving two months and a half of illness and an out-of-pocket expense of over six thousand pounds. This instead of the prosperous winter season which had already seemed assured.

II

A little more than a year afterwards, February 1898, came the burning of the storage, which I have already described, and the effect of which was so permanently disastrous in crippling effort. Eight months after that came the greatest calamity of his life.

The disasters of these three years, 1896-7-8, seemed cumulative and consistent to the

> " Unhappy master,
> Whom unmerited disaster
> Follows fast and follows faster."

The first struck his activity; the second crippled his resources; the third destroyed his health.

III

To any human being health is a boon. To an actor, *quâ* actor, it is existence. During the provincial tour in the autumn of 1898 all was going well. We had got through the earlier weeks of the tour when we had, through very hot weather, played some of the lesser places and were now in the big cities. Birmingham and Edinburgh had shown fine results of the week's work in each place, and we were in the midst of the first week in Glasgow—always a stronghold of Irving. On the Thursday night, 13th October, we were playing *Madame Sans Gêne* to a fine house and all was going splendidly. Just before the curtain went up on the second act, in which Napoleon makes his appearance, Irving sent for me to my office. I came at once to his dressing-room. I found him sitting down dressed for his part. His face was drawn with pain at each breath. When I came in he said :

"I think there must be something wrong with me. Every breath is like a sword-stab. I don't think I ought to be suffering like this without seeing some one." As I saw that he was really ill, I asked if I might go and dismiss the audience. But he would not hear of it. Never in his life have I known him let any pain of his own keep him from his work. He said :

"I shall be able to get through all right ; but when I have seen a doctor we may have to make some change for to-morrow." I hurried off to send for a doctor, and as his call came he went on the stage. The doctor arrived during the last act, but he could not see him till the end of the play. Then the doctor said he feared he was seriously ill, and hurried him off to his hotel—and to bed. A careful examination showed that he had both pneumonia and pleurisy. Two nurses of special excellence were picked out and preparations were made for a lengthy illness.

The bill for next night was *The Merchant of Venice* and Norman Forbes, almost without preparation, played Shylock. The tour went on by Irving's wish, for the livelihood of some seventy people depended on it. The ten weeks which it lasted cost him a very considerable sum of money.

The cause of his illness was a chill received the previous Sunday. That day the Company went from Edinburgh to Glasgow, but he remained as he had an engagement to lunch at Dalmeny with Lord Rosebery. In the afternoon he drove back to Edinburgh and took train. At that time, however, the new station of the North British Railway was in process of erection and had reached a stage in which the road from Princes Street down to the level of the line was blocked during reconstruction; so that it was necessary to walk down. There had been a good deal of rain that afternoon and the torn roadway was full of water-pools. In walking through the imperfectly lighted way he got his feet wet and had to sit in this condition in a carriage without a foot-warmer during the hour's journey to Glasgow. He did not feel the ill effects immediately, but the seeds of the disease, or rather the diseases had been laid.

Of course during his illness he had every help and care that could be. But his case was a bad one. For seven weeks he lay ill in Glasgow during which time I almost lived in trains, seeing the work started and finished in each town and in the meantime travelling to Glasgow and to London, where immense and responsible work for the future had to be done. Forbes-Robertson had then the Lyceum for an autumn season, but his tenancy expired at Christmas. So we arranged that the Carl Rosa Opera Company should play for six weeks. Then Martin Harvey would produce a play, *The Only Way,* a version of Charles Dickens' *A Tale of Two Cities,* dramatised by Freeman Wills. Our negotiations for letting the theatre were very difficult, for as we did not know when it would be possible for Irving to play, we had in every case to have the option of bringing the temporary tenancy to an end at any time to suit us. This involved that every arrangement made by any one renting the theatre should make similar conditions with his own people. Nevertheless, through all difficulties we arranged for the provisional occupy-

"LIKE GREGORY BREWSTER" 329

ing the theatre at a good rental right up to the end of July.

As I used to see Irving every few days I could note his progress—down or up. At first, of course, he got worse and worse; weaker, and suffering more pain. He had never in his life been anything but lean, but now as he lost flesh the outline of his features grew painfully keen. The cheeks and chin and lips, which he had kept clean shaven all his life, came out stubbly with white hair. At that time his hair was iron-grey, but no more. I remember one early morning when I came into the sitting-room and found his faithful valet, Walter, in tears. When I asked him the cause—for I feared it was death—he said through his sobs:

"He is like Gregory Brewster!"—the old soldier in *Waterloo*. Walter did not come into the room with me; he feared he would break down and so do harm. When I stole into the room Irving had just waked. He was glad to see me, but he looked very old and weak. Poor Walter's description was sadly accurate. Indeed he realised the pathetic picture of the dying Sir John Falstaff given by Mrs. Quickly:

"His nose was as sharp as a pen."

It was not till 7th December that he was well enough to get back to London. On 15th at Manchester, where I then was with the Company, I got a wire from him asking to see me at once on urgent business. I saw him next morning. The business was regarding a speculative offer made to him, against which I strongly advised him. The business did not, however, require much thought;

it came to an end before it was well started. That day he left for Bournemouth. He was looking well when he left though still very weak. He felt much even the going *down* stairs from his second floor in Grafton Street. For the remainder of his life he could never with ease go *up* stairs.

On Wednesday morning, 21st December, I got a wire asking me to come down to Bournemouth by the 2.15 train. I arrived at five at the Bath Hotel where he was staying. The note in my diary says:

"H. I. looking well. Much stronger, self-possessed and evenly balanced. Arranged to tour at Easter. Lyceum season in September and October. American tour in autumn."

This was just what I had already advised, and in which Loveday had thoroughly acquiesced. We had arranged for a rack-rental of the Lyceum for the season. We should have a tour of three months with small expenses, as we should only take a few plays with light casts and would mainly play in places in which he had never appeared. The satisfactory result was a foregone conclusion.

Then would come a holiday of two months to recuperate and get strong, and then a season of eight weeks in London. This, too, promised more than well. He had already arranged with Sardou and Moreau to produce *Robespierre* that year (1899); and as he had paid a thousand pounds advance royalties he would have no fees to pay for five or six weeks. He had then also an offer of ten thousand pounds for his lease of the Lyceum to come into operation after October. This offer was still open in case he should wish to avail himself of it. The American tour promised a rich reward.

A CHANGE OF POLICY

Irving's judgment was at high tide when with fresh hope and vigour he accepted this policy. I left him the next morning to join the tour at Brighton where it was to finish on Saturday, Christmas Eve. We were both in good spirits, hopeful and happy.

IV

It was an unfortunate thing for his own prosperity that Irving did not adhere to the arrangement then made. I fear that the chagrin which he felt at the check to his plans had too operative a force with him. When the offer made by the parent Lyceum Theatre Company was put before him he jumped at it; and before he had consulted with me about it, or even told me of it, he had actually signed a tentative acceptance. It was now three weeks since he had agreed as to the policy of the immediate future. Loveday and I had been during that time engaged in working out the provincial and American tours, so that it was a surprise when he sent to us both to come down to Bournemouth to see him regarding the new proposal. We went down on the 12th January and stayed a few days. We discussed the matter of the Company's proposition, and I laid before him some memoranda comparing this with the scheme already in hand. The advantage was all to the latter. It was easy to see, however, that Irving's mind was made up. The new scheme was attractive to him in his then condition and circumstances. He had been recently very, very ill and was still physically weak. He had for over two years felt the want of capital or such organised association of interests as makes for helpfulness; and here was something which would share, if it did not lift, the burden. At any rate, whatever may have been the cause or the prevailing argument or interest with him, he had in this matter made up his mind. When a man of his strong nature makes up his mind to a course of action he generally goes on with it despite reasons or arguments. So far as facts and deeds go he is like a horse that has taken the bit between its teeth. He listened, as ever, attentively and courteously and with seeming thoughtfulness, to all I had to say—and then shifted conversation to details, as though the main principle had been already accepted. On the 14th Comyns Carr came down on behalf of the Company as had been agreed before Irving sent for us. Together we all went over the scheme. As Irving had accepted the principle and was determined to go on, we could only discuss details. I tried hard to get a betterment of the sharing terms; but without avail. The only change of importance I could effect was that Irving should be put down for the same salary—almost nominal to an actor of his position—which had always been entered on our books. Even this was to be only the provincial salary, not the American which was three times as much. This concession, however, as to salary was eventually to him an addition of some five thousand pounds. A few lesser matters, such as the Company sharing the cost of storage, were to his betterment.

In the original proposition it had been, I believe, suggested that Irving should be a director of the

Company, but when he told me of this I said such a decided " No " that he acquiesced. I impressed on him that he must not have his name in any form as a participant in the venture mentioned. He was selling to the Company and sharing his outside profits with them ; and that such being the measure of his association, he should not be implicated beyond it.

According to our previous plan of policy I was already in treaty with Charles Frohman regarding the tour in America, to begin in the autumn of that year. There was to be no change in this arrangement, as after the London season with *Robespierre* was to come this tour. The correspondence with Frohman had now reached a point when it was absolutely necessary that one or other of us should cross the Atlantic. A multitude of details had to be discussed, and as this was our first business transaction with Frohman, all had to be gone over carefully so as to insure a full understanding of our mutual and individual interests and responsibilities. This could not possibly be done by cable, and there was no time for letters ; already we were nearly a year later than was usual with such arrangements. As we had to settle things face to face, and as his own affairs would not allow of Frohman's leaving America at that time, I had to go to New York. I left London on 31st January 1899, and arrived at New York in the *Germanic* on 11th February—after coming through the greatest storm in the North Atlantic ever recorded. I left New York in the *Teutonic* on 22nd February, and arrived in London on 1st March. During the time of my absence everything in which

Irving was concerned had been completed. The contract between him and the Syndicate Company had been finally settled by the solicitors. The Syndicate Company had sold its rights to the Lyceum Theatre Company, which had been effectively floated and of which the whole capital had been subscribed. There was not anything left to me to do in the matter.

On my return I was surprised to hear that, in addition to the amount of capital originally mentioned in the provisional contract with Irving as that of the final Company to which his agreement was to be transferred on its flotation—namely, £170,000 in £100,000 6 per cent. preference and £70,000 ordinary shares—there appeared a sum of £120,000 mortgage debentures given to the original freeholders as a part of the purchase money. This made the responsibility of the Company up to £290,000.

Later on I learned that Irving's name had appeared in the prospectus as "Dramatic Adviser," a thing against which I had cautioned him. As a matter of fact he was never called by the directorate of the Company to fulfil the function. Once, he *offered* advice as to an engagement—which advice was happily taken to considerable advantage to the Company. But so far as I know he was never asked for his advice, nor were the Company's prospective arrangements ever made known to him in advance of the public intimation. I mention this here as it is, I think, advisable for his sake that it should be known.

With the one exception of Gillette's engagement, he never had knowledge of, or act or part in any of the business of the Lyceum Theatre Company outside those matters dependent on or arising from his own agreement with them.

As to myself: for right or wrong, when once I had communicated to him my views on the advisability of his contracting with the Company at all, I had no part in the matter and no responsibility.

After that illness of 1898 Irving's health was never the same as it had been before it. There was always a certain shortness of breath which, if it did not limit effort, made him careful how he exerted himself. It may have been partly this; it may have been partly the wound to a proud nature which was entailed by the long series of misfortunes with their consequent losses; but there was a certain shrinkage within himself during the last seven years of his life which was only too apparent to the eyes of those who loved him. To the outer world he still bore himself as ever: quiet, self-contained, masterful in his long purpose. Perhaps the little note of defiance which was added was the conscious recognition of the blows of Fate. But outside his own immediate circle this was not to be seen; he was far too good an actor to betray himself. The bitterness was all for himself. He did not vent it on any one; he did not blame any one. He took it as a good fighter takes a hard blow: he fought all the more valiantly. When he was stricken with pleurisy and pneumonia he was in his sixty-first year. He had been working hard for forty-two years; strenuously for twenty-seven of them. Growing age more or less limits the resilient power; labour so exacting and so prolonged increases vastly the wear and tear of life.

So we may, I think, take it that he was actually older than his years. Thus every little ailment told on him with undue force. Things that he used not to mind had now to be carefully considered. He had when working to give up many of his old pleasures so as to save himself for his work. Amongst these pleasures was that of sitting up late. Work had to be considered first, and last, and between; and whatever would take from his strength had to be rigorously put aside. Thus life lost part of its charm for him. He felt it deeply; and, all unknowing, was fostered that bitterness which had struck root already. It is the nature of strong men to fight harder through evil hours, and this was indeed a strong man. He would not give way on any point. Well he knew, with that deep, true instinct of his which is always the superior to mere logical thought, that to give way in anything however small is the beginning of the end—

"—the little rift within the lute
That by and by will make the music mute,
And ever widening slowly silence all."

His bearing through the last seven years was truly heroic. Now that it may be spoken of and known, I may say that I can recall in my own experience nothing like it. Each day, each hour, had its own tally of difficulty to be overcome—of pain or hardship to be borne—of some form of self-denial to be exercised. For a long time before this he had a complaint which always goes on increasing—a complaint common to actors and to all men and women who have to speak much; the complaint which is called "clergyman's sore throat."

CAUSE OF ILLNESS DISCOVERED

Doctors classify it as *Follicular Pharyngitis*. It is as well as an irritating and often painful malady, a lowering condition from its constant loss of those secretions which make for perfect health. After his illness this seemed to grow to alarming proportions. Month by month, and year by year the weakening expectoration increased, till for the last three years he used some *five hundred* pocket-handkerchiefs in each week. Such a detail is a somewhat sickening one even to read—what must it have been to the poor brave soul who through it all had to so bear himself as to conceal it from the world. He who lived with the fierce light of publicity on him had eternally to play his part day and night, bearing his old brave front so that none might know. Whoso is worthy to wear the crown must have the courage and the patience to endure. I ask no pity for him. He would have scorned even with his dying breath to ask for himself pity from any of the sons of men. But to ask for pity and to deserve it are different things. It is my duty—my privilege now that in the perspective of history, recent though it be, I am writing the true inwardness of his life—to speak the exact truth so that those who loved him, even those who were content to accept him unquestioned, should learn how unfalteringly brave he was. It was not till February 1905 when after a hard night's work he fell fainting in the hall-way of the hotel at Wolverhampton that the true cause of his weakness was diagnosed. Fortunately he fell into the hands of one of the most able doctors in England, Dr. W. A. Lloyd-Davies of that town—a man to whom grateful thanks are due for his loving care of my dear friend.

He it was that discovered that for more than six years—ever since his attack of pleurisy and pneumonia—Irving had been coughing up pus from an unhealed lung. I ask no pardon for giving these medical details. It was prudent to be silent all those years; but the time has gone for such reticence. It is well that the truth should be known.

Many and many a time; day or night; in stillness; in travel; in tropic heat such as now and again is experienced in early summer in America; through raging blizzards; in still cold when the thermometer registered down to figures below zero which would kill us in a breath did we have it in our moist atmosphere; in dust-storms of rapid travel; in the abounding dust of many theatres, the man had to toil unendingly. For others there was rest; for him none. For others there was cessation, or at worst now and again a lull in the storm of responsibility; for him none. Others could find occasional seclusion; for him there was no such thing. His very popularity was an added strain and trial to increasing weakness and ill-health. But in all, and through all, he never faltered or thought of faltering. For the well-meaning friend or stranger there was the same ever-ready hand of friendship, the same old winning smile of welcome. He might have later to pay for the added strain entailed by his very kindness of heart, but he went on his way all the same.

Henry Irving had undertaken to play the game of life; and he played it well. Right up to the very last hour of his life, when he was at work he *would not* think of himself. He would play as he had ever played: to the best of his power;

in the fulness of his intention ; with the last ounce of his strength.

If those who make it their business to direct the minds of youth knew what I know about him they would take this man—this great Englishman —as a shining light of endeavour ; as a living embodiment of that fine principle, " Whatsoever thy hand findeth to do, do it with all thy might." All his life long Irving worked for others—for his art ; never for himself. If rewards came—and they showered upon him—he took them meekly without undue pride, without arrogance ; never as other than tributes beyond his worth. He made throughout years a great fortune, but nearly all of it he spent as it came on his art, and in helping his poorer brethren. His own needs were small. He lived in a few rooms, ate sparingly, drank moderately. He had no vices that I know of ; he was not extravagant ; did not gamble, was not ostentatious even in his charities. There are many widows and orphans who mourn his loss ; if only for his comforting sympathy and the helping of his kindly hand. In the sacred niche of many, many hearts there is a blank space which only a memory—no longer an image—fills.

Requiescat in pace !

V

In those last seven years of his life I was not able to see so much of him as I had been in the habit of doing throughout the previous twenty. We had each of us his own work to do, and the only way I could help him was to take on my own shoulders all the work I could. As he did not come to his office in the theatre regularly every day as he was accustomed to do, I used to go to him; to his flat in Stratton Street when in London, to his hotel when we travelled. He did not often have supper in the old way. He still entertained to a reasonable amount, but such entertainments were generally in the shape of dinners on Sunday, the only day possible to him. When the play was over at night he would dress slowly, having a chat as he did so, for he loved to talk over his work past, present and future. When travelling he would often be reluctant to take his way to his lonely home; if indeed a hotel can be called a home. When in London he would linger and linger; the loneliness of his home made it in a degree a prison house. But all that while, night by night and year by year, he would stick to his purpose of saving himself for his work—at any cost to himself in the shape of loss of pleasure, of any form of self-abnegation.

Thus it was that through those last seven years I saw less of his private life than I had hitherto done. My work became to save him all I could. Of course each day during working months, each night except at holiday times—I would see him for hours; and our relations were always the same. But the opportunities were different. Seldom now were there the old long meetings when occasion was full of chances for self-development, for self-illumination; when idea leads on idea till presently the secret chambers of the soul are made manifest.

Seldom did one gather the half-formed thoughts and purposes which tell so much of the inner working of the mind. It was, of course, in part that hopes and purposes belonged to an earlier age. There is more life and spring in intentions that have illimitable possibilities than in those that are manifestly bounded, if not cramped, by existing and adverse facts. But the effect was the same. The man, wearied by long toil and more or less deprived by age and health of the spurs of ambition, shrank somewhat into himself.

This book is no mere panegyric; it is not intended to be. For my own part, my love and admiration for Irving were such that nothing I could tell to others—nothing that I can recall to myself—could lessen his worth. I only wish that, so far as I can achieve it, others now or hereafter may see him with my eyes. For well I know that if they do, his memory shall not lack. He was a man with all a man's weaknesses and mutabilities as well as a man's strong qualities. Had he not had in his own nature all the qualities of natural man how could he have for close on half a century embodied such forces—general and distinctive—in such a long series of histrionic characters whose fidelity to natural type became famous. I have the feeling strong upon me that the more Irving's inner life is known, the better he must stand in the minds and hearts of all to whom his name, his work, and his fame are of interest.

The year 1899 was so overwhelmingly busy a one for him that he had little time to think. But the next year despite the extraordinary success which attended his work he began to feel the loss of his own personal sway over the destinies of the Lyceum. There was in truth no need for worrying. The work of that year made for the time an extraordinary change in his fortunes. In the short season of fifteen weeks at the Lyceum the gross receipts exceeded twenty-eight thousand pounds. Five weeks tour in the Provinces realised over eleven thousand pounds. And the tour in America of twenty-nine weeks reached the amazing total of over half a million dollars. To be exact $537,154.25. The exchange value in which all our American tour calculations were made, was $4.84 per £1. So that the receipts become in British money, £110,982, 4s. 9d.—leaving a net profit of over thirty-two thousand pounds.

But the feeling of disappointment was not to be soothed by material success. Money, except as a means to an end, never appealed to Irving. We knew afterwards that the bitterness that then came upon him, and which lasted in lessening degree for some three years, was due in the main to his surely fading health. To him any form of lingering ill-health was a novelty. All his life up till then he had been amazingly strong. Not till after he was sixty did he know what it was to have toothache in ever so small a degree. I do not think that he ever knew at all what a headache was like. To such a man, and specially to one who has been in the habit of taxing himself to the full of his strength, restriction of effort from any cause brings a sense of inferiority. So far as I can estimate it, for he never hinted at it much less put it in words, Irving's tinge of bitterness was a sort of protest against Fate, for he never visited it on any of those around him.

HENRY IRVING ON SHIPBOARD

HENRY IRVING, 1905

Indeed in any other man it would hardly have been noticeable; but Irving's nature was so sweet, and he was so really thoughtful for his fellow-workers of all classes, that anything which clouded it was a concern to all.

As his health grew worse the bitterness began to pass away; and for the last two years of his life his nature, softened however to a new tenderness, went back to its old dignified calm.

VI

In the spring of 1905 came the beginning of the end. He had since his illness gone through the rigours of two American winters without seemingly ill effect. But now he began to lose strength. Still, despite of all he would struggle on, and acted nightly with all his old self-unsparing energy and fire. The audiences saw little difference; he alone it was who suffered. Since the beginning of the new century his great ventures had not been successful. *Coriolanus* in 1901 and *Dante* in 1903 were costly and unsuccessful. Both plays were out of joint with the time. The public in London, the Provinces and America would not have them; though the latter play ran well for a few weeks before the public of London made up their minds that it was an inferior play. In both pieces Irving himself made personal success; it was the play in each case that was not popular. This was shown everywhere by the result of the change of bill; whenever any other play was put up the house was crowded. But a great organisation like Irving's requires perpetual sustenance at fairly high pressure.

The five years of the new century saw a gradual oozing away of accumulation. The "production account" alone of that time exceeded twenty-five thousand pounds.

Had he been able to take a prolonged rest, say for a year, he might have completely recovered from the injury to his lung. But it is the penalty of public success that he who has achieved it must keep it. The slightest break is dangerous; to fall back or to lose one's place in the running is to be forgotten. He therefore made up his mind to accept the position of failing health and strength and set a time limit for his further efforts.

VII

The time for his retirement he fixed to be at the conclusion of his having been fifty years on the stage. He made the announcement at a supper given to him by the Manchester Art Club on June 1, 1904. This would give him two years in which to take farewell of the public. The time, though seeming at the first glance to be a generous one, was in reality none too long. There were only about forty working weeks in each year, eighty altogether. Of these the United States and Canada would absorb thirty. The Provinces would require three tours of some twelve weeks each. London would have fourteen or fifteen weeks in two divisions, during which would be given all the available plays in his repertoire.

At the conclusion of the tour we arranged with Mr. Charles Frohman, who secured for us the American dates for which we asked. We had

A TOUCHING FAREWELL

made out the tour ourselves, choosing the best towns and taking them in such sequence that the railway travel should be minimised. All was ready, and on 19th September we began at Cardiff our series of farewell visits. The Welsh people are by nature affectionate and emotional. The last night at Cardiff was a touching farewell. This was repeated at Swansea with a strange addition: when the play was over and the calls finished the audience sat still in their places and seemingly with one impulse began to sing. They are all fine part-singers in those regions, and it was a strange and touching effect when the strains of Newman's beautiful hymn, " Lead kindly light," filled the theatre. Then followed their own national song, " Hen fwlad fen Hadne "—" Land of my fathers."

Irving was much touched. He had come out before the curtain to listen when the singing began ; and when after the final cheering of the audience he went back to his dressing-room the tears were still wet on his cheeks.

During that tour at half the places the visit was of farewell. For the tour had been arranged before Irving had made up his mind about retiring and it was the intention that the last tour of all, before the final short season in London, should be amongst the eight provincial cities.

VIII

In one of the towns then visited and where the visit was to be the final one, there was a very remarkable occasion. At Sunderland he had made his first appearance in 1856, and now the city wished to mark the circumstance of his last appearance in a worthy way. A public banquet was organised at which he was presented with an Address on behalf of the authorities and the townspeople. The function took place on the afternoon of Friday, October 28, 1904. The occasion was of special interest to Irving. For weeks beforehand his mind was full of it for it brought back a host of old memories. He talked often with me of those old days, and every little detail seemed to come back vividly in that wonderful memory of his which could always answer to whatever call was made upon it. Amongst the little matters of those days when all things were of transcendent importance was one which had its full complement of chagrin and pain : In the preliminary bill regarding the New Lyceum Theatre, where the names of all the Company were given, his own name was wrongly spelled. It was given as " Mr. Irvine." At that time the name in reality did not matter much. It was not known in any way ; it was not even his own by birthright, or as later by the Queen's Patent. But it was the name he hoped and intended to make famous ; and the check at the very start seemed a cruel blow. Of course the error was corrected, and on the opening night all was right.

In his early life he was very unfortunate regarding the proper spelling of his name. I find in the bill of his first appearance in Glasgow at the Dunlop Street Theatre his name thus given in the cast of the great spectacular play, given on Easter Monday, April 9, 1869, *The Indian Revolt :*

> " Achmet, a Hindoo attached to the Nana, by Mr. Irwig (his first appearance)."

I do not think that these two mistakes ever quite left his memory—certainly he was always very particular about his name being put in the bill exactly as he had arranged it.

The Sunderland function went off splendidly. Everything went so well that the whole affair was a delight to him and gave the city of his first appearance a new and sweet claim on his memory.

IX

Another provincial tour was arranged for the spring of 1905. It began at Portsmouth on 23rd January and was to go on to 8th April, when it would conclude at Wigan. But severe and sudden illness checked it in the middle of the fifth week. The passage through the South and West had been very trying, for in addition to seven performances a week and many journeys there were certain public hospitalities to which he had been pledged. At Plymouth, lunch on Wednesday with the Admiral, Sir Edward Seymour; and on Thursday with the Mayor, Mr. Wyncotes, and others in the Plymouth Club. At Exeter, on Wednesday a Public Address and Reception in the Guildhall. Two days later at Bath a ceremony of unveiling a memorial to Quin the actor, followed by a civic lunch with the Mayor, Mr. John, in the Guildhall. On the following Tuesday, 21st February, a Public Address was to be presented in the Town Hall of Wolverhampton under the auspices of the Mayor, Mr. Berrington.

But by this time Irving had become so alarmingly ill that we were very seriously anxious. After the performance of *The Lyons Mail* at Boscombe on 3rd February he had been very ill and feeble, though he had so played that the audience were not aware of his state of health. The note in my diary for that day is :—

"H. I. fearfully done up, could hardly play. At end in collapse. Could hardly move or breathe."

His wonderful recuperative power, however, stood to him. Next day he played *The Merchant of Venice* in the morning and *Waterloo* and *The Bells* at night.

The function at Bath was very trying. The weather was bitterly cold, yet he stood bareheaded in the street speaking to a vast crowd. This required a great voice effort. It was a striking sight, for not only was the street packed solid with people, but every window was full and the high roofs were like clusters of bees. Our journey on the following Sunday was from Bath to Wolverhampton. Much snow had fallen and there was intense frost. So difficult was the railroading that our "special" was forty-five minutes late in a scheduled journey of three hours and ten minutes. In that journey Irving got a chill which began to tell at once on his strength. On Monday night he played *Waterloo* and *The Bells*. My note is :—

"H. I. very weak, but got through all right."

But that night in going into the hotel he fainted— for the first time in his life! He did not know he had fainted until I told him the next morning. When the doctor saw him in the morning he said that he would not possibly be able to go to the Town Hall in the afternoon and play at night; that he was really fit for neither, but he might get through *one* of them. *Becket* was fixed for that night, and it was comparatively light work for him. That night he played all right, but at the end was done up, and short of breath. The next night he played *The Merchant of Venice,* and at the end of the play made his speech of farewell to Wolverhampton. But his condition of illness was such that we decided that the tour must be abandoned. Dr. Lloyd-Davies was with him in the theatre all the evening and did him yeoman's service. The next day Dr. Foxwell of Birmingham came over for consultation. After their examination the following bulletin was issued :

> "It is imperatively necessary that Sir Henry Irving shall not act for at least two months from this date.
> "Arthur Foxwell, M.D.
> "W. Allan Lloyd-Davies, L.R.C.P., F.R.C.S."

On 17th March I visited Irving at Wolverhampton. He was looking infinitely better and we had a drive before luncheon. The two doctors had another consultation and it was decided that Irving must not go to America as arranged for the following autumn. Loveday came down by a later train, and he and Irving and I consulted as to future arrangements. We returned to London next day and a few days later Irving left Wolverhampton for Torquay, where he remained till 19th April.

In the meantime I had seen Charles Frohman and postponed our American tour for a year.

X

A short season of six weeks had been arranged for Drury Lane. This began on 29th April. There were three weeks of *Becket* and two of *The Merchant of Venice*. In the last week were three nights of *Waterloo* and *Becket* and three nights of *Louis XI*. All went well for the six weeks. The plays chosen were the least onerous in Irving's repertoire; he was none the worse for the effort.

The last night of the season, June 10, 1905, was one never to be forgotten by any one who was present. It almost seemed as if the public had some precognition that it was the last time they would see Irving play. The house was crowded in every part—an enormous audience, the biggest Irving ever played to in London—and full of wild enthusiasm. An inspiring audience! Irving felt it and played Louis XI. magnificently; he never played better in his life. The moment of his entrance was the signal for a roar of welcome, prolonged to an extraordinary degree. Something of the same kind marked the close of each act. At the end the audience simply went mad. It was a scene to be present at once in a lifetime. The calls were innumerable. Time after time the curtain had to be raised to ever the same wild roar. It was marvellous how the strength of the audience held out so long.

It had been arranged that on that night at the close of the play the presentation of a Loving Cup by the workmen of all the theatres throughout the kingdom should take place on the stage. The representatives of the various theatres assembled in due course, a mass of some hundred of them. As there were to be some speeches, a moment of quiet was necessary; we tried turning down the lights in the theatre, for still the audience kept cheering. It never ceased—that prolonged insistent note of perpetual renewals which once heard has a place in memory. After a while we did a thing I never saw done before: the lights were turned quite out. But still the audience remained cheering through the black darkness of the house.

Irving with his usual discernment and courtesy recognised the right thing to do. He ordered the curtain to go up once more, and stepping in front of the stage said, so soon as the wild roar of renewed strength, stilled on purpose, would allow him:

> "Ladies and gentlemen,—We have a little ceremony of our own to take place on the stage to-night. I think, however, it will be the mind of all my friends on the stage that you should join in our little ceremony. So with your permission we will go on with it."

Another short sharp cheer and then sudden stillness.

The presentation was made in due form and then — the curtain still remaining up, for there was to be no more formal barrier that night—the audience, cheering all the time, melted away.

It was a worthy finish to a lifetime of loving appreciation of the art-work of a great man.

This was Irving's last regular London performance, and with the exception of his playing *Waterloo* for the benefit of his old friend, Lionel Brough, at His Majesty's Theatre on 15th June, the last time he ever appeared in London.

XI

The autumn tour of that year, 1905, was fixed for ten weeks and a half, to commence at Sheffield on 2nd October. The tour commenced very well. There were fine houses despite the fact that it was the week of the Musical Festival. On Tuesday, 3rd, the Lord Mayor, Sir Joseph Jonas, gave a great luncheon for him in the Town Hall. Irving was in good form and spoke well. There was nothing noticeable in his playing or regarding his health all that week. On Saturday night there was a big house and much enthusiasm. Irving seemed much touched as he said farewell. From Sheffield we went on to Bradford.

The Monday and Tuesday night at Bradford went all right. Irving did not seem ill or extremely weak. We had by now been accustomed to certain physical feebleness—except when he was on the stage. On Wednesday the Mayor, Mr. Priestley, was giving a big lunch for him in the Town Hall at which he was to be presented with a Public Address. I joined him at his hotel at a little past one o'clock and we went together to the Town Hall. He seemed very feeble that morning, and as we went slowly up the steep steps he paused several times to get his breath. He had become an adept at concealing his physical weakness on such occasions. He would seize on some point of local or passing interest and make inquiries about it, so that by the time the answer came he would have been rested. There was a party of some fifty gentlemen, all friends, all hearty, all delightful. On

HENRY IRVING AND JOHN HARE

The last photograph of Henry Irving, taken in John Hare's garden at Overstrand by Miss Hare, 1905

HE WANTED TO KNOW 353

the presentation of the Address he spoke well, but looked sadly feeble.

That night we played *Louis XI*. He got through his work all right, but was very exhausted after it. The bill of the next night was the one we dreaded, *The Bells*. I had been with him at his hotel for an hour in the morning and we had got through our usual work together. He seemed feeble, but made no complaint. There was a great house that night. When Irving arrived he seemed exceedingly feeble though not ill. In his dressing-room I noticed that he did that which I had never known him do before: sit down in a listless way and delay beginning to dress for his part. He seemed tired, tired; tired not for an hour but for a lifetime. He played, however, just as usual. There was no perceptible diminution of his strength —of his fire. But when the play was over he was absolutely exhausted. Whilst he was dressing I went in and sat with him, having previously given instructions to the Master Machinist to send *The Bells* back to London. When I told Irving what I had done he acquiesced in it and seemed relieved. He had played *The Bells* against the strong remonstrances of Loveday and myself. Knowing him as I did, I came to the conclusion that his doing so was to prove himself. He had felt weak but would not yield to the suspicion; he wanted to *know*.

It may be wondered at or even asked why Henry Irving was allowed to play at all, being in his then state of weakness.

In the first place, Irving was his own master, and took his own course entirely. He was of a very masterful nature and took on his own shoulders the full responsibility of his acts. He would listen to the advice of those whom he trusted naturally, or had learned to trust; but he was, within the limits of possibility, the final arbiter of matters concerning himself in which there was any power of choice. The forces of a strong nature have to be accepted *en bloc;* these very indomitable forces of resolution and persistence—of the disregard of pain or weariness to himself which had given him his great position—ruled him in weakness as in strength. His will was the controlling power of his later as of his earlier days.

Moreover, he *could not* stop. To do so would have been final extinction. His affairs were such that it was necessary to go on for the sake of himself in such span of life as might be left to him, and for the sake of others. The carrying out of his purpose of going through his farewell tours would mean the realisation of a fortune; without such he would begin the unproductive period of age in poverty. Accustomed as he had been for now many years to carry out his wishes in his own way: to do whatever he had set his heart on and to help his many friends and comrades, to be powerless in such matters would have been to him a never-ending pain of chagrin. All this, of course over and above the ties and duties of his family and his own personal needs. He was a very proud man, and the inevitable blows to his pride would have been to him worse than death—especially when such might be obviated by labour, howsoever arduous or dangerous the same might be. We who knew him well recognised all this. All that we could do was to keep our own counsel, and to help him to the best of our respective powers.

XII

The next morning, 13th October, I went to Irving at half-past twelve. Loveday as had been arranged came at one o'clock. We three discussed matters ahead of us fully. We decided on the changes to be made in the bill for the following week when we were to play in Birmingham. Irving seemed quite calm, and, under the circumstances, cheerful. He endorsed the decision of the previous evening as to leaving *The Bells* out of the repertoire for the remainder of the tour; he seemed pleased at not having to play the piece for the present. We then decided on such other arrangements as were consequently necessary. In the course of our conversation Irving said:

"Of course the American tour is absolutely impossible! It will have to be abandoned! But time enough for that; we can see to it later."

That morning he was undoubtedly feeble. He was so unusually amenable in accepting the changes of his plans that when we were walking back I commented on it to Loveday, saying:

"He acquiesced too easily; I never knew him so meek before. I don't like it!"

When he came down to the theatre that night Irving seemed much better and stronger, and was more cheerful than he had been for some time.

He played well; and though he was somewhat exhausted, was infinitely less so than he had been on the previous evening. There was no speech that night, so that the last words he spoke on the stage were Becket's last words in the play :—

"Into Thy hands, O Lord! into Thy hands!"

I sat in his room with him while he dressed. He was quite cheerful, and we chatted freely. I thought that he had turned the corner and was already, with that marvellous recuperative power of his, on the way to get strong again. I told him that it was my opinion that now he was rid of the apprehension of having to play *The Bells* he would be himself soon :

"You have been feeling the taking up of your work again after an absence of it for four months, the longest time of rest in your life. Now you have got into your stride again, and work will be easy!"

He thought for a moment and then said quietly :

"I really think that is so!" Then he seemed to get quite cheery.

Percy Burton, who arranged our advance matters, had in answer to my telegram come over from Birmingham, so that he might be fully told of our prospective changes. He was coming home to supper with me before he got the train back to Birmingham. I had asked Irving if he wanted to see him; but he said he did not, as Burton quite knew what to do. Then, always thoughtful of others, he added :

"But if he is going by the one o'clock train you must not wait here. He will want time to take his supper." I stood up to go and he held out his hand to say good-night. Afterwards, the remembrance of that affectionate movement came back to me with gratitude, for it was not usual; when men meet every day and every night, handshaking is not a part of the routine of friendly life. As I went out he said to me:

"Muffle up your throat, old chap. It is bitterly cold to-night and you have a cold. Take care of yourself! Good-night! God bless you!"

Those were the last words that I heard Henry Irving speak!

Burton and I were at supper when a carriage drove rapidly up to the door of my lodging. I suspected that it was something for me and opened the door myself at once. Mr. Sheppard, one of my assistants who always attended to Irving's private matters, stepped in saying quickly:

"I think you had better come down to the Midland Hotel at once. Sir Henry is ill. He fainted in the hall just as he did at Wolverhampton. When the doctor came I rushed off for you!" We all jumped into the carriage and hurried as fast as we could go to the hotel.

In the hall were some twenty men grouped round Irving who lay at full length on the floor. One of the doctors, there were three of them there then, told me quietly that he was dead. He had died just two minutes before. The clock in the hall showed the time then as eight minutes to twelve. So that he died at ten minutes to twelve.

It was almost impossible to believe, as he lay there with his eyes open, that he was really dead.

I knelt down by him and felt his heart to know for myself if it was indeed death. But all was sadly still. His body was quite warm. Walter Collinson, his faithful valet, was sitting on the floor beside him, crying. He said to me through his sobs:

"He died in my arms!"

His face looked very thin and the features sharp as he lay there with his chest high and his head fallen back; but there was none of the usual ungracefulness of death. The long iron-grey hair had fallen back, showing the great height of his rounded forehead. The bridge of his nose stood out sharp and high. I closed his eyes myself; but as I had had no experience in such a matter I asked one of the doctors, who kindly with deft fingers straightened the eyelids. Then we carried him upstairs to his room and laid him on his bed.

I had to send a host of telegrams at once to inform the various members of his family and the press. The latter had to go with what speed we could, for the hour of his death was such that there was no local information. Loveday arrived at the hotel after we had carried him to his room. He was indeed greatly distressed and in bitter sorrow.

The actual cause of Irving's death was physical weakness; he lost a breath, and had not strength to recover it.

Sheppard told me that when Irving was leaving the theatre he had said to him that he had better come to the hotel with him, as was sometimes his duty. When he got into the carriage he had sat with his back to the horses; this being his usual custom by which he avoided a draught. He was quite silent during the short journey. When he got out of

LYING DESOLATE AND LONELY 359

the carriage he seemed very feeble, and as he passed through the outer hall of the hotel seemed uncertain of step. He stumbled slightly and Sheppard held him up. Then when he got as far as the inner hall he sat down on a bench for an instant.

That instant was the fatal one. In the previous February at Wolverhampton, when he had suffered from a similar attack of weakness, he had fallen down flat. In that attitude Nature asserted herself, and the lungs being in their easiest position allowed him to breathe mechanically. Now the seated attitude did not give the opportunity for automatic effort. The syncope grew worse; he slipped on the ground. But it was then too late. By the time the doctor arrived, after only a few minutes in all, he had passed too far into the World of Shadows to be drawn back by any effort of man or science. The heart beat faintly, and more faintly still. And then came the end.

Before I left the hotel in the grey of the morning I went into the bedroom. It wrung my heart to see my dear old friend lie there so cold and white and still. It was all so desolate and lonely, as so much of his life had been. So lonely that in the midst of my own sorrow I could not but rejoice at one thing: for him there was now Peace and Rest.

I was at the hotel again at 7.30, and then went to meet his eldest son, H. B. Irving, at the Great Northern Station at 9.35. He had received my telegram in time to start by the newspaper train. His other son, Laurence, with his wife arrived later in the day; my telegram to him had not arrived in time to allow his coming till the morning train. The undertaker had come in the morning at nine, and the embalming was done before Irving's sons had arrived.

That afternoon all the Company, including the workmen, came to see him. It was a very touching and harrowing time for all, for he was much beloved by every one.

At seven o'clock in the evening the body was laid in the lead coffin. I was present alone with the undertakers and saw the lead coffin sealed. This was then placed in the great oak coffin—which an hour later was taken privately through the yard of the Midland Hotel by a devious way to the Great Northern Station so as to avoid publicity; for the streets were thronged with waiting crowds. At Bradford, Saturday is a half day, and large numbers of people are abroad. The ex-Mayor, Mr. Lupton, who had entertained Irving in the Town Hall at his previous visit, kindly arranged with the Chief Constable that all should be in order in the streets. All day throughout the City the flags had been at half-mast, and there was everywhere a remarkable silence through which came the mournful sound of the minute-bells from seemingly all the churches.

At half-past nine we left the hotel to drive to the railway station. The appearance of the streets and the demeanour of the crowd I shall never forget; and I never want to. Everywhere was a sea of faces, all the more marked as all hats were off as we drove slowly along. Street after street of silent humanity; and in all that crowd nothing but grief and respect. One hardly realised its completeness till when, now and then, a sob broke the stillness.

To say that it was moving would convey but a poor idea of that attitude of the crowd; it was poignant — harrowing — overwhelming. In silence the crowd stood back; in silence, without hurry or pushing or stress of any kind, closed around us and followed on. It was the same at the railway station; everywhere the silent crowd, holding back respectfully, uncovered.

For a quarter of a century I had been accustomed when travelling with Irving to see the rushing crowd closing in with cheers and waving of hats and kerchiefs; to watch a moving sea of hands thrust forward for him to shake; to hear the roar of the cheering crowd kept up till the train began to move, and then to hear it dying away from our ears not from cessation but from mere distance. And now this silence! No nobler or more loving tribute than the silence of that mighty crowd could ever be paid to the memory of one who has passed away. Were I a Yorkshireman I should have been proud of Bradford on that day. It moves me strangely to think of it yet.

XIII

The Dean and Chapter of Westminster Abbey were memorialised by a number of persons of importance to have a Public Funeral with burial in the Abbey. So important were the signatories that no difficulty was experienced. The only condition made was that the body should be cremated, as a rule had been established that henceforth no actual body should be buried in the Abbey. The ground had in the past been so broken that for new graves it would be necessary to go down into the concrete, which might injure the structure. The Abbey authorities were most kind in all ways. Dean Armitage Robinson gave from his sick bed his approval, and Sub-Dean Duckworth and Archdeacon Wilberforce made all arrangements. Indeed the Dean on the day of the funeral got up in order to perform the burial service.

The Baroness and Mr. Burdett-Coutts, knowing that Irving's flat in 17 Stratton Street was not suited to receive the crowds who would wish to pay their respects, kindly placed at the disposal of his family their spacious house in Piccadilly and Stratton Street. Here on Thursday 19th he lay in state. The great dining-room was made a *Chapelle ardente*, and here were placed the many, many flowers that were sent. There was a veritable sea of them—wreaths, crosses, symbolic forms of all kinds. On the coffin over the heart lay the floral cross sent by the Queen. Attached to it was a broad ribbon on which she had written as her tribute to the Dead the last words he had spoken on the stage :

" Into Thy hands, O Lord ; into Thy hands."

On a little table in front of the coffin lay the wreath sent by Ellen Terry. Behind, hung high along the end wall of the lofty room, was the Pall —" sent anonymously " as the card on it declared. Surely such a pall was never before seen. It was entirely wrought of leaves of fresh laurel. Thousands upon thousands of them went to its making up. It was so large that at the funeral when fourteen pall-bearers marched with the coffin it covered all the space and hung to the ground, before, behind, and on either side.

Through that room all day long passed a silent and mournful crowd of all classes and degrees; and at any moment of the time a single glance at their faces would have shown what love and sorrow had brought them there.

XIV

I

The Public Funeral took place on Friday, 20th October. It would be impossible in a book of this size to give details of it, even if such belonged to the scope of my work. Suffice it that all the honours which can be paid to the illustrious dead were observed. The King had sent to represent him, according to the custom of such ceremonies, Irving's old and dear friend, General the Right Hon. Sir Dighton Probyn, V.C. The Queen's formal representative was Earl Howe; but her personal tribute was the beautiful cross of flowers which lay on the actor's coffin. The Prince and Princess of Wales were also represented. Others were there also whom men call " great "—chiefs of all great endeavours. Ministers and soldiers, ambassadors and judges, peers and great merchants, and many sorrowing exponents of all the Arts. To name them would be impossible; to try to describe the ceremony unavailing. But the place for all this is not here; it belongs now to the history of the Age and Nation.

II

All the previous night the coffin had lain in the little chapel of St. Faith between the South Transept—wherein is the Poets' Corner where Irving was to be laid, and the Chapter-House—where the mourners were to assemble. The funeral had been arranged for noon, but hours before that time every approach to the Abbey was thronged with silent crowds. There was a hush in the air through which the roar of the traffic in the streets seemed to come modified, as though it had been intercepted by that belt of silence. Slowly, imperceptibly, like shadows in their silence, the crowds gathered; a sombre mass closing as if with a black ring the whole precincts of the Cathedral.

Noon found the interior of the edifice a solid mass of people, save where the passage-way up the Nave and Choir was marked with masses of white flowers. Wreaths and crosses and bunches of flowers must have been sent in hundreds—thousands, for in addition to those within, both sides of the Cloister walks were banked with them.

Who could adequately describe that passing from the Chapter-House whence the funeral procession took its way through the South and West Cloister Walk, down the South Aisle and up the Nave and Choir till the coffin was rested before the Sanctuary; the touching music, in which now and again the sweet childish treble—the purest sound on earth—seemed to rend the mourners' very hearts; the mighty crowd, silent, with bowed heads; everywhere white faces with eyes that wept.

Oh that crowd! Never in the world was greater tribute to any man. The silence! The majestic silence, for it transcended negation and became positive from its dormant force. "Not dead silence, but living silence!" as the dead man's old companion, Sir Edward Russell, said in words that should become immortal. All thoughts of self were forgotten; the lesser feelings of life seemed to have passed away in that glory of triumphant sorrow. Eye and heart and brain and memory went with the Dead as to the solemn music the mournful procession passed along. Surely a lifetime of devotion must have gone to the crowning of those long-drawn seconds. To one moving through that divine alley-way of sympathetic sorrow it seemed as though the serried ranks on either hand, seen in the dimness of that October day, went back and back to the very bounds of the thinking world.

As from the steps of the Sanctuary came the first words of the Service for the Burial of the Dead, a bright gleam of winter sunshine burst through the storied window of the Southern Transept and lit up the laurel pall till it glistened like gold.

And then for a little while few could see anything except dimly through their tears.

When the last words of the Benediction had been spoken over his grave, there came from the Organ-loft the first solemn notes of Handel's noble *Dead March*. The great organ had been supplemented by military music, and as the mournful notes of the trumpets rose they seemed to cling to the arches and dim corners of the great Cathedral, tearing open our hearts with endless echoes. And then the solemn booming of the muffled drums seemed to recall us to the life that has to be lived on, howsoever lonely or desolate it may be.

> " The song of woe
> Is after all an earthly song."

The trumpets summon us, and the drums beat the time of the onward march—quick or slow as Duty calls.

March! March!

INDEX

INDEX

ABBEY, Edwin A., R.A., i. 321 ; ii. 79-85
Abbey, Henry E., i. 317
Aberdeen, Countess of, i. 322
Aberdeen, Earl of, i. 322, 340-341
Absolute, Captain, i. 1-5
"Acting, an Art," ii. 247, 263, 265
"Acting and Actors," ii. 157-158
Acting, Old School and New, i. 12-24
"Actor-Managers," i. 47
"Actors and Acting," ii. 265
Actor's Note," "An, ii. 157-158
Adams, Judge, i. 318
Addresses by Irving, ii. 244-265
Ade, George, i. 318
Adventures, ii. 266-296
Agnew, Sir Wm., Bart., i. 318
Aide, Hamilton, i. 323
Aitken, J. A., R.S.A., i. 323
Albermarle, Earl of, i. 320
Albery, James, i. 7, 315
Alcester, Lord, i. 319
Aldrich, Thomas Bailey, i. 316; ii. 53
Aldworth, i. 212-221, 232-239
Alexander, Geo., i. 322 ; ii. 130
Alexandra, Queen, i. 173-174, 175, 268 ; ii. 213-214, 225, 362
Allingham, Mrs. H., i. 234, 318
Alma-Tadema, Sir Laurence, R.A., i. 325 ; ii. 65-72, 152, 245
Amber Heart, The, ii. 301
America, Visits to, i. 285-288 ; ii. 229-237
American Reporters, i. 297-303
Ames, Col., i. 320
Anderson, Mary, i. 325
Applause, Effect of, i. 74
Arlton, Frank, ii. 188-189
Arnott, A., i. 63-69, 142-143
Arnold, Sir Arthur, ii. 240
Arnold, Sir Edwin, i. 227, 326
Arnold, W. T., i. 316
Arrowsmith, J. W., i. 326
Art du Comédien," "L', ii. 158
Art of Acting, The, ii. 158, 253-260, 264
Art-sense, i. 144-147

Arthur, Gen. Chester A. (President, U.S.A.), ii. 229
Arthur, Robert, i. 319
Ashbourne, Lord Chancellor, i. 323
Asif Kadr Saiyid Wasif Ali Mirza, i. 339
Ashwell, Lena, i. 255, 322
Asquith, Rt. Hon. H. H., i. 316
Athenæum Club, i. 243
Aubertin, Mr., i. 352
Austin, Alfred (Poet Laureate), i. 323 ; ii. 255
Austin, L. F., i. 316
Ayling, John, i. 317

BABA Khem Singh Bedi, i. 339
Baby in *Henry VIII.*, i. 116-117
Bach, Walter, ii. 146
Bacon and Shakespeare, Tennyson on, i. 235
Baghos Pacha Nubar, H.E., i. 317
Bailey, Lieut. (U.S.N.), i. 326
Bailey, Sir William, i. 322
Baillie-Hamilton, Sir Wm., i. 335
Baker, Bernard N., i. 322
Balance of Comfort, The, ii. 137, 301
Baldwin, Admiral (U.S.A.), i. 322
Balfour, Rt. Hon. A. J., i. 316
Ball, John Meredith, i. 112-113
Ballantine, Serjeant, i. 317
Bancroft, George, i. 317
Bancroft, Lady, i. 318
Bancroft, Sir Squire, i. 318 ; ii. 141, 186, 240
Banks, Sir W., i. 321
Baring's Bank, i. 192-193
Barnato, Barney, i. 318
Barnay, Ludwig, i. 318 ; ii. 151-156
Barnes, General (U.S.A.), i. 315
Barnum, P. T., i. 318
Baroda, The Gaekwar of, i. 320
Barr, Robert, ii. 138
Barrett, Lawrence, i. 315 ; ii. 152-153
Barrett, Wilson, i. 323 ; ii. 118, 153
Barrie, J. M., i. 316 ; ii. 137
Barron, Elwyn, i. 323
Barrows, B. H., i. 323

INDEX

Barry, Lord Justice, i. 324
Barry, Sergeant, ii. 60
Barrymore, Ethel, i. 321
Bartlett, Frank, i. 319
Bartlett, W. H., i. 324
Bass, Col. (U.S.A.), i. 324
Bassanio, i. 276
Bastien-Lepage, Jules, ii. 163–165
Bateman, Col., i. 141–144 ; ii. 307
Bateman, Mrs. H. L., i. 53, 75 ; ii. 175, 307
Bates, General (U.S.A.), ii. 232
Bates, W. O., i. 319
Bath, Quin Memorial. Civic Lunch, ii. 347
Bayard, T. F. (U.S. Ambassador), i. 321
Beaconsfield, Lady, ii. 39–40
Beaconsfield, Earl of, i. 168–169 ; ii. 37–42
Beatrice, i. 101–103
Beaufort, The Duke of, i. 325
Becke, Louis, i. 318
Becket, i. 209–211, 221–242 ; Windsor, ii. 216–222, 301, 302
Becket, Reading, Canterbury Cathedral, i. 242–245
Becket, Reading, King Alfred Millenary, i. 245–246 ; ii. 233
Beckett, Arthur à, i. 319
Bective, The Countess of, i. 324
Bedford Street, Irving's office at, i. 273
Beecher, Henry Ward, i. 322
Behenna, Sarah, i. 103
Beit, Alfred, i. 319
Belasco, David, i. 320
Belfast, Samaritan Hospital, i. 57–60
Belgians, The King of the, i. 364
Bell, C. Moberley, i. 325
Bell, E. Hamilton, i. 324
Bell, Mackenzie, i. 325
Bellevue Gardens, ii. 125–127
Belle's Stratagem, The, i. 5–7, 89 ; ii. 301
Bells, The, i. 12, 141–144, 152–153 ; ii. 301, 302 ; Irving's last performance in, 353
Belmont, Perry, i. 325
Belmore, Lionel, ii. 226–227
Bendall, Ernest A., i. 91, 318
Benedict, Sir Julius, i. 95, 322
Benedict, Mrs. and Miss Stone, i. 325
Bennett, Joseph, i. 326
Benvolio, i. 87
Beresford, Admiral Lord C., i. 316
Bernhardt, Maurice, i. 317
Bernhardt, Sarah, i. 317 ; ii. 53, 161–166

Berrington, Mr. (Mayor of Wolverhampton), ii. 347
Beveridge, J. D., i. 326
Bierstadt, Albert, i. 315
Bigelow, Mr., i. 362
Bigelow, Poulteney, i. 322
Bigelow, Prescott, i. 320
Billings, Dr. (U.S.A.), i. 315
Bikaner, Maharaja of, i. 338
Bimetallism, ii. 34–35
Birkbeck Institute, i. 304–306, 368
Bishop, J. B., i. 287–288, 319
Blackie, Prof., i. 319
Blaine, J. G., i. 316
Blake, Sir Henry, i. 326
Blanchard, G. R., i. 325
Blashfield, E., i. 323
Bliss, Cornelius, i. 323
Bliss, Wm., i. 325
Blomfeld, Lady, i. 326
Bloody Marriage, The, ii. 137
Blyth, Henry A., i. 324
Blyth, Sir James, Bart., i. 318
Boarding School, The, ii. 301
Bobbili, Raja of, i. 339
Bobbs, W. C., i. 316
Bodley, John Edward Courtenay, i. 319
Boito, i. 318 ; ii. 140–141
Bolton, T. H., M.P., i. 316
Book III. Chapter V., ii. 301
Booth, Edwin, i. 2, 86–92, 318 ; ii. 152
Booth, O., ii. 137
Booth, Wilkes, ii. 103
Boothby, Guy, i. 316
Boots at the Swan, i. 16
Borrajo, E. M., i. 321
Boston, *Faust*, i. 183 ; *Dante*, i. 274
Boston, Tremont Theatre, Harvard Night at, ii. 260–261
Bourchier, Arthur, i. 323 ; ii. 227
Boucicault, Dion (the Elder), i. 138–139, 315 ; ii. 136
Boucicault, Dion (the Younger) i.326
Boughton, Geo., R.A., i. 317 ; ii. 80, 89
Bournemouth, i. 330–331
Bowker, Alfred (Mayor of Winchester), i. 246
Bowles, Samuel, i. 319
Boyd-Carpenter, Right Rev. Wm. (Bishop of Ripon), i. 324 ; ii. 253
Bradbury, Mr., ii. 44
Braddon, Miss (Mrs. Maxwell), i. 1 319
Bradford : Irving's last performances—his sudden death, ii. 352–361
Bradshaw, Christopher, i. 315

INDEX

Brady, Judge (N.Y.), i. 317
Braithwaite, Lilian, i. 323
Brereton, Austin, i. 315
Bresnin, Fire Chief, ii. 275
Brewster, Hon. Benjamin H., i. 315; ii. 192–193
Bride of Lammermoor, The, see *Ravenswood*
Bridal Chambers, Variants of, i. 100
Bridge, Sir John F., i. 241
Bright, J. F., D.D. (Master of University), ii. 252
Bright, Jacob, i. 324
Bright, John, i. 28
Brisson, Adolphe, i. 316; ii. 140
Bristol, Prince's Theatre, i. 249; ii. 203
British Legion, The, i. 16
Broadfield, E. J., i. 322
Brodribb, Samuel, i. 129
Brodribb, Thomas, i. 129
Brodrick, Hon. G. C. (Warden of Merton), ii. 252
Brodsky, Prof., i. 325
Bromley, " Uncle " George, i. 318
Brooke, The Ranee, Lady, i. 315
Brooklyn : *Dante,* i. 274
Brooks, Sydney, i. 317
Brough, Lionel, ii. 183
Brougham, Lord, i. 28
Broughton, Phyllis, i. 322
Brown, Ford Madox, i. 119
Brown, Mrs. Hannah, ii. 308–310
Browne, Dr. Edgar, i. 316
Browning, Robert, ii. 87–91
Bryant, W. E., i. 320
Bryce, Annan, i. 317
Bryce, Prof. James, i. 368
Brydges-Willyams, Mr., i. 317; ii. 176
Buck, Col. E. A., i. 289, 362
Buffalo Liberal Club, ii. 265
Bull, W. L., i. 323
Burbank, A. P., i. 316; ii. 160
Burdett-Coutts, The Baroness, i. 84, 319; ii. 147–148, 234, 308, 362
Burdett-Coutts, W.A., M.P., i. 319, 362; ii. 69, 153, 362
Burgin, G. B., i. 318
Burlesque of the *Corsican Brothers,* i. 169–170
Burnand, Sir Francis C., i. 91, 320, 362, 364; ii. 87, 137, 153
Burne-Jones, Sir Edward, Bart., i. 253–255, 319; ii. 73–78
Burne-Jones, Sir Philip, Bart., i. 325
Burnham, Daniel, i. 320
Burnham, Lord, i. 283–284, 315; ii. 175

Burns, Rt. Hon. John, i. 323; ii. 55
Burton, Lady, i. 324, 350–361
Burton, Percy, ii. 356–357
Burton, Sir Richard, i. 324, 350–361; ii. 118
Butler, Richard, i. 320
Byegones, i. 164; ii. 301
Byles, W. P., M.P., i. 325
Byron, H. J., i. 325
Byron, Lord, ii. 90

CADWALLADER-JONES, Mrs. and Miss, i. 318
Cahn, Julius, i. 322
Caine, Hall, i. 26, 318; ii. 53–54; 115–124, 130, 141–142
Caine, Ralph Hall, i. 325
Caird, Dr., ii. 250
Caldecott, R., i. 317
Calmour, A. C., i. 317
Calvé, i. 316
Calvert, i. 91–92
Cambridge University, i. 241; "Rede" Lecture, D.Litt., ii. 247–249
Cameron, Sir Charles, i. 316
Campbell, Angus, i. 318
Campbell, Lord Archibald, i. 324
Canterbury Cathedral, i. 242–245; ii. 184–186
Captain of the Watch, The, ii. 301
Captive, The, i. 352
Cardiff : Farewell visit, ii. 45
Carey, Wm., i. 324
Carleton, H. Guy, i. 319; ii. 137
Carl Rosa Opera Company, ii. 328
Carr, J. Comyns, i. 323; ii. 125, 154, 332
Carr, Mrs. Comyns, i. 323; ii. 154
Carr, Philip, i. 326
Carrington, Earl of, i. 323
Carroll, Howard, i. 318
Carson, John B., i. 325
Casella, The Misses, ii. 51, 146
Casella, Mr., i. 320
Cassel, Sir Ernest, i. 315
Cassio, i. 16, 87
Castle, Capt. Egerton, i. 319; ii. 137
Catholic Social Union, ii. 265
Catling, Thomas, i. 318
Cawdor, Earl of, i. 325
Cecil, Arthur, i. 91
Chambers, Haddon, i. 316
Chance, H. T., i. 321
Chandler, Senator, i. 322
Chappell, Arthur, i. 324
Charcot, Dr., i. 316
Charles I., i. 12, 138–139; ii. 301, 302

372 INDEX

Chicago and *Faust*, i. 184
Chicago, Illinois Theatre, i. 132–134
Chicago, Twentieth Century Club, ii. 264
Chicago, University of, ii. 263
Chicago Times Herald, i. 250
Chicago, U.S. Cruiser, i. 327–331
Childs, G. W., i. 323 ; ii. 110
Chinese Ambassador, i. 78–79
Choate, Joseph B. (U.S. Ambassador), i. 320 ; ii. 234
Christie's, i. 152 ; ii. 91
Christmas, i. 308–309
Churchill, Lady Randolph, i. 317
Churchill, Lord Randolph, i. 317 ; ii. 35
Chute, J. Macready, i. 319
Claire, Louise, i. 7
Claretie, Jules, i. 153–155, 318 ; ii. 140, 162
Clarke, J. I. C., i. 256, 325 ; ii. 137
Clarke, Lady Campbell, i. 283, 316
Clarke, Senator, i. 317
Clarke, Sir Campbell, i. 316 ; ii. 160
Clayton, John, i. 91
Cleland, Baillie, i. 316
Clemens, S. L., *see* Twain, Mark
Clement, E. H., i. 323
Clery, Jules, i. 154
Cleveland, Grover (President U.S.A.), ii. 229–230
Clifford, Mrs. W. K., i. 317
Clover Club, ii. 92
Coatbridge, i. 17
Cody, Genl. Hon. W. F. (U.S.A.), i. 324 ; ii. 142
Coitier, i. 131
Coleridge, Lord, L.C.J., i. 316
Coleridge, Hon. Stephen, i. 321
Collins, Arthur, i. 322
Collins, Col., i. 324
Collinson, Walter, ii. 224, 279, 329, 358
Collis, General (U.S.A.), i. 324
Colman, Geo., i. 83
Colonial Conference, i. 314
Colonial Premiers, The, i. 252, 334, 340–341
Colonial Troops, i. 251–252
Columbia (College) University, ii. 262–263
Colvin, Sidney, i. 322
Comédie-Française, The, i. 153–155 ; ii. 158, 161, 162–163
Commercial, " Only a," i. 49–50
Connaught, Duke of, i. 38
Conreid, Heinrich, i. 320
Cook, Dutton, i. 326
Cook, E. T., i. 317
Cooke, Geo. Frederick, i. 74

Cooke, Sir C. Kinloch, i. 315
Cool as a Cucumber, ii. 301
Cooper, Lady Agnes, i. 321
Cooper, Sir Alfred, ii. 146
Copperfield, i. 42
Coquelin, Cadet, i. 315, 316 ; ii. 141
Coquelin, Constant (Aîné), ii. 157–160
Coquelin, Fils, i. 318 ; ii. 158
Coriolanus, i. 83 ; ii. 65–70, 343
Coronation, The King's (1902), it 334–342 ; ii. 243
Corpse, The way to carry a, i. 97–98
Correspondence, i. 61–62
Corry, " Monty " (Lord Rowton), i. 168
Corsican Brothers, The, i. 159–172 ; ii. 275, 301
Coudert, Mr., i. 325
Count, The, ii. 137
Courier of Lyons, The, i. 17
Courtney, W. L., i. 320 ; ii. 137, 138, 252–253, 256
Craig, Edith, i. 326 ; ii. 53
Craigie, Mrs., i. 317
Cramp, Charles, i. 318
Cramp, Edwin, i. 315
Craven, Hawes, i. 75, 85–86, 94, 104, 110, 179, 205, 255, 317 ; ii. 86, 212
Crawford, Earl of, i. 323
Crawford, Marion, i. 316 ; ii. 318
Crawford, Robert, i. 324
Creelman, James, i. 323
Crewe, Earl of, ii. 210
Critchett, Sir Anderson, i. 322
Critic, The, i. 17
Cronegk, i. 323 ; ii. 153
Crosby Hall, i. 187
Cunningham, David, i. 58
Cup, The, i. 89, 162, 202–208 ; ii. 301
Curan, i. 118
Currie, Lady (" Violet Fane "), i. 321
Currie, Lord, i. 321
Cuthbert, W., i. 86, 205
Cymbeline, ii. 72, 301, 325
Cyrano de Bergerac, ii. 160

Dabbs, Dr., i. 240–241, 321
Daily News, The, i. 287–288
Daily Telegraph, The, i. 187, 283, 287 ; ii. 324
Daisy's Escape, i. 164 ; ii. 301
Dalhousie, The Earl and Countess of, ii. 253–257
Daly, Augustin, i. 322, 369
Daly, Judge (New York), i. 320
Damala, i. 321 ; ii. 166
Damrosch, Walter, ii. 140
Dana, Charles A., i. 316

INDEX

Dangle, i. 17
Dante, i. 211 ; ii. 32
Dante, i. 271-275 ; ii. 318, 343
Darbyshire, Alfred, i. 316
D'Arcy Knox, i. 319 ; ii. 186
Darmont, i. 320 ; ii. 53, 166
Davenport, Colonel, i. 16
Davis, Clarke, i. 319
Davis, Dr., i. 316
Davis, E. D., i. 129
Davis, Fay, i. 324
Davis, Judge N. (New York), i. 317
Davis, Richard Harding, i. 315
Davis, Will J., i. 323
Dead Heart, The, ii. 301
De Bornier, i. 361 ; ii. 118, 120
Deemster, The, ii. 117-118
De Lara, Isidore, i. 321
de la Rue, Sir Andros, Bart., i. 320
del Balzo, Duca and Duchessa, i. 324
Demon Lover, The, ii. 123-124
Depew, Senator Chauncey, i. 315
Derlacher, George, i. 326
Devonshire, The Duchess of, i. 254, 317
Devonshire, The Duke of, i. 317
Dewar, Sir James, i. 317 ; ii. 323
Dexter, Wirt, i. 316
Dexter, Mrs. and Miss Wirt, i. 316
De Young, M. H., i. 321
Diamond Jubilee (1897), i. 251-252, 333-334
Dicey, Edward, i. 318
Dickens, Chas., ii. 280, 282 ; ii. 177
Dickens, Chas. (the younger), i. 91, 280, 315
Dickens, Henry Fielding, i. 280-282, 315
Dickens, Kate (Mrs. Perugini), i. 280, 317
Dickens, The Misses, i. 315
Dicksee, Frank, R.A., i. 318
Diderot, D., *Paradox of Acting*, i. 48-49 ; ii. 18, 157-158
Didier, i. 17
Dillon, Valentine (Lord Mayor of Dublin), ii. 208-211
Dixey, Mr., i. 321
Dixon, A. J., i. 324
Dixon, J., ii. 137
Dixon, Misses Hepworth, i. 326
Dolat Singh, Maharaja Kunwar, i. 339
Dolgoruki, Princess, ii. 52
Domville, Dr., i. 321
Donaldson, Thomas, i. 321 ; ii. 92-93, 100, 102, 105, 106, 110, 111
Don Quixote (J. J. C. Clarke), i. 256 ; ii. 137

Don Quixote (W. G. Wills), i. 255-258 ; ii. 137, 301
Doricourt, i. 278
Dornton, Young, i. 6-7
Dorsheimer, Governor, i. 320 ; ii. 259
Dowden, Edward, i. 27, 321 ; ii. 95-99
Doyle, Sir Arthur Conan, i. 248, 249, 321 ; ii. 138
Dramatists, ii. 131-139
Dream of Eugene Aram, The, i. 28-32, 43 ; ii. 178
Drew, John, i. 321
Drew, Mrs. Harry, i. 321
Drexel, A. ("Tony"), ii. 110
Drury Lane Theatre, i. 273-274 ; ii. 151, 203 ; Irving's last performances in London, 350-351
Dublin, Theatre Royal, 1867, i. 1-7 ; 1871, 7-8 ; 1872, 11 ; 1877 ; 47-50 ; Early Experiences at the Queen's Theatre, 14-18 ; Public Reception and Address, 1894, ii. 208-211
Dublin University, 1876, Honours from, i. 35-41 ; 1877, a Reading at Trinity College, 42-44 ; 1892, D.Litt., ii. 244-247
Du Bois, Dr. (U.S.N.), i. 325
Dubourg, A. W., i. 317
Du Chaillu, Paul B., i. 369
Duckworth, Sub-Dean Robinson, ii. 362
Dufferin and Ava, The Marquis of, ii. 246, 248-249
Du Maurier, George, i. 323
Dumont, General, i. 325
Dunn, J. Nicol, i. 322
Dunne, F. P., ii. 166
Dunraven, The Earl of, i. 323
Dunton, Theodore Watts, i. 321
Duplat, General, i. 325
Durham, Arthur, i. 321
Duse, i. 324
Duval, H. C., i. 320
Dyall, Charles, i. 321

EDINBURGH, i. 118, 277-278
Edinburgh, H.R.H., the Duke of, *see* Saxe-Coburg-Gotha, Duke of
Edinburgh Philosophical Institute, 1881 and 1891, ii. 264
Edinburgh, Queen's Theatre, i. 276
Edinburgh Theatre Royal, i. 3
Edgar and Lucy, see *Ravenswood*
Edison, i. 176
Educational value of the Stage, i. 183
Edward VII., i. 161-162, 173-174, 175, 268, 284, 310-311 ; ii. 186, 212-215, 219, 238, 242, 243, 363
Edwards, Col. C. (U.S.A.), i. 324

INDEX

Edwards, J. Passmore, i. 320
Edwards, Wm., i. 316
Egerton, Lady Alix, i. 326
Egerton, Lady Mabel, i. 325
Eibenschutz Ilona, i. 318
Elderkin, John, i. 318
Eliot," "Max (Mrs. Ellis), i. 323
Elliot, Maxine, i. 325
Elliot, Mr. (President of Harvard), ii. 259–260
Elliott, Gertrude, i. 318
Elliott, Sir George, Bart., ii. 38–39
Elliott, Samuel, i. 326
Ellis, Sir Whittaker, i. 317
Ellis, Walter, i. 323
Elsler, Fanny, i. 8
Emery, Capt. (U.S.A.), i. 325
Emin Pasha, i. 370
Emlyn, Lord, i. 326
Emmott, W. T., i. 315
End of the Hunting, The, ii. 137
Engel, Lewis, i. 326
"English Actors," ii. 253–255
Enoch Arden, i. 211
Erben, Admiral (U.S.A.), i. 325, 327–331
Escott, T. H. S., i. 325, 362
Esher, Lord, i. 321
Eugene Aram, i. 12, 127–128; ii. 296, 301
Eugénie, The Empress, i. 372
Eustace, Jennie, i. 322
Evarts, Senator, i. 320
Exeter, ii. 347

Fahnstock, H. C., i. 325
Fairchild, Charles, i. 324
Fairchild, Gen. L. (U.S.A.), i. 317
Fairplay, Frank, i. 16
Fardell, Sir Thomas, i. 325
Farjeon, B. L., i. 321
Farquhar, Gilbert, i. 317
Farquhar, Lord, i. 322
Farrar, Dean, i. 29, 243–244, 322
Farrell, John, i., 315
Farren, Nellie, i. 323
Farringford, i. 212, 224–232
Fateh Ali Khan, Nawab, i. 339
Faudel-Phillips, Lady, i. 283, 319
Faudel-Phillips, Sir George, Bart., i. 319
Faust, i. 109, 146–147, 175–184; ii. 275, 301, 302
Fawcett, Edgar, i. 319
Fawsitt, Amy, i. 7
Fearing, C. F., i. 317
Febvre, i. 319
Ferment, i. 175
Fernandez, James, i. 317

Field, Eugene, i. 322
Field, Marshall, i. 318
Field, Roswell, i. 319
Fife, The Duke of, i. 316
Fildes, Sir Luke, R.A., i. 325
Finance, i. 62–63; ii. 304–320
Fires, ii. 269–279, 297–303, 325–326
First Nights, i. 124, 242, 314
Fisher, Joseph, i. 319
Fiske, John, i. 231, 246, 324
Fiske, Stephen, i. 315
Fitz-George, Col., i. 323
Fitzgerald, Dr. C. S., i. 321
FitzGerald, Edward, i. 318
FitzGerald, Percy, i. 321
FitzGerald, Sir Maurice (The Knight of Kerry), i. 318
Fitzgibbon, Lord Justice, i. 317
Fladgate, W. F., i. 325
Floods, ii. 279–285
Florence, W. J., i. 91, 316
Florizel, i. 16
Flower, C. E., ii. 128
Flying Dutchman, The, ii. 124, 130, see also *Vanderdecken*
Foord, John, i. 325
Foote, General (U.S.A.), i. 321
Forbes, James Staats, i. 323
Forbes Norman, i. 322; ii. 327
Forbes, Wm., i. 244
Forbes-Robertson, Johnston, i. 255, 266, 318; ii. 241, 328
Ford, E. Onslow, R.A., i. 325; ii. 59–64
Ford, Isaac N., i. 319; ii. 166
Foreign Warships, Visits of, i. 327–332
Ford, Wolfram Onslow, ii. 63
Forrest, Edwin, i. 8; his watch, ii. 92
Foresters, The, i. 211, 247
Fowler, Thomas P., i. 321
Fox, John, jun., i. 325
Foxwell, Dr. Arthur, ii. 349
Francis, J. M., i. 319; ii. 294
Frankau, E., i. 321
Franklin, Mrs., i. 326
Franqueville, Comte de, i. 316
Frederic, Harold, i. 320
Freeman's Journal (Dublin), i. 16
Freiberger, E., i. 318
French, Samuel, i. 144
Friendship of Irving with Bram Stoker, i. 25–34, 60
Frith, W. P., R.A., i. 318
Frohman, Chas., i. 319; ii. 333, 344, 349
Frohman, Daniel, i. 321
Froude, J. A., ii. 32
Fuji, The, i. 331–332
Fulda, Ludwig, ii. 137

INDEX

Fulvius, Titus Quintus, i. 16
Furness, H. H., jun., i. 319
Furness, Horace Howard, i. 318
Furniss, Harry, i. 319
Fussy, ii. 279
Fyles, Franklin, i. 320

GAIETY Theatre, i. 99-100, 154, 169-170 ; ii. 161
Galdemar, Ange, i. 321
Galitzin, Prince Nicholas, ii. 58
Gamester, The, i. 82
Gangadhar Madho Chitnavis, i. 339
Garden, E. W., i. 320
Gardner, Mrs. Jack, i. 315
Garnett, Richard, C.B., i. 325
Garnier, i. 315 ; ii. 166
Garrick Club, ii. 91
Garrick, David, his malacca cane, ii. 90
Gaskell, The Misses, i. 322 ; ii. 144
Gaston, Duke of Orleans, i. 128-130
Gatti, S., i. 318
Gemini et Virgo, i. 42, 352
Gennadius, Signor, i. 316
George Washington, ii. 137
Gerbel, Count de, ii. 170-171
Gerbel, Countess de, *see* Ward, Miss Geneviève
Gerische, ii. 143
German, Edward, i. 320
Germany, Crown Prince of (Frederick III.), i. 179
Germany, Emperor William I. of, ii. 239
Germany, Emperor William II. of, ii. 222-223, 225
Germany, Empress Frederick of, ii. 219
Giffard, R. Swain, i. 323
Gilbert, Alfred, R.A., i. 148, 152-153, 318 ; ii. 140
Gilbert, Mrs., i. 322
Gilbert, W. M., i. 325
Gilbey, Henry, i. 324
Gilbey, Sir Walter, Bart., i. 315
Gilder, R. Watson, i. 321
Gillette, Wm., i. 318 ; ii. 316, 334
Gillespie, Mrs., i. 316
Gilman, Daniel (President, Johns Hopkins University), i. 316
Gisippus; or, the Forgotten Friend, i. 16
Gladstone, Mrs. W. E., i. 325 ; ii. 32, 35-36
Gladstone, Rt. Hon. W. E., i. 123-124 ; as an actor, 166-168, 325 ; ii. 26-36
Gladstone, W. H., ii. 31
Glaister, Prof., ii. 251

Glasgow, i. 60-61
Glasgow Theatre Royal, ii. 68-69
Glasgow, Irving's Illness, ii. 326-329
Glasgow University, LL.D., ii. 250-252
Gleichen, Count, ii. 41
Glenesk, Lord, i. 319
Glimpse of America, A, i. 368
Glover, Mrs., i. 317
Goddard, Moses B. I., i. 321
Godkin, E. L., i. 321
Godwin, Parke, i. 320
Goetz, Ludovic, i. 317
Goetz, Miss Alice, i. 317
Goetz, Mrs., ii. 141
Gollanz, Prof. T., i. 322
Goodall, Frederick, R.A., i. 315
Goodwin, Nat, i. 315 ; ii. 166
Gordon, Admiral, i. 318
Gordon, Lady Marjorie, i. 326
Goschen, Lord, i. 325
Got, ii. 239
Gough, Vice-Admiral, i. 321
Gounod, i. 325 ; ii. 148-150
Gouraud, Col., i. 176
Gower, Lord Ronald, i. 319
Graham, J. F., i. 324
Grain, Corney, i. 318
Grand Theatre, Islington, i. 369
Grant, Digby, i. 7-11
Grant, Gen., i. 294 ; ii. 105
Grau, Maurice, i. 326
Graydon, Dr., i. 316
Greenfell, W. H., i. 323
Greenwood, Arthur, i. 322
Grego, Joseph, i. 324
Griffin, Gerald, i. 16
Griffin, Sir Lepel, i. 326
Griffiths, Major Arthur, i. 320
Griggs, J. W. (Attorney-General, U.S.A.), i. 323
Griscom, W., i. 318
Grossmith, Geo., i. 316
Grossmith, Weedon, i. 320
Grosvenor, Countess, i. 318
Grove, Archibald, i. 323
Grove, F. C., ii. 174
Grove, Sir George, i. 174
Grundy, Sydney, i. 321
Gunter, Archibald Clavering, i. 319
Guthrie, F. Anstey, i. 318 ; ii. 87
Gwalior, Maharaja of, i. 338

HAASE, Frederick, ii. 239
Hackett, Henry, i. 318
Hackney, Mabel (Mrs. L. Irving), ii. 224
Hagenbach's Menagerie, ii. 128-132
Haines, F.M. Sir Frederick, i. 324

INDEX

Hall, T. W., i. 110
Hallé, Chas., i. 321
Halstead, Murat, i. 322
Halswelle, Keeley, A.R.S.A., i. 109-110, 325
Hamill, C., i. 316
Hamilton, Lady Cicely, i. 321
Hamilton, Angus, i. 317
Hamilton, J. McLuer, i. 318
Hamilton-Gordon, Hon. Lady, i. 324
Hamlet i. 12, 16, 25-27, 75-82, 87; A Reading, 304-306; Hall Caine's Criticism of, ii. 115-116, 273-275, 300
" Hamlet " (An Address), ii. 264
Hampton Court, i. 90-92
Handy, M. P., i. 323
Handwriting, Character by, ii. 22
Hann, W., i. 86, 94; ii. 212
Hanna, Senator Mark, i. 322; ii. 230
Hapgood, Norman, i. 320-321
Hardman, Lady, i. 324
Hardman, Sir William, i. 324
Hardwicke, Earl of, i. 318
Hardy, Thomas, i. 323
Hare, Gilbert, i. 326
Hare, John, i. 145, 317; ii. 87, 138, 140
Harker, J., i. 110, 255
Harlem Opera House, i. 288
Harmsworth, Alfred, *see* Lord Northcliff
Harper, Henry, i. 318
Harper, W. R. (President, Chicago University), i. 316
Harper's Magazine, ii. 80, 157
Harraden, Beatrice, i. 324
Harris, John, i. 25; ii. 168
Harris, Sir Augustus, i. 321; ii. 154
Harrison, Judge, i. 316
Hart, John, i. 325
Hartford, *Dante*, i. 274
Harvard, Sander's Theatre, ii. 259-260
Harvard University, ii. 258-262
Harvey, Col., i. 324
Harvey, Martin, i. 318; ii. 328
Harvey, Mrs. Martin, i. 318
Hassard, Sir John, i. 244, 326
Hatton, Joseph, i. 324, 362
Hauck, Minnie, i. 324
Haverland, Fraulein, i. 316
Haweis, Rev. H. R., ii. 114
Hawkes, Wells J., i. 322
Hawkins, Anthony Hope, i. 316
Hawkins, F. W., ii. 19, 160
Hawkesley, Ernest, i. 315
Hawthorne, Julian, i. 322
Hay, Helen, ii. 155

Hay, Col. John (U.S. Ambassador), i. 323; ii. 155, 232
Haydon, Judge, i. 322
Hearn, James, i. 317
Heilbron, David, i. 324
Heilbut, Samuel, i. 325
Heinemann, Wm., i. 317
Henderson, Sir James, i. 319
Hennell, E. W., ii. 145
Henry VIII., i. 113-117; ii. 300, 302
Henschel, Georg, i. 316; ii. 143-144
Hentschel, Carl, i. 321
Herbert, Miss, i. 1-7, 175
Herkomer, Prof. Hubert von, R.A., i. 202
Hetherington, C., i. 318
Heward, A. G. R., i. 318
Hichens, Robert, i. 266, 325
Hicks, Seymour, i. 317
High Life Below Stairs, ii. 301
Hill, Vice-Chancellor, of Cambridge, ii. 247
Hill, Frank, i. 316
Hinkle, A. Howard, i. 316
Hisses, i. 15-18
Hodges, Commander (U.S.N.), i. 326
Hoey, Mrs. Cashel, i. 322
Hogarth, Miss Georgina, i. 280, 315
Hohenlohe - Langenburg, Prince Ernest of, i. 321
Hollingshead, John, i. 169, 317
Holloway, W. J., i. 120-123
Holmes, John Henry, i. 315
Holmes, Oliver Wendell, i. 149
Homer, Tennyson on, i. 235
Home Rule Bill, ii. 33
Home Sweet Home, ii. 124
Honey, Geo., i. 7
Horton, H. C., i. 326
Hoskins, Wm., i. 129
Hosmer, C. R., i. 324
Houghton, Lord, i. 321, 353-355
Howard, J. B., i. 68-69, 321
Howard, Joseph, jun., i. 316
Howe, Earl, ii. 363
Howe, Henry, i. 324; ii. 216
Howells, W. D., i. 323; ii. 234
Hoyt, Henry Martyn (Solr.-Gen. U.S.A.), i. 319
Huddleston, Baron, i. 324
Hughes, Col., i. 318
Hughes, Tom, i. 325
Hulse, Hon. Lady, i. 324
Hulse, Sir Edward, Bart., i. 324
Hume, Fergus, ii. 137
Hunted Down, i. 281
Hunter, Colin, A.R.A., i. 326
Hutton, Laurence, i. 322

INDEX

Hypercriticism, i. 104-105, 205-207

IAGO, i. 89
Ibraham, H.H. Prince, i. 315
Idar, Maharaja of, i. 338
Inderwick, F., Q.C., i. 323
Indian and Colonial Troops, i. 251-252
Indian Princes, i. 252, 334, 338-340, 342
Indian Revolt, The (" Mr. Irwig "), ii. 346
Interviewers, i. 297-301
Iolanthe, i. 137 ; ii. 301
Irish Famine, i. 28-29
Irish Times, The, i. 7
Iron Chest, The, i. 83 ; ii. 301
Irving, Henry :
    Note.—For appearances in individual Plays and Rôles and at London Theatres *see* under their respective names ; at Provincial and other Theatres, under name of town or cities ; *see also* America, visits to
Early experiences in Dublin, i. 3-7, 11, 14-18
A blaze of genius, i. 28-32
Honours from Dublin University, i. 35-41
Carriage dragged by Students, i. 40
A Reading at Trinity College, Dublin, i. 42-44
" Chaired," i. 43-44
Takes over management of the Lyceum, i. 60-63, 72
Joined by Bram Stoker, i. 60-61
Lyceum Productions, i. 70-71
Mastery and decision of character, i. 79-81
Not ill for seven years, i. 82
Respect for feelings of others, i. 105-106
A lesson in collaboration, i. 111-113
Influenza during run of *King Lear*, i. 119-123
His method, i. 127-140
First appearance on the stage, i. 128-130
Skill in " make-up," i. 139-140
Love for children, i. 140
Generosity to Mrs. L. Lewis, i. 144
Love of sincerity i. 146, 148

Irving—(*continued*)
Devotion and zeal of his staff, i. 148-150
Presentation, twenty-fifth anniversary *The Bells*, i. 152-153
Entertainment French Authors, i. 154-155
A good friend to supers, i. 158
His stage doubles, i. 170
A narrow escape, i. 183
Fiftieth birthday—a record house, i. 183
A gift for reading, i. 186-187
On Tennyson, i. 197 199
Knowledge of character, i. 199 ; ii. 310
Tennyson's plays, i. 197-246
Fifty-fifth birthday — *Becket* produced, i. 242
Reading, *Becket*, Canterbury Cathedral, i. 242-245
King Alfred Millenary, i. 245-246
Early days, i. 277-278
Visits to America, i. 285-288
Last performance in America, i. 288
Care in speaking, i. 298-299
Reading, *Hamlet*, Birkbeck Institute, i. 304-306
A heavy bill, i. 306
Energy and nervous power, i. 306-307
Christmas, i. 308-309
A social force, i. 310-326
His house at Brook Green, i. 312
Last reception at the Lyceum, i. 333-342
Politics, i. 343
Two favourite stories, i. 346-349
His Philosophy of his Art :
    Key-stone, ii. 1-3
    Scientific process, ii. 3-6
    Character, ii. 6-14
    The play, ii. 14-15
    Stage perspective, ii. 16-18
    Dual consciousness, i. 149, 265, ii. 18-21, 296
    Individuality, ii. 22
    Beauty, the aim of art, ii.23
    Summary, ii. 24-25
As Hamlet, Onslow Ford Statue of, ii. 61-62
His hands, i. 234 ; ii. 63-64, 119
Artistic co-operation with E. A. Abbey, ii. 81-83
Last portraits, ii. 87

378   INDEX

Irving—(continued)
  Danger from a monkey:
    Manchester, ii. 125-126
    Stratford-on-Avon, ii. 127-128
  His love of animals, ii. 128-130
  Dramatists—his search for plays, ii. 131-139
  Musicians, ii. 140-150
  Order of the Komthur Cross, ii. 155
  Friendship with Toole, ii. 177-189
  Ellen Terry, ii. 190-207
  Public reception and address, Dublin, 1894, ii. 208-211
  Performances at Sandringham and Windsor, ii. 212-228
  Presidents of the United States, ii. 229-237
  Knighthood, ii. 238-243
  Presentation from his fellow players, ii. 240
  Universities:
    Dublin, 1876, Honours from, i. 35-41; 1892, D.Litt., ii. 244-247
    Cambridge, 1898, "Rede" Lecture, D.Litt., ii. 247-249
    Glasgow, 1899, LL.D., ii. 250-252
    Oxford, 1886, "English Actors," ii. 252-257
    Manchester, "Macbeth," ii. 257-258
    Harvard, 1885 and 1894, two addresses, ii. 258-262
    Columbia, 1895, "Macbeth," ii. 262-263
    Chicago, 1896 and 1900, two lectures, ii. 263
    Princeton, 1902, "Shakespeare and Bacon," ii. 264
    Other learned bodies and institutions, ii. 264-265
  Adventures:
    Over a mine bed, ii. 266-269
    Fires, ii. 269-279
    Floods, ii. 279-285
    Train accidents, ii. 285-288
    Storms at sea, ii. 289-293
    Falling scenery, ii. 293-296
  Instances of fearlessness, ii. 21, 273-274, 280-281, 294-296
  Finance, i. 62-63; ii. 304-320

Irving—(continued)
  A bequest, ii. 309-310
  Lyceum Theatre Company, ii. 315-320
  The turn of the tide:
    Strenuous life, ii. 321-322
    Accident to knee, i. 126; ii. 322-325
    Burning of the Lyceum Storage, ii. 297-303, 325-326
    Illness at Glasgow, ii. 326-330
    Lyceum Theatre Company, ii. 331-335
    Failing health, ii. 335
    Fortitude and patient suffering, ii. 336-339
    Last years, ii. 339-359
    Determination to retire, ii. 344
  Farewell Visits:
    Cardiff: A touching farewell, ii. 345
    Swansea: *Lead, Kindly Light*, ii. 345
    Sunderland: Public banquet and address, ii. 345-347
    Exeter: Public address and reception, ii. 347
    Bath: Unveils Quin Memorial—Civic lunch, ii. 347
    Wolverhampton: Public address—serious illness —tour abandoned, ii. 347-349
  Last Performances in London, ii. 350-351
  Workmen present a loving-cup, ii. 350-351
  His last tour:
    Sheffield: Civic luncheon, ii. 352
    Bradford: Public address —last performances, ii. 352-356
  Sudden death, ii. 357-359
  Public funeral in Westminster Abbey, ii. 361-366
Irving, Henry Brodribb, jun., ii. 85, 359
Irving, Laurence, i. 265, 267, 272; ii. 359
Isle of St. Tropez, ii. 137
Iwamoto, Captain, i. 320

JACK, Prof., i. 320
Jackson, Dr., ii. 248

INDEX

Jacobs, W. W., i. 325
Jagannath Barua, Rai Bahadur, i. 339
James, David, i. 321, 325 ; ii. 296
Jeejeebhai, Sir Jamsetjee, i. 339
Jefferson, Joseph, i. 316 ; ii. 230
Jeffery, John B., i. 316
Jekyll and Hyde, i. 137
Jerome, Jerome K., i. 317
Jerome, "Larry," i. 321
Jerome, Leonard, i. 316
Jester King, The, ii. 137
Jeypore, Maharaja of, i. 338
Jingle, ii. 301
Joel, Solly, i. 318
Joel, Wolf, i. 325
John, Mr. (Mayor of Bath), ii. 347
Johnson, R. Underwood, i. 319
Johnson, H. T., ii. 137
Johnston, Sir Harry, i. 369
Jonas, Sir Joseph (Lord Mayor of Sheffield), ii. 352
Jones, Henry Arthur, i. 322 ; ii. 138
Jones, Senator, i. 318
Jowett, Benjamin (Master of Balliol), ii. 252-253
Joy, Albert Bruce, i. 317
Julius Cæsar, ii. 144

Kapurthala, H.H. The Raja of, i. 318
Kaye, Lady Lister, i. 319
Kean, Chas., i. 134, 161-162 ; ii. 90, 217-218
Kean, Edmund, i. 20 ; relics of, ii. 90
Kean, Mrs. Chas., ii. 201
Keeley, Dr., i. 315
Keeley, Mrs., i. 322
Keenan, T. J., i. 321 ; ii. 166
Kelly, Chas., i. 162
Kelvin, Lord, ii. 246
Kemble, Henry, i. 319
Kenney, Charles Lamb, i. 323
Keppel, Admiral Sir Harry, i. 315
Kerr, Fred, i. 320
Keyser, Miss Agnes, i. 320
King, T. C., i. 16
King, Wilson, i. 324 ; ii. 169
King, Alfred Millenary, i. 245-246
King and the Miller, The, ii. 301
King Arthur, i. 211
King Arthur (J. Comyns Carr), i. 253-255 ; ii. 74, 261-262, 300, 302
King Arthur (W. G. Wills), i. 253 ; ii. 137
King Lear, i. 118-124, 128 ; ii. 56-57, 182, 301

Kingston, W. Beatty, i. 317, 358 ; ii. 146
Kinsmen," "The, ii. 80
Klein, Chas., i. 317
Knight, Joseph, i. 322
Knighthood, ii. 238-243
Knollys, Lord, i. 324
Knowles, Sir James, i. 44-47, 201, 320, 351 ; ii. 31
Kohlapur, Maharaja of, i. 339
Kohlsaat, H. H., i. 250-251, 319
Kooch Bahar, Maharaja of, i. 339
Kuhe, W., i. 326

Labouchere, Mrs. (Henrietta Hodson), i. 318
Labouchere, Henry, M.P., i. 318
Lady Audley's Secret, i. 1-7
Lady of Lyons, The, i. 156-158, 187 ; ii. 301
Lady Torfrida, The yacht, ii. 41-52
Laertes, i. 16, 87
Laffan, W. M., i. 321
Lambdin, Dr., i. 318
Lancashire Lass, The, i. 281
Langdon, Woodbury, ii. 319
Langmaid, Dr., i. 321
Langtry, Mrs., i. 319
Lankester, Prof. Ray, i. 322
Lanyon, General Sir Owen, i. 315
Lathrop, Mr. and Mrs. Bryan, i. 317
Law, David, i. 322
Lawrence, F. R., i. 317
Lawrence, Gerald, i. 324
Lawrence, Sir Henry, Bart., i. 317
Lawson, F. W., i. 320
Lawson, The Hon. Harry, i. 321
Leaves of Grass, ii. 93-96, 107-108
Leaf, Walter, i. 233, 234-236
Le Clerc, ii. 140
Le Clerc, Rose, i. 323
Lee, Col. Arthur, M.P., i. 323
Lee, Sidney, i. 321
Lefroy, Edward, i. 44
Lehmann, Rudolph, i. 114, 324
Leighton, Lord, ii. 245, 246-247
Leighton, Sir Baldwin, Bart., i. 321
Leiningen, H.S.H. Prince, i. 325
Le Sage, J. M., i. 319
Leslie, Fred, i. 325
Leslie, Miss Amy, i. 318
Lestocq, W., i. 318
Lever, Chas., i. 355
Levy, J. M., i. 283-284, 287
Levy, Miss Matilda, i. 283, 321 ; ii. 176
Lewanika, King, i. 339
Lewis, Arthur, i. 319 ; ii. 90

380 INDEX

Lewis, Mrs.Arthur (Kate Terry), i. 319 ; ii. 90
Lewis, Sir George, Bart., i. 323 ; ii. 186
Lewis, George, J. G., i. 316
Lewis, Leopold, i. 144
Leycester, Rafe, i. 323
Leyden, Count de, i. 319
Libotton, ii. 163
Librarians, Conference of, i. 314
Lincoln, Abraham, ii. 103-104, 108-109, 111
Lincoln, Robert (U.S. Ambassador), i. 322
Lindsay, Sir Coutts, Bart., i. 321
Linton, Sir James D., P.R.I., i. 315
Linley, Tinsley, i. 323
Liszt, Abbé Franz, i. 319 ; ii. 145-148
Littleton, Alfred, ii. 146
Littleton, Augustus, ii. 146
Livadia, The, ii. 48-52
Liverpool *Town Crier,* ii. 115
Livingstone, David, i. 366
Lloyd, Frank, i. 320
Lloyd, John Uri, i. 321
Lloyd-Davies, William Allan, i. 319 ; ii. 337-338, 349
Lockwood, Sir F., M.P., i. 315
London and County Bank, ii. 308
London County Council, ii. 318
Londesborough, Earl of, i. 323
Long, Edwin, R.A., i. 139, 317
Lord Chamberlain's Department, The, ii. 120-121, 132-134, 275
Louis XI., i. 131-134 ; ii. 301, 302 ; Irving's last performance in London, 350, 353
Loveday, H. J., i. 42, 63, 69, 81, 84-85, 96-97, 115, 150, 177, 222-223, 247, 266, 343 ; ii. 44, 162, 213, 219, 270-271, 280, 330, 331, 349, 353, 355, 358
Low, Seth, i. 316 ; ii. 234, 262-263
Lowe, D. F. (of Heriots'), i. 317
Lowell, James Russell (U.S. Ambassador), i. 321
Lowne, C. M., i. 325
Lowne, E. Y., i. 323
Lucas, Seymour, R.A., i. 114-115, 318
Lucy, H. W. (" Toby, M.P. "), i. 324
Lupton, Mr. (Ex-Mayor of Bradford), ii. 360
Lyceum Audience, i. 73-75, 285-286
 Productions, i. 70-71
 Storage, Burning of the, ii. 297-303

Lyceum Theatre, Irving's first season i. 72-82; Hospitalities, i. 310-342, Irving's last reception, 333-342 ; ii. 161-162, 313 ; Enlarged and improved 311 ; Cash takings, 312
Lyceum Theatre Company, i. 70, 71, 268 ; ii. 315-320, 325-326, 331-335, 342
Lyell, J. L., i. 323
Lyon, Major, i. 317
Lyons Mail, The, i. 134-138 ; ii. 21, 301, 302, 348
Lytton, Earl of (Owen Meredith), i. 320

MACARTNEY, Sir Haliday, i. 78
Macbeth, i. 12, 107-113 ; ii. 300, 302
Macbeth," " The character of, ii. 257-258, 262-263, 265
McCarthy, Justin, M.P., i. 318
McCarthy, Justin Huntly, i. 325
McClure, Col., i. 323
McConnell, Judge, i. 315
McCormick, Robert Sanderson (U.S. Ambassador), i. 319
McCullough, John, i. 90, 316 ; ii. 152, 153
Macdona, J. C., M.P., i. 320
Macdonald, Gen. Sir H., i. 322
McDowell, James, ii. 223-224, 228
McHenry, James, i. 8, 9, 318, 358 ; ii. 40-41
McIlvaine, C. W., i. 315
Mackail, Mrs. (Miss Burne-Jones), i. 318 ; ii. 75
Mackail, J. W., i. 318
Mackay, John, i. 323
Mackellar, Duncan, i. 322
McKelway, St. Clair, i. 317
McKenna, Theodore, i. 325
Mackenzie, Sir Alexander C., i. 323 ; ii. 140, 146
Mackenzie, Sir James, ii. 241
Mackenzie, Sir Morell, i. 316 ; ii. 146
McKinley, Wm. (President U.S.A.), ii. 230-233
Maclaren, Ian, ii. 8
McMichael, Clayton, ii. 229
McMichael, Morton, i. 318
McMichael, Walter, i. 317
MacMillan, Fredk., i. 317
McNally, John, i. 318
MacQuoid, Katherine S., i. 326
MacQuoid, Thomas, i. 326
Macready, i. 138, 281 ; Relics of, ii. 66, 181
Macready, Miss, ii. 44
McVeagh, Wayne (Attorney-General, U.S.A.), i. 320; ii. 232-233

INDEX

Madame Sans-Gêne, i. 259-265 ; ii. 326
Madden, Judge, i. 324
Mahan, Capt. (U.S. Navy), i. 327-331
Mahomed Aslam Khan, Lieut.-Colonel Nawab, i. 339
Mahomet, ii. 118-121
Mail, The (Dublin), i. 13
Major, Charles, i. 316, 324
"Make-up," i. 139-140
Management :
  Responsibility and difficulties, i. 61-63, 149-152, 185
  Public pulse, i. 189-193
  Hazard of, i. 275
  Rain of plays, ii. 131-138
  Finance, i. 62-63; ii. 304-320
Manchester, Art Club, ii. 344
Manchester, Theatre Royal, 1860, i. 86-87
Manchester, Victoria University of, i. 108 ; ii. 257-258
Manchester, Dean of, i. 319
Manchester, Duchess of, i. 318
Manchester, Duke of, i. 91
Manchester Guardian, ii. 307
Mancinelli, i. 320
Mandeville, Lord, *see* Manchester, Duke of
Mansfield, Richard, i. 316, 358
Mansfield, Mrs. Richard, i. 316
Mapes, Victor, i. 324
Marbury, Miss Elizabeth, i. 268, 271, 317
Margetson, Mr. and Mrs., i. 315
Marion, W., ii. 274
Marius, ii. 166
Marlow, Julia, i. 317
Marlow, Young, i. 6-7
Marquand, John P., i. 323
Marquette, ss., ii. 289, 290
Marryat, Capt., i. 296
Marshall, Frank A., i. 42, 83, 322 ; ii. 128, 133-137
Marshall, Mrs. Frank A. (Ada Cavendish), i. 322
Marshall, Dr. John, i. 325
Marston, Edward, i. 369
Martin, Bradley, i. 321
Martin, Carlaw, i. 521
Martin, Lady (" Helen Faucit "), i. 325
Martin, Sir Theodore, i. 325
Massingham, H. W., i. 315
Mathew, Rt. Hon. Lord Justice, i. 320
Mathews, C. W., i. 278, 322
Mathews, Chas., i. 277-279
Mathews, Mrs. Chas., i. 278, 324

Mathews, Prof. Brander, ii. 234
Matthews, Mrs. Frank, i. 7
Matthison, Arthur, i. 170
Maude, Cyril, i. 325
Maung On Gaing, i. 339
Maunsell, Dr., i. 13
Maurel, Victor, i. 323 ; ii. 160
Maxwell, Gerald, i. 326
Maxwell, W. B., i. 326
May, Phil, i. 317
Mayer, Gaston, i. 325
Mayer, M. L., i. 317 ; ii. 157-159
Mead, Tom, i. 135-137
Medicine Man, The, i. 71, 266
Meherban Ganpatrao Madhavrao Vinchwikar, i. 339
Meiningen Company, The, ii. 151-154
Meissonier, J. L. E., ii. 72
Mellor, Col., M.P., i. 315
Meltzer, J. H., i. 324
Mempes, Mortimer, i. 316
Mensdorff, Count Albert, i. 316
Mephisto, ii. 137
Merchant of Venice, The, i. 82-86 ; as in Shakespeare's time, 293 ; ii. 203, 296, 300, 327
Merivale, Herman, i. 185-189, 324 ; ii. 174
Merrill, General Louis (U.S.A.), i. 323
Merritt, Genl.Wesley (U.S.A.), i. 320
Metcalfe, J. S., i. 318
Methven, James, i. 321
Meysey-Thompson, Sir Henry, ii. 34
Michie, Col. Peter (U.S.A.), i. 291-292, 322
Midian Gold Mines, i. 357
Milburn, Dr. (Chaplain, American Senate), ii. 9
Miles, General (U.S.A.), i. 317
Millet, Frank D., i. 323
Milner, Rt. Hon. Sir Fred., Bart., i. 320
Mimra, Capt., i. 316, 331-332
Minnehaha, ss., ii. 292
Minton, Maurice, i. 320
Miranda, Count, ii. 176
Mitchell, Langdon, i. 320
Molloy, Fitzgerald, i. 315
Monckton, Lady, i. 317
Monckton, Sir John, i. 317
Montague, H. J., i. 7
Montgomery, Col. (U.S.A.), ii. 231
Montgomery, Lieut. (U.S.A.), i. 322
Moore, Ernest, i. 315
Moore, F. Frankfort, i. 322
Moore, Mary, i. 318
Moreau, Emile, i. 271-273, 321 ; ii. 330

INDEX

Morris, Lord, i. 319
Morritt, Miss Greta, i. 316
Morrow, Judge, i. 323
Morse, Prof., ii. 234
Mortimer, James, i. 326
Moscheles, Felix, i. 319
Mouillot, Fred., i. 321
Mounet, Jean Paul, i. 318
Mounet-Sully, i. 155, 323 ; ii. 163
Much Ado about Nothing, i. 100–106, 193 ; ii. 198–199, 300
Mudie, Andrew, i. 322
Muhamad Faiyaz Ali Khan, Nawab, i. 339
Mullen, Mr., i. 353
Müller, Rt. Hon. Frederick Max, ii. 146, 252
Muncacksy, Madame, ii. 146
" Municipal Theatres," ii. 264
Munro, David A., i. 323
Murray, Dr. A. S., i. 205, 206–207
Murray, David, R.A., i. 320
Murray, Gaston, i. 7
Musicians, ii. 140–150
Myers, Frederick, i. 325 ; ii. 248–249

Nance Oldfield, i. 194–196
Nansen, Dr., i. 319
Napier, Lord, i. 294
Narjac, Countess, i. 322
Nast, Thomas, i. 326, 329
Nazro, Commander (U.S.A.), i. 319
Nerval, Lucien de, i. 17
Nesper, i. 320
Nettleship, Mrs., i. 319
Nevada, Emma, i. 315
Nevill, Lady Dorothy, i. 323
New, Col. John C. (U.S.A.), i. 324
New Haven : *Dante*, i. 274
Newman, Dr. David, i. 318
Newton, H. Chance, i. 324
New Way to Pay Old Debts, A, i. 87 ; ii. 90
New York : *Faust*, i. 184 ; *Dante*, 274
 Goethe Society, ii. 264
New York Tribune, i. 289 ; ii. 259–260
Nihilists, ii. 48–49, 51–52, 53–58
Nilsson, Christine, ii. 176–177
Nineteenth Century, The, i. 44–47 ; ii. 32
Norman, Henry, M.P., i. 316
Normand, Jacques, i. 154, 319
North, Col., i. 323
Northbrook, Earl of, ii. 27
Northcliff, Lord, i. 320
Northcott, John, i. 317

Ober-Ammergau Play, ii. 253
Ochiltree, Col. Tom (U.S.A.), i. 325 ; ii. 166
O'Connor, T. P., M.P., i. 319
Ogilvie, Stuart, i. 323
Olivia, i. 145 ; ii. 301, 302, 325
Only Way, The, ii. 328
Onslow, Earl of, i. 324
Orchardson, W. Q., R.A., i. 324
O'Rell, Max, i. 324
Orrock, James, R.I., i. 315
Osborne, General (U.S.A.), i. 316
Osgood, James R., i. 325
Othello, i. 12, 42, 86–89 ; ii. 300
Otis, C. A., i. 318
Owens College, *see* Manchester, Victoria University of,
Oxford University, An Address at, ii. 252–257

Paderewski, i. 315 ; ii. 141–142
Padgett, W., i. 318
Page, Thomas Nelson, i. 322 ; ii. 232, 233
Palliser, Esther, i. 322
Palmer, A. M., i. 322
Palmer, Edmund Henry, i. 318
Palmer, Sir Walter, Bart., i. 316
Panglima Kinta, The Datoh, i. 339
Paradox of Acting, i. 48–49 ; ii. 18–19
Paris, i. 95
Parke, Dr., i. 369
Parker, Louis N., i. 325
Parker, Sir Gilbert, i. 318
Parkinson, J. C., i. 319
Parnell, Chas. Stewart, ii. 27, 31
Parry, Judge, i. 324
Parsons, Alfred, A.R.A., i. 325
Parsons, W. B., i. 322
Partridge, J. Bernard, i. 317 ; ii. 86–88
Partridge, W. Ordway, i. 316
Patti, i. 316
Pauline ; or, A Night of Terror, i. 17
Pauncefote, Lord, ii. 232–233
Pawling, Sydney S., i. 325
Pearce, Sir William, Bart., i. 324 ; ii. 43–52
Pearce, Sir Wm. Geo., Bart., ii. 44
Peixotto, i. 316
Pellegrini, Carlo, i. 325
Pemberton, Edgar, i. 316
Penberthy, Capt. Isaac, i. 103
Penberthy, John, i. 102–103, 125
Pencoast, A., i. 321
Perak, The Sultan of, i. 339
Perkins, i. 110
Perry, E. A., i. 320
Perry Bar Institute, ii. 264

INDEX

Perugini, Mr., i. 317
Peter the Great, i. 265
Petrie, J. N., i. 320
Pettie, John, R.A., i. 324
Phelps, E. J. (U.S. Ambassador), i. 322
Philadelphia : *Faust*, i. 184 ; *Dante*, 274
Contemporary Club, ii. 265
Philip, i. 12
Phister, Montgomery, i. 315
Pigott, E. F. S., i. 316
Pinches, E. E., i. 322
Pinero, A. W., i. 164, 324 ; ii. 138-139
Pirbright, Lord (Baron de Worms), i. 317
Pirrie, Lord, i. 324
Pitou, Augustus, i. 317
Pittsburgh, i. 309
Playfair, Dr., i. 324
Plays : difficulties of obtaining, ii. 131-132 ; sources of, 132 ; bought but not produced, 132-137
Plowden, A. C., ii. 87
Plymouth, ii. 347
Poland, Sir Harry, i. 316
Politics in the theatre, i. 138-139
Pollock, Lady, i. 319
Pollock, Sir Frederick, Bart., i. 319
Pollock, Walter Herries, i. 48-49, 319 ; ii. 19, 137
Polo, Marco, i. 371
Ponsonby, Sir Henry, ii. 214, 216-221
Ponsonby-Fane, The Hon. Sir S., i. 315 ; ii. 275-276
Popoff, Admiral (Russian Navy), ii. 48
Porel, M., i. 325
Porter, H.E. General Horace (U.S.A.), i. 235, 317 ; ii. 104
Porteus, Dr., i. 324
Potter, Flag-Lieut. (U.S.A.), i. 326
Potter, Cora Urquhart (Mrs. Brown Potter), i. 322
Praed, Mrs. Campbell, i. 325
Price, Prof., ii. 234
Priestly, Mr. (Mayor of Bradford), ii. 352
Primrose, Sir John Ure, Bart., i. 322
Princess's Theatre, i. 87-88
Princeton University, ii. 264
Prinsep, Val, R.A., i. 324
Pritchard, Hesketh, ii. 137
Pritchard, K., ii. 137
Probyn, Genl. Sir Dighton, V.C., i. 317 ; ii. 363

Proctor, Joseph, i. 317
Prodigal Son, The, ii. 130
Professor's Love Story, The, ii. 137-138
Pryde, Dr., i. 324
Pullman, Geo., i. 318 ; ii. 264
Pullman, Mrs., i. 318
Purrington, W. A., i. 316

QUAIN, Sir Richard, Bart., i. 322
Queen Mary, i. 12, 152, 197
Queen Victoria's Jubilee (1887), i. 333
Queen's Theatre, i. 280 ; ii. 191
Quin Memorial, ii. 347

RADNOR, Earl of, i. 324
Raising the Wind, ii. 301
Raleigh, Mr. and Mrs. Cecil, i. 326
Ralph, Julian, i. 326
Ramaswami Mudaliyar, Sir Savalai, Raja, i. 339
Randegger, i. 317
Ravenswood, i. 185-193 ; ii. 301, 302
Raymond, John T., i. 326
Reade, Chas., i. 134
" Rede " Lecture, Cambridge, ii. 247-248
Redford, G. A., i. 316
Reed, T. (Speaker, U.S.A.), i. 320
Reeves, Sims, i. 319
Reform Club, i. 343
Rehan, Ada, i. 322
Reid, Sir Wemyss, i. 316
Reid, Thomas, i. 324
Reid, H. E. Whitelaw (U.S. Ambassador) i. 91, 319
Rejane, i. 322
Remsen, Professor, i. 321
Renan, Ernest, ii. 114
Renaud, ii. 140
Revue Illustrée, ii. 158
Reynolds, T., i. 326
Rhoades, J. H., i. 325
Ribblesdale, Earl of, i. 325
Ricarde-Seaver, Major, i. 192, 324, 329 ; ii. 160
Richard II., ii. 79-85
Richard III., i. 42, 44, 49, 124-126 ; ii. 81, 301, 322-325
Richards, Frank, i. 320
Richardson, H. H., i. 320
Richelieu, i. 12, 128-130 ; ii. 301
Richmond, Sir David, Bart., i. 322
Richter, Hans, ii. 144-145
Rideing, W. H., i. 320
Rienzi, ii. 137
Riggs, Mrs. (Kate Douglas Wiggin), i. 320

384 INDEX

Riley, J. Whitcomb, i. 318; ii. 112-113, 160
Ripon, Bishop of, *see* Boyd-Carpenter
Ristori, Madame, ii. 169-170
Ritchie, Mrs. Richmond (Miss Thackeray), i. 317
Ritchie, Richmond, i. 317
Ritchie, Sir James, i. 322
Rivals, The, i. 1, 3-7
Rival towns, i. 345
Rives, G. L., i. 320
Riviere, Henri, i. 320
Road to Ruin, The, i. 5-7
Robert Emmett, i. 83; ii. 132-136
Robert Macaire, ii. 301
Robertson, Graham, i. 321
Robespierre, i. 268-271; ii. 330
Robin Hood, i. 211
Robinson, Dean Armitage, ii. 361-362
Robinson, Professor, i. 321
Robinson, Sir John R., i. 325
Robinson, Sir William, i. 315
Rockman, Ray, i. 321
Rogers, Frederick, ii. 55
Romeo and Juliet, i. 87, 93-100
Roose, Dr. Robson, i. 321
Roosevelt, Theodore (President, U.S.A.), ii. 233-237
Root, Elihu (Sect. of State, U.S.A.), i. 323; ii. 232
Rosa, Carl, i. 322
Rosebery, Earl of, ii. 238, 327
Ross, C. H., i. 325
Ross, Callender, i. 320
Rossetti, Wm. Michael, ii. 93
Rothschild, Alfred de, i. 320
Routledge, Edmund, i. 318
Rowe, Mrs. Jopling, i. 325
Royal Academy Banquet, i. 314
    College of Music, i. 173-174; ii. 245
    Institution, ii. 241, 242, 247, 265
Russell, Judge (N.Y.), i. 321
Russell, Charles, i. 320
Russell, Henry, i. 279
Russell, of Killowen, Lord, L.C.J., i. 322
Russell, Sir Edward R., i. 26, 315; ii. 365
Russell, Sir W. H., i. 317
Russia, Czar Alexander II. of, ii. 48-52
Russia, Grand Duke Nicholas of, ii. 49-50

ST. ALBANS, Duchess of, i. 318, 369
St. Gaudens, Augustus, i. 322; ii. 108-109

St. Helier, Lord and Lady (Sir F. and Lady Jeune), i. 320
St. James's Company, i. 1-7
St. James's Hall, i. 327
St. James's Theatre, i. 175, 278, 280, 281
St. John, Sir Spencer, i. 319
Sala, George Augustus, i. 91, 324, 362; ii. 153
Salvini, i. 316
Salvini, Alexander, i. 315
Sambourne, Linley, i. 325
Sandhurst, Lord, i. 324
Sandringham, 1889, ii, 212-215; 1902, 222-228
Santley, Charles, i. 315
Sarasate, i. 316
Sarcy, Francisque, i. 154, 316
Sardou, Victorien, i. 268, 271-273; ii. 330
Sargent, John, R.A., i. 324; ii. 80
Saviolo, ii. 137
Saunders, John, i. 249
Saxby, Howard, i. 322
Saxe-Coburg-Gotha, Grand Duke of, ii. 155
Saxe-Meinengen, H.S.H. Grand Duke of, i. 320; ii. 154-156
Saxe-Weimar, Prince Edward of i. 324
Scenery, accidents from falling, ii. 293-296
Schley, Admiral (U.S.A.), i. 323
Schmalz, Herbert, i. 326
Schneider, Mdlle, ii. 175
School for Scandal, The, i. 5-7
School of Reform, i. 175
Schröeder, Admiral (German Navy), i. 320
Schuldig, ii. 137
Schwab, G. H., i. 321
Scoones, W. B., i. 320
Scott, Clement, i. 319, 362; ii. 19, 324
Scotter, Sir Charles, i. 315
Scott-Gatty, Alfred, i. 325
Seattle, i. 345
Seddon, Rt. Hon. Richard, i. 340-341
Sedelia Rab, The Datoh, i. 339
Seton, Sir Bruce, Bart., i. 323
Seymour, Admiral Sir Edward, ii. 347
"Shakespeare and Bacon," ii. 264
"Shakespeare and Goethe," ii. 264
"Shakespeare as a Playwright," ii. 264
Shakespeare's Plays, i. 75-126
Shaw, Edward J., i. 316
Shaw, George F., i. 323

INDEX

Shea, Judge (New York), i. 316
Sheffield, ii. 352
Sheppard, J. W., ii. 357, 359
Sherlock Holmes, ii. 316
Sherman, General (U.S.A.), i. 323
Sherwood, Mrs., i. 324
She Stoops to Conquer, i. 5-7
Shelton, George, i. 326
Siam, H.R.H. The Crown Prince of, i. 339
Silent Voices, The, i. 241
Simmons, J. G., i. 323
Simpson, Palgrave, ii. 172
Sinclair, Archdeacon, i. 319
Sinclair, Col., i. 323
Skelmersdale, Lord, i. 321
Sketchley, Arthur, i. 353
Skipsey, Joseph, i. 319
Smalley, G. W., i. 317
Smiles, Samuel, i. 321
Smith, Ballard, i. 324
Smith, C. Stewart, i. 316
Smith, Chas. Emery (U.S.A.), ii. 232
Smith, Pamela Colman, i. 326
Smith, Sir Charles Euan, i. 321 ; ii. 140
Smithsonian Institute, ii. 109
Snake's Pass, The, ii. 27-29
Snape, W., i. 320
Sorley, Baillie, i. 316
Soulsby, Sir W. J., i. 320
Sprague, H. W., i. 322
Springfield : *Dante*, i. 274
Stage," " The, ii. 264
Stage Art, Philosophy of :
  Key-stone, ii. 1-3
  Scientific process, ii. 3-6
  Character, ii. 6-14
  The play, ii. 14-15
  Stage perspective, ii. 16-18
  Dual consciousness, i. 149, 265 ; ii. 18-21, 296
  Individuality, ii. 22
  Beauty, the aim of Art, ii. 23
  Summary, ii. 24-25
  Ellen Terry, ii. 196-203
Stage as it is," " The, ii. 264
Stagecraft :
  Macbeth, i. 23-24
  Hamlet, i. 76
  Lessons in illusion, i. 114-116
  Stage jewellery, i. 115-116
  Richard III., i. 125-126
  A marching army, i. 157-158
  Some great sets, i. 159-161
  Stage snow, i. 161
  A stage supper, i. 171-172
  Application of Science, i. 176
  Stage fire, i. 176-177
  Steam and mist, i. 177

Stagecraft—(*continued*)
  Division of stage labour, i. 177-178
  A "ladder" of angels, i. 180-182
  Stage perspective, i. 205-206, 261-263
  Camma's dress, i. 207
  Limelight and electric light, i. 302
Stage Manager, Irving a, i. 3
Stanford, H. B., i. 326
Stanford, Sir Chas. Villiers, i. 223, 232, 321 ; ii. 140
Stanlaws, Penrhyn, ii. 137
Stanley, Sir Henry M., i. 323, 362-370
Stannard, Mrs. (John Strange Winter), i. 319
Stanwood, F. M., i. 319
State Subsidy for theatres, ii. 153-154, 163, 313
Statue of Irving as Hamlet, ii. 61-62
Stavenhagen, ii. 146-147
Steel, Mrs., ii. 138
Stepniak, S., ii. 53-58
Sterling, Antoinette, i. 321 ; ii. 148
Sterner, Albert, i. 319
Stirling, Arthur, i. 324
Stirling, Mrs. (Lady Gregory), i. 315
Stock Companies, i. 1
Stoker, Abraham, i. 20
Stoker, Bram :
  Earliest recollections of Irving, 1867, i. 1-7
  Friendship with Irving, i. 25-34, 60
  Coming events, i. 53-54
  Joins Irving, i. 60-61
  A Triton amongst minnows, i. 165-166
  and Tennyson, i. 201-202, 215-221, 224-239
  An angry reporter, i. 301-302
  A visit to the *Chicago*, i. 328-331
  "England and Japan ! " i. 331-332
  Walt Whitman, ii. 92-111
  First meets Ellen Terry, ii. 190-191
  Their friendship, ii. 206-207
  Irving's last words to, ii. 357
Stoker, Dr. Geo., C.M.G., i. 97-98, 323, 357
Stoker, Sir Thornley, i. 58, 60, 321
Stoker, T., C.S.I., i. 322
Stone, Marcus, R.A., i. 320
Stone, Melville, i. 317
Storms at Sea, ii. 289-293

INDEX

Story, Principal, of Glasgow University, i. 315 ; ii. 250-252
Story, Samuel, M.P., i. 323
Story of Waterloo, A, see *Waterloo*
Stoyle, J. D., i. 170
Straggler of '15, A, see *Waterloo*
Straight, Sir Douglas, i. 323
Stranger, The, i. 83
Stratford-on-Avon, ii. 127-128
Strathcona, Lord, i. 325
Students :
    Irving's carriage dragged by, i. 40 ; "chaired," i. 43-44
    Seized and carried by, ii. 246 ;
    Wild enthusiasm, 258
    As supers—a challenge, ii. 261-262
Sunderland, Lyceum Theatre ; Irving's first appearance on the stage, i. 129 ; Farewell visit, ii. 345-347
Sullivan, Barry, i. 20-24
Sullivan, Sir Arthur, i. 111-113, 324
Sullivan, T. Russell, i. 325
Supers, i. 98-99, 157-158, 171 ; ii. 261
Surface, Joseph, i. 6-7
Sutherland, Duke and Duchess of, i. 322
Swan, John, R.A., i. 321
Swansea, farewell visit, ii. 345

TABER, Robert, i. 266, 316
Tacoma, i. 345
Tagore, Maharaja Kunwar, i. 389
Tailer, W. H., i. 325, 369
Tait, Lawson, i. 325
Talbot de Malahide, Lord, i. 351
Talma, ii. 18-20
Tamagno, i. 325
Tarkington, Booth, i. 324
Taylor, Goodenough, i. 318
Tayor, Tom, i. 316
Teazle, Lady, i. 6
Teck, H.R.H. Duchess of, i. 311
Teck, H.S.H. Duke of, i. 311
Teck, Princess May of, *see* Wales, Princess May of,
Telbin, W., i. 86, 94, 180-181, 205, 326
Teller, Leopold, i. 319 ; ii. 153
Templar, Col., i. 320
Temple, Archbishop, i. 200
Tennant, F., i. 326
Tennant, Mrs., i. 326
Tenniel, Sir John, i. 317
Tennyson, Lady (Alfred), i. 214, 233, 241, 321 ; ii. 220
Tennyson, Lady (Hallam), i. 219, 233 ; ii. 220

Tennyson, Alfred Lord, i. 49 ; His plays, i. 197-246 ; on Irving's *Hamlet*, 201 ; "Irving will do me justice," 241 ; Death—burial in the Abbey, 240-241, 321 ; Walt Whitman, ii. 98-100
Tennyson, Hallam, Lord, i. 214, 220, 223, 224, 228, 233, 234, 236
Tennyson, Lionel, i. 233
Terriss, William, i. 15, 120 ; ii. 153, 220
Terry, Edward, i. 318
Terry, Ellen :
    Note.—*See also* under various plays
    Under John Hare's Management, i. 145
    As a Dramatist, i. 194-196
    On the *Lady Torfrida*—motherhood, ii. 44-47
    Stepniak on, ii. 57
    A prime consideration in Irving's arrangements, ii. 69-70, 191-193, 197-199
    Frightened by a monkey, ii. 127
    Early playing with Irving, ii. 191
    Knighting an Attorney-General, ii. 192-193
    A generous player, ii. 193-194
    Her Ophelia, ii. 195
    Real flowers, ii. 195-196
    Her Art, ii. 196-203
    Last performance with Irving, ii. 203
    Separation, ii. 203
    Comradeship, ii. 203-205
    Dublin, 1894, ii. 208-211
    At Sandringham and Windsor, ii. 212-222
Terry, Mr. and Mrs. Fred., i. 319
Terry, Marion, i. 323
Thaddeus, Mr. and Mrs., i. 318
Thesiger, Gen. Hon. C., i. 317
Theatre, The, ii. 19
Théâtre Français, *see* Comédie-Française
"Theatre in its relation to the State," The, ii. 247-248
Thomas, Brandon, i. 325
Thomas, Moy, i. 320
Thompson, Superintendent, ii. 296
Thompson, Alfred, i. 94
Thompson, Sir Henry, i. 322
Thompson, Slason, i. 323
Thomson, Frank, i. 318
Thomson, Sir Wm., C.B., i. 315
Thorne, Thomas, i. 315
Threlfall, T., i. 323

INDEX

Tilghman, B., i. 317
Todhunter, Dr., i. 326
Toole, J. L., i. 17, 91, 173, 317, 329, 358, 362 ; ii. 53, 138, 140, 142, 153, 153–154, 158 ; lifelong friendship with Irving, 177–189
Tosti, i. 317
Tower, H. E. Charlemagne (U.S. Ambassador), i. 319
Traill, H. D., i. 266, 323, 362
Train accidents, ii. 285–288
Tree, Herbert Beerbohm, i. 321
Tree, Mrs. Beerbohm, i. 321
Trelawny, i. 353
Tristan, i. 131
Trower, Seymour, i. 324
Truax, Judge (N.Y.), i. 315
Tseng, The Marquis, i. 78–79
Tucker, W. W., i. 91
Turnbull, Mr., ii. 223
Twain," " Mark (S. L. Clemens), i. 324 ; ii. 166
Twelfth Night, ii. 300
Two Roses, i. 7–11 ; ii. 301
Tyars, Frank, i. 86, 319, 326
Tybalt, i. 95
Tyrrell, Prof. R. Y., i. 322
Tyson, Mrs., i. 316

UNIVERSITIES :
    Cambridge, i. 241 ; ii. 247–248
    Chicago, ii. 263
    Columbia, ii. 262–263
    Dublin, i. 35–41, 42–44 ; ii. 244
    Glasgow, ii. 250–252
    Harvard, ii. 258–262
    Manchester, i. 108 ; ii. 257–258
    Oxford, ii. 252–257
    Princeton, ii. 264
United States Military Academy, *see* West Point
Presidents of, 299–237

VALENTINE, Sydney, i. 325
Value of Individuality," " The, ii. 260–261
Vambery, Arminius, i. 321, 371–372
Van Aucken, Mrs., i. 324
Vanbrugh, Irene (Mrs. Boucicault), i. 325
Vanbrugh, Violet (Mrs. Arthur Bourchier), i. 323 ; ii. 227
Vandenhoff, i. 276
Vanderbilt, W. H., ii. 72
Vanderdecken, i. 55–57
Vanderpoel, Judge, i. 316
Van Horne, Sir Wm., i. 318
Van Tellen, Mrs., i. 355
Van Wart, Ames, i. 324

Vaudeville Company, i. 7–11
Vaudeville Theatre, i. 9
Vaughan, Benjamin, M.P., i. 269
Vaughan, Cardinal, ii. 265
Vestal, The, ii. 137
Vezin, Hermann, i. 119–120, 145, 322
Victoria, Queen, i. 179 ; 1889, Irving's first appearance before, ii. 212–215 ; 1903, 215–222, 238, 243
Villon, ii. 137
Vincent, Mr., i. 16
Volk, ii. 108–109
Volunteers, The, i. 16
Voss, Richard, ii. 137

WAGNER, H. L., i. 319
Waite, Alfred, i. 325
Wales, Albert Edward, Prince of, *see* Edward VII.
Wales, Prince George of, ii. 363
Wales, Princess Alexandra of, *see* Alexandra, Queen
Wales, Princess May of, i. 311, 363
Walker, Genl. Francis A. (U.S.A.), i. 318
Walker, Lord Chancellor, i. 315
Walker, R. Stodart, i. 319
Waller, Lewis, i. 322
Wallis, Whitworth, i. 325
Walrus, The yacht, i. 84
Walsall Literary Institute, ii. 264
Wandering Heir, The, ii. 202
Ward, Col., ii. 171
Ward, Edwin A., i. 315
Ward, Geo., i. 287
Ward, Miss Geneviève, i. 255, 314 ; ii. 167–176, 220
Ward, Mrs., i. 318
Ward, Mrs. Humphry, i. 324
Wardell, Chas., ii. 190–191
Warner, Charles, i. 326
Warner, Chas. Dudley, i. 323 ; ii. 234
Warren, Arthur, i. 321
Warren, T. H. (President of Magdalen), ii. 252
Warren, Wm., i. 317
Warwick, Earl and Countess of, i. 320
Washington : *Dante*, 274
Waterloo, i. 247–253 ; Sandringham, ii. 222–228
Watkins, Archdeacon, i. 321
Watson, Alfred E. T., i. 317
Watson, Malcolm, i. 319
Watterson, Henry, i. 321
Webb, Harry, i. 15
Webb, Miss Betty, i. 321

INDEX

Webster, Ben., i. 317
Webster, Mrs. Ben., i. 317
Webster, Sir Richard, i. 227-228
Weightman, R., i. 319
Wellborn, i. 87
Werner, ii. 301
Westminster Abbey, i. 7 ; Tennyson burial, 241
Irving's burial, ii. 361-366
West Point, U.S., Military Academy, i. 291-296
Wharncliffe, Earl of, ii. 146
Whistler, James McNeil, i. 151-152, 322
White, Sir Arnold, i. 204, 326
White, Stanford, i. 323
White House, Washington, ii. 231, 233, 236
Whiteside, James, i. 28
Whitman, Walt, i. 214 ; ii. 92-111
Whittier, C. A., i. 91
Wicks, Frederick, i. 323
Widener, Peter A. B., i. 316
Wikoff, Chevalier, i. 8-11
Wilberforce, Archdeacon, ii. 362
Wiley, Major W. H., i. 318
Wilkins, Miss Mary, ii. 138
Willard, E. S., ii. 138
Willard, Mrs. E. S., i. 319
Williams, Montagu, Q.C., i. 316
Williams, Talcott, i. 319 ; ii. 106
Wills, Rev. Freeman, i. 319, 328
Wills, W. G., i. 55, 255, 257, 326 ; ii. 137
Wilson, Dr. Andrew, i. 324 ; ii. 123
Wilson, Francis, i. 315
Winchilsea, Earl and Countess of, i. 326

Winchester, i. 245-246 ; ii. 233
Windsor Castle, ii. 215-222
Windyer, Sir William, i. 324
Wingfield, Hon. Lewis, i. 91
Winslow, Forbes, i. 326
Winter, William, i. 289-290, 319, 358 ; ii. 259-260
Winter's Tale, A, i. 16
Winton, Gen. Sir F. de, i. 319
Wise, John Sargent, i. 321 ; ii. 230
Wolf, Elsie de, i. 316
Wolseley, F.M. Viscount, i. 321
Wolverhampton, Irving's illness at, ii. 337-338, 347-349, 359
Wolverhampton Literary and Scientific Institute, ii. 264
Woodall, Wm., M.P., i. 317
Worcester, Marquis of, i. 315
Worms, i. 320
Wortley, A. S., i. 321
Wrestling match, A, i. 50-53
Wright, James, ii. 223
Wyllie, Sir Wm. Curzon, i. 335
Wyncotes, Mr. (Mayor of Plymouth), ii. 347
Wyndham, Fred., i. 323
Wyndham, Rt. Hon. George, i. 318
Wyndham, Sir Charles, i. 316 ; ii. 160

YATES, Edmund, i. 91, 315, 362, 364
Yerkes, Mr., i. 325
Young, John Russell, i. 294, 322
Yturbe, Signor, i. 317

ZANGWILL, Israel, i. 31